TWAYNE'S WORLD AUTHORS SERIES

A Survey of the World's Literature

Sylvia E. Bowman, Indiana University

GENERAL EDITOR

CHINA

William Schultz, University of Arizona

EDITOR

Liang Chien-wen Ti

TWAS 374

LIANG CHIEN-WEN TI

By JOHN MARNEY

Oakland University

TWAYNE PUBLISHERS

A DIVISION OF G. K. HALL & CO., BOSTON

Copyright © 1976 by G. K. Hall & Co.

All Rights Reserved

First Printing

Library of Congress Cataloging in Publication Data

Marney, John.
  Liang Chien-wen Ti.

  (Twayne's world authors series : TWAS 374 : China)
  A later version of the author's thesis, University of Wisconsin, 1972.
  Bibliography: pp. 205–12
  Includes index.
  1. Liang T'ai-tsung, Emperor of China, 503–551.
PL2668.L47Z8   895.1'1'2   75–22198
ISBN 0–8057–6221–3

MANUFACTURED IN THE UNITED STATES OF AMERICA

Contents

98578

About the Author

John Marney was born in London and spent the first part of his career touring the world as a professional orchestral violinist. After several visits to the Far East he became attracted to oriental affairs, and this interest led to the award of degrees from the London University School of Oriental and African Studies and Oxford University. He received his doctorate in medieval Chinese literature from the University of Wisconsin. He spent two years at Kyoto University, Japan, on Fulbright and Ford fellowships, and has studied for extended periods in Taiwan and Hong Kong. Currently he teaches Asian Studies at Oakland University, Rochester, Michigan. His forthcoming publications include a volume of translations of some 250 poems by Emperor Chien-wen of Liang (A.D. 503–551); a study of medieval Chinese folklore; a series of articles on the literary-salon games of the period; and a handbook of modern Chinese grammar for classroom use.

Preface

For many reasons, and in spite of their important influences, the history and literature of third- to sixth-century China have largely been neglected. Source material is locked in the difficult, if not entirely incomprehensible, elliptical and allusive parallel-prose style of the time; modern studies which have been attempted are for the most part in Japanese. The Chinese themselves have to a great extent ignored the period, regarding the "palace-style" literature and the philosophical vogue for metaphysical speculation as an offense against Chinese ethics and a black spot in the Chinese tradition. Many of the social and political organizations and institutions of the era, too, are unique in Chinese history, and scholars have generally preferred to investigate the more typically Chinese societies of the great dynasties. This biography of an eminent political and literary personality, a gentleman of his times, may help, then, in creating an interest in the West in Six Dynasties studies.

In accordance with Twayne World Authors Series objectives, this study has been prepared for a general audience, which does not have access to original sources. Thus, source references and bibliography have been much curtailed, a policy which further accommodates the necessary economy of space. The specialist scholar is directed to an earlier version of the text, submitted in 1972 at the University of Wisconsin in partial fulfillment of the requirements for the Ph.D., which includes full references.

The work was financed by grants from the Department of Health, Education and Welfare in Washington, D.C.; the Fulbright-Hays program; the Ford Foundation; and the University of Wisconsin graduate scholarship program. I am grateful to these institutions for their generous support.

Thanks are also due to Professors Wang Ling and Wen Ts'ung-wen, who discussed the basic texts with me; to the late

Professor Richard H. Robinson for his help with the Buddhist texts; to Professor Albert E. Dien for his patient instruction and interest; to the staff at the Research Institute for Humanistic Studies of Kyoto University for their many kindnesses. I am deeply grateful to Professor Chow Tse-tsung of the University of Wisconsin for his scholarly criticism and encouragement as my doctoral adviser. Special thanks go to Professor William Schultz of the University of Arizona for his careful preparation of the manuscript; and to Marian Wilson of Oakland University who typed the manuscript more than once and helped solve innumerable technical and literary problems.

JOHN MARNEY

Oakland University

Chronology

502	April 30	Liang dynasty established.
503	December 2	Hsiao Kang born. Third son of Emperor Wu.
506	February 26	Enfeoffed as Prince of Chin-an.
509–530		Provincial appointments.
531	May 7	Crown Prince Chao-ming dies at age twenty-nine.
	June 27	Hsiao Kang promoted, out of turn, to the heir-apparency. Moved to East Palace at the capital. Salon composition becomes known as "palace-style."
548	September	Hou Ching rebels against the Liang; besieges capital. Hsiao Kang given command of defense.
549	April 24	City falls to Hou Ching's forces.
	June 12	Emperor Wu dies at age eighty-six.
	July 7	Emperor's death announced; Hsiao Kang enthroned.
551	November 15	Hsiao Kang murdered by Hou Ching's men. Canonized as Emperor Ming; temple-name Kao-tsung.
552	June 5	Interred at Chuang-ling. Unauthorized posthumous names revoked by the Prince of Hsiang-tung; renamed Emperor Chien-wen, with the temple-name T'ai-tsung.
552	January 1	Hsiao Kang's successor, Hsiao Tung, forced to abdicate; Hou Ching establishes self as Emperor of Han.
552	March-April	Hou Ching driven out by Prince of Hsiang-tung's general, Wang Seng-pien.
	May 16	Eighth brother, Hsiao Chi, proclaims self emperor.

	May 26	Hou Ching assassinated while escaping North.
	December 13	Prince of Hsiang-tung proclaims self emperor.
553	August	Emperor Yüan (Prince of Hsiang-tung) kills brother, Hsiao Chi. Transfers capital to Chiang-ling.
554		Chiang-ling sacked by Northern Wei.
555	January 27	Emperor Yüan sandbagged to death by nephew, Hsiao Ch'a.
	February 7	Hsiao Ch'a becomes puppet emperor for Wei.
	July 1	Hsiao Yüan-ming proclaimed emperor of Liang by Wang Seng-pien.
	October 29	Wang Seng-pien killed by colleague Ch'en Pa-hsien; Hsiao Yüan-ming deposed; Emperor Yüan's son, Hsiao Fang-chih, established as emperor.
557	November 16	Hsiao Fang-chih deposed. Ch'en Pa-hsien becomes first emperor of the Ch'en dynasty.

Introduction

In many ways the Liang dynasty (A.D. 502–557) represents the culmination of the era which began with the flight of the Chin nobility from Tartar invaders southward across the Yangtze river in 317 and ended with the unification of North and South China under the Sui in 589. The Sung, Ch'i, and Liang regimes were all based at the Eastern Chin (317-420) émigré capital of Chien-k'ang (modern Nanking); throughout the century and a half of their duration, little real change was effected in administrative, social, or cultural patterns.

The first emperor of Liang, Hsiao Yen, known posthumously as Emperor Wu of Liang (464–549), overthrew the sovereign of the Ch'i dynasty, to whom he was distantly related, and founded a dynasty. In the early stages of his fifty-year reign, some attempt at social and economic reform was made. Civil and military systems of ranks and duties were reorganized; the penal code was reviewed; mercantile standards were brought into uniformity; and new coinage was minted, together with the introduction of a number of short-term emergency measures, in a desperate fight against the endemic disasters caused by shortage and debasement of currency and the decline of trade. But these efforts at reform were too superficial and lacked the thrust of genuine concern for the improvement of social conditions that might have carried them through. Society quickly settled down to much the same sort of existence that had prevailed during the previous century.

The nobility was confirmed in its pride, wealth, status, and privilege. At the highest level, the imperial scions were enfeoffed in their infancy with princeships, dukedoms, baronies, and marquisates commensurate with their relationship to the throne. They were entitled to the income from the taxation of a specified number of households in a given locality, though the recipient of such a fief did not necessarily reside there, nor did he exercise political or administrative control of the region.

11

Apart from these imperial commissions, large areas of public land were also exploited by the aristocracy for their own private interests. This aristocracy was formed of the long-established families who had appropriated great estates during the semi-colonizing period that followed the arrival of the émigré nobility in 317. Members of these families were intimately connected, and more often than not identical, with the official bureaucracy of the southern dynasties. Jealous of their status and of the privileges available to them as a result of their official and economic power, they manipulated recruitment into the official hierarchy, and so into their own ranks, to their own advantage. Government commissions throughout the South were charged with grading the populace into nine ranks according to moral and intellectual qualities (the so-called "rectification of the nine grades") for the selection of candidates for official positions. In practice, of course, family background was the decisive qualification, and in this way the oligarchy was preserved and perpetuated.

From the very beginning of his reign, Emperor Wu implemented a policy of consolidating the highest administrative powers in the hands of his immediate family. Within a decade of the founding of the dynasty, most civil and military governorships (the highest rank in the nine-rank system) of the twenty-three provinces under Liang control were held by his young sons, his brother, and his nephews. As a means of curbing the ambitions of the hereditary nobility, the tutors and advisers for these young princes were recruited from the lower ranks of the literati. These were the so-called "cold gates"—that is, families which for one reason or another had not been included in high office for several generations. Excluded for so long, it was difficult for them to gain reinstatement. The intention now was to satisfy their frustrated ambitions and enlist their allegiance to the new dynasty. The actual chores of government were delegated to them, and it was common for their ranks to become hereditary; yet they found themselves blocked in subordinate positions. More fortunate were the arrivistes, primarily minor figures in provincial administration attached to Emperor Wu's entourage, who came to eminence upon Emperor Wu's accession to the throne.

Thus the royalty held the reins of government in their personal grip. The lower echelons of the bureaucratic hierarchy did the day-to-day work. The arrivistes, secure in Emperor Wu's favor, controlled entrée into the metropolitan court. The hereditary families—whose pedigrees stemmed from far back into former regimes, and who were welcomed by the royal patrons of the literary salons for their aristocratic culture—degenerated into elegant dilettantes, snubbed their lesser colleagues, and became disgruntled at having to share privilege with poor upstarts.

Fifty years of relative peace brought the peasantry to a low ebb of poverty and oppression. Levies were constantly assessed from them for the construction of palaces and temples and for the largely abortive military adventures against the North. They suffered the inequitable imposition of harsh laws and penalties that aroused the sympathy even of members of the royalty, and their labor brought them little profit in the discriminatory and unstable markets. As a general result, in an unexpected skirmish with an initially insignificant band of renegade northern soldiery, the Hsiao found themselves deserted by nobleman and peasant alike, enervated by a faction-torn war council, and supported only by those officers who had found personal favor with their masters.

A particular feature of high society in the South was the salon. Under Emperor Wu, salon culture flourished among the aristocracy as never before or after. The salons were based on the metropolitan and provincial courts of the Hsiao royalty or on the private courts of the great families and the arrivistes and were attended by officials of the court and literate gentry. In time they became the focus of strong regional and factional loyalties. The emperor exercised little control over the provincial salons, but as long as he could keep his governors constantly on the move and maintain a continual turnover in personnel the salons posed little of the threat to the metropolitan court that might have appeared under a full-fledged feudal system. However, in time of strife, the regional courts closed in upon themselves and sought only to eliminate their rivals. Rather than rallying around the throne, they stood aloof in the crisis, hoping to profit from the collapse of the regime and seize supreme authority for themselves.

In the salon culture, literature was the prime interest. Clannish and snobbish, unwilling or unable to sully their hands with practical affairs or associate with lesser officials, the great nobles withdrew to their literary parlor games. The romantic folk songs indigenous to the South caught the fancy of the languid aristocrat poets. New poetic techniques involving a lately rationalized tonality were tried. Literary theory became the basis of court rivalries and factionalism, and the dynasty saw the completion of the most influential canons of Chinese literary criticism, the *Wen-hsin tiao-lung* of Liu Hsieh and the *Shih-p'in* compiled by Chung Hung. Palace-style verse came to flower in the latter half of the regime and supplied the greater part of the content of the *Yü-tai hsin-yung* anthology, the very antithesis, at least in intent, of the sterner *Wen-hsüan*, compiled a decade or two earlier.

The Liang scholars inherited the concern felt in former southern dynasties for consolidating things Chinese, whose obliteration at the hands of the barbarian tribes occupying the North was a perennial threat. Perhaps because so many of the achievements of the period have been lost, the Liang is not renowned for scholarship as is, say, the Han dynasty. Yet close reading of the historical records reveals that antiquarian and classical studies, as well as cultured leisure-time activities, were pursued with great diligence and genuine enthusiasm. Historical research by no means lagged behind literary interests. A copy of the *Dynastic History of the Han*, dating from the first century, was a prized possession and was the subject of massive exegeses. A vast number of histories was produced during Liang, several of which number among the official *Twenty-Five Dynastic Histories*. Important geographical surveys were conducted. Archaeological discoveries were treasured. Theories of military technique, painting, chess, music, and calligraphy were popular, and their devotees among the highest royalty, we are informed, were in no way inferior to those of other eras. Court bibliophiles scoured the kingdom for ancient texts; rare manuscripts were loaned to friends who copied or memorized them. Substantial libraries were established and comprehensive bibliographies were compiled. A court scholar could gain a reputation through the elucidation of an uncommon graph, and such philological interests eventually produced the *Yü-p'ien* lexicon with its rationalization of the *fan-ch'ieh* system of phonetics. Ancient Chinese precedents for court and ritual etiquette, upon which rested sanctions for imperial authority, were the subject of much inquiry, and biographies in the dynastic histories of the period are frequently choked with a scholar's researches on a point of protocol. The National Academy was reinstituted and disciplines were established in the various classics. Countless exegeses of the classics and philosophies were published. Public lectures on these subjects, given in the idyllic palace gardens by favorite courtiers and even members of the royal family, were popularly attended.

The Liang lays claim to particular distinction among the Southern courts for the devotion paid during this time to the Buddhist cause. There was no one among its gentry adherents to outdo Emperor Wu himself in demonstrations of religious fervor. If the genuine piety of these dilettante aristocrats be doubted, at least the competitive patronage required of them assured the metropolitan temples of unprecedentedly lucrative support. Translations of Indian Buddhist documents, exegeses, systematization of doctrine, and more lasting contributions to Buddhist learning were accomplished less ostentatiously in the mountain retreats of the provincial monastic communities, who shunned the temporal glitter that marked the activities of their brethren at the capital.

Militarily, the Liang recorded a rapid decline. Poor leadership in the field, where reportedly inept noblemen were appointed to supreme command over professional soldiers; factional disputes; and the long-standing reluctance on the part of the comfortably ensconced southern nobility to venture North aborted Emperor Wu's campaigns against the North and his dreams of unifying the empire. Even the efforts to exploit the collapse of the Toba-Wei house in the North ended in ignominy. In 534 the Wei regime finally disintegrated into Western and Eastern Wei. This split became a primary factor in the overthrow of the Liang, since it precipitated the initially successful bid for the Southern throne by the Tartar general Hou Ching.

Hou Ching was soon routed, but not before the Southern capital at Chien-k'ang had twice been laid waste and the flower of the resident Hsiao royalty murdered. The remnants of over two hundred and fifty years' accumulation of cultural treasures were transported upstream to the Prince of Hsiang-tung Hsiao I's court at Chiang-ling (modern Hupei province). With the fall of Chiang-ling to Western Wei in 555, even those treasures that had survived the sack of Chien-k'ang were lost.

The destruction of a whole era was thus perpetrated in less than a decade. Little remained of the great libraries and collections or even of the palaces and temples that had housed them. The great families, too, had been virtually wiped out, together with much of the ethic they had represented. Despite the conscious lavishness of the succeeding Ch'en courts and, for a while, the unabated popularity of palace-style verse, the Southern tradition of the aristocratic salon was dealt its death-blow with the fall of the Liang.

CHAPTER 1

The Provincial Administrator

THE imperial annals of the dynastic history of the Liang record four accredited emperors. Hsiao Kang, posthumously known as Emperor Chien-wen, reigned as the second of these monarchs, and he was succeeded by a younger brother and a nephew, respectively emperors Yüan and Ching. In terms of effective political control, however, the Liang dynasty began and ended with the reign of its first emperor, Hsiao Kang's father, Emperor Wu, the Martial Emperor Hsiao Yen. Emperor Wu's biography in these same imperial annals traces his ancestry, as befits his status as an emperor, back some four centuries to Hsiao Ho, an illustrious official of Han times. In the form of "Ho begat Yen; Yen begat Piao," etc., a lineage of no less than twenty-four generations is determined. Tendentious and contrived as this genealogy may be, Emperor Wu was nevertheless a member of the old Hsiao clan which had fled south following the fall of the Western Chin capital at Loyang to barbarian tribes and the subsequent collapse of the regime in the early fourth century. The émigré Chinese nobility appropriated for themselves vast tracts of undeveloped land south of the Yangtze River; the Hsiao established themselves at South Lan-ling, near Chien-k'ang, the metropolitan district of the newly established Eastern Chin dynasty (in modern Nanking district, Kiangsu province), nostalgically named after the old Western Chin district of Lan-ling, north in Shantung. Thus, the Hsiao became part of the hereditary landed aristocracy who exercised control over the South during the Six Dynasties period. In the second half of the fifth century they became powerful enough to seize—and hold—the Southern throne, and in 479 they assumed imperial dignity as the Ch'i dynasty. It

17

was his own kin, then, that Emperor Wu overthrew when, in 501, he destroyed the Ch'i and established the Liang.

By the time Emperor Wu ascended the throne he was nearly forty years old and as yet had produced no male progeny. His first wife, Hsi Hui, had been one of the most sought-after ladies of three successive dynasties. In spite of inauspicious omens accompanying her birth, she was famed both for her maidenly and scholarly accomplishments, and was originally to have been betrothed to the young Hou-fei, emperor of the Sung regime. However, this lad was stabbed to death by political assassins before he had reached his fifteenth birthday. Later, a prince of the Ch'i begged her hand in marriage, but her family declined on the pretext that the girl was unwell. Finally, in 482, Emperor Wu, at the time still a relatively low-ranking provincial administrator in Hsiang-yang (modern Honan province), took her as his consort. She bore her husband three daughters, but soon, in late August or September of the year 499, she died. She was thirty-one years old.

Only a matter of months earlier, in 498, typifying the taste of the Southern nobility for very young girls, regardless of their social status, Emperor Wu had taken a local thirteen-year-old girl, Ting Ling-kuang (485–526), into his household. As a person who later achieved eminence, records of her nativity are embellished with the apocrypha of historical hindsight; her official biography states that her birth was attended by a supernatural aura, and it was on this account that she was given the name Ling-kuang (Splendid Radiance). Physiognomists predicted an unusual future for her. Furthermore, she suffered from a red macula on her left arm, which refused to heal; strangely, this disappeared completely on her marriage to the man who would within three years become emperor.

Little Miss Ting is officially represented as Emperor Wu's first overt excursion into extramarital relations, and the respective dates of her arrival and Madam Hsi's early demise might give rise to some speculation. Indeed, the histories assign traditional roles to the two women: Madam Hsi is seen as the harsh principal wife, so jealous of her younger rival that she forced the girl to perform prodigious domestic tasks—her daily chores including hulling five large measures of grain. And never having borne a son herself, rarely did she permit Miss Ting to share her lord's couch. Diplomatically, however, Ting Ling-kuang remained cheerfully submissive and solicitous of the older woman's welfare, and there is no concrete evidence on record on which to base any dark conclusion.[1]

In September or October 501, Lady Ting gave birth to Emperor Wu's first son, Hsiao T'ung. (Since Emperor Wu was not yet emperor, no record was made of the precise date of the boy's birth.) Some seven months later, on April 30, 502, the Liang regime was formally established. In the accompanying distribution of honors, Madam Hsi was posthumously awarded the rank of empress; Lady Ting was given the title Noble Personage (*kuei-jen*). Three months later, however, before she had been formally instated, she was given the superior title Noble Consort (*kuei-pin*). This court title, instituted some three centuries earlier, at the beginning of the Wei regime, was the first of the five ranks below that of empress, and meant that Lady Ting was now given charge of all the palace women. Thereupon, together with her son, she took up residence in the Hsien-yang Palace, the central court of the imperial palace complex at the capital, Chien-k'ang.

On December 24, 502, Lady Ting's fourteen-month-old son, Hsiao T'ung, was established as heir apparent (and hence is traditionally referred to by his posthumous title Crown Prince Chao-ming). At once it was mooted that according to protocol the rank of the mother of the crown prince should be raised commensurately. The claim rested on a precedent from Sung times, about half a century earlier, and implied that Lady Ting should be honored as empress. The move was a timely one: just at this time, another imperial concubine, the Virtuous Lady Wu, of whom the new emperor was said to be the thrall, gave birth to the emperor's second son, Hsiao Tsung. Lady Ting must have hoped to secure her position at court over her rivals for the emperor's favor by pressing for instatement as empress. Poor Lady Wu was slandered and aspersions were cast on the fatherhood of her son so that mother and child fell from grace. Nevertheless, the emperor demurred over Lady Ting's advancement. He is said to have been plagued by ghostly visitations from his first wife, Hsi Hui, jealous even in death. Whatever the reason, he never set any living woman in that supreme rank. Thus, still as Noble Consort, at the age of eighteen Lady Ting bore Hsiao Kang, Emperor Wu's third son.[2] The boy was born in the Hsien-yang Palace on December 2, 503, two years after the crown prince.[3]

Hsiao Kang officially became a member of the nobility at a little over two years of age. Crown appointments were usually conferred at the Chinese New Year (February-March in the Western calendar), and in accord with this custom, on February 26, 506, Hsiao Kang was enfeoffed as Prince of Chin-an, with an appanage of eight thousand households.[4] This enfeoffment secured his income, but, in the quasi-feudal system of the Southern Dynasties, Hsiao Kang was not required to reside in the Chin-an area (modern Fukien province) nor was he allowed political, military, or administrative control over its inhabitants. The fief was formerly held by Hsiao Pao-i, the eldest son of Emperor Ming (r. 494–499) of the Ch'i dynasty. After the establishment of the Liang, perhaps to make way for Hsiao Kang, a prince of the new royal household, Hsiao Pao-i, was removed from Chin-an and enfeoffed as Prince of Pa-ling (modern Hunan province). Crippled in his youth by a debilitating disease, he died within a year or two after his new enfeoffment. His incumbency as Prince of Chin-an had carried an appanage of three thousand households; thus, Hsiao Kang's appanage of eight thousand households represents an enormous increase of personal appropriation from the tax income of this area. It appears even more lucrative in contrast with the appanage of two thousand households uniformly granted to Hsiao Kang's brothers.[5] Hsiao Kang's generous fortune in this respect can be cited as part of the manifold evidence that he was Emperor Wu's favorite son.

Some three years later, in 509, Hsiao Kang acquired a tutor. Formal education for the young prince began during his fifth year. Emperor Wu asked a minister, Chou She, to recommend a man of high moral character, dignified in deportment and highly qualified in literary scholarship, to be personal companion to Hsiao Kang. Chou She suggested his own younger brother-in-law, Hsü Ch'ih (472–551). Hsü Ch'ih had from early youth been fond of literary pursuits and was learned in the classics, histories, and philosophies. The recommendation was approved, and Hsü Ch'ih was ratified as imperial tutor. From this time, Hsü followed Hsiao Kang on his tours of the provinces, and his own official titles advanced with the promotions of his young ward. He exercised immense influence upon Hsiao Kang and upon other members of Hsiao Kang's entourage. Hsiao Kang was endowed with his own literary brilliance, but one is led to believe that to a great extent it was Hsü Ch'ih who was the driving force behind Hsiao Kang's activities and achievements.

Hsiao Kang's studies must have progressed well; he gained an early reputation for being extraordinarily clever and perceptive. It was said that by the age of six he was already writing literary pieces. Emperor Wu was surprised at the reports of his precocity and had the boy brought before him to be tested. "Hardly had the child taken up his pen than the piece was completed." "So exquisite was the phraseology that Emperor Wu sighed and remarked, "This son is the Tung-a of our family' " (*LS* 4.8b). (Another version has Emperor Wu say, "I have always thought of Tung-a as nothing but an empty reputation, but now I can believe in it" (*NS* 8.3b). Emperor Wu's reference was to one of the greatest poets in Chinese history, Ts'ao Chih (192–232), Prince of Tung-a during the Wei dynasty, who at the age of ten surprised his father, the redoubtable statesman, general, and poet Ts'ao Ts'ao (d. 220), Emperor Wu of Wei, with his literary ability. There will be occasion later to comment on the Hsiao royalty's appreciation of their affinity with the earlier Ts'ao poet-rulers. In any case, Emperor Wu's epigram concerning Hsiao Kang had already been uttered by yet another Emperor Wu (r. 483–493), of the Ch'i dynasty, in respect of his eighth son, Hsiao Tzu-lung.

Reports like this in the exemplar dynastic histories must be treated with caution, if not skepticism, but there is other evidence that Hsiao Kang "grew up expansive in manner and never exhibited excessive mirth or anger" (*ibid.*). Less convincing is the idealized description of his physical characteristics:

He had the dignified and stern appearance of a god. The hair at the temples was full, and the jaw beneath was square, just like a painting. Straight hair reached toward the ground; twin eyebrows glinted

kingfisher-blue. The hair at the nape coiled clockwise, like a string
of cash reaching down the back. The jade sceptre he clasped was
indistinguishable from the hand that held it, and his sidelong glances
illumined others with the brilliance of his eyes.[6] (*NS* 8.3b)

The description of whiskers as being "like a painting" is
common in the official histories of the period. It was applied
to monarchs and officials alike, including a Sung emperor and
noblemen, a Liang official, and Hsiao Kang's ninth son, Hsiao
Ta-wei. A modern commentator understands the phrase in this
context to mean that individuals hairs could be seen running
in regular, minutely separated parallel lines in the stylized
manner of portraits done at the time. It is doubtful if any
painting survives from these times, but copies done by T'ang art-
ists, and later copies of these copies, exemplify this feature. A
very famous example is the "Scroll of the Emperors," attributed
to the seventh-century artist, Yen Li-pen. A portrait purporting
to be that of Hsiao Kang, perhaps by the thirteenth-century
artist, Ma Lin, survived into the twentieth century in the Palace
Museum collection at Peking, but this seems to have been lost
in the disturbances of the Chinese civil war during 1947–1949.
Whatever the source, the subject appears altogether clean-
shaven.[7]

Hsiao Kang's first administrative appointment was conferred
in 509, when he became Cloud Canopy general and was given
command of the garrison at Shih-t'ou ch'eng, to the west of the
imperial city, guarding the riparian approaches to the capital.
In this capacity he would have continued to reside in the
imperial palace. The titles, ranks, and offices assigned to the
imperial princes in their childhood were, of course, little more
than sinecures or, at best, training for the administrative
responsibilities that would fall to them later. It is certain,
however, that during Liang even the imperial incumbents of
provincial appointments did actually reside in the area over
which they had administrative command. In fact, appointees
to provincial governorships and magistracies were obliged to
pay their respects at the palace altars and depart for their posts
the very next day after the announcement. Thus, from the age
of five until he was twenty-eight, Hsiao Kang was constantly

on the move; during these years he traveled to and from almost a dozen metropolitan and provincial posts, covering most of the twenty-three provinces under which the Liang regime was administered at this time.

There seems to be no special rationale for the sequence of provincial appointments or for the transfer of a particular person to a particular locale. Perhaps Emperor Wu wished merely to keep his close relatives on the move to prevent their establishing a secure base in the provinces from which they could launch an attack on the throne. Indeed, Emperor Wu himself had come to power in this way, and this was to happen again in the later years of the dynasty after the princes had ceased to move around in provincial appointments. A metropolitan posting was obviously preferred to a distant provincial office, lucrative positions were awarded in recognition of exemplary service, and banishments in the form of rustication to distant magistracies are recorded; but for the most part the politics behind the Liang appointments are not mentioned.

The ranks themselves had been reorganized by Emperor Wu soon after his accession to the throne. He instituted one hundred twenty-five generalships in twenty-four ranks, the twenty-fourth counting as the highest, corresponding to ten grades. Of these, Hsiao Kang's Cloud Canopy or Cloud Banner generalship (canopies and banners were symbols of rank) ranked a relatively high eighteenth. For civil appointments, the traditional nine-grade system, with the first grade counting as highest, still held good; but in 508 this too was extended to include eighteen ranks, the eighteenth counting as highest. Official salary, as recompense for service, was paid out of the treasury, in addition to any tax appanage received from an enfeoffment, and corresponded to the grade of the office. The first grade entitled its incumbent to a salary of ten thousand piculs of grain (*tan*). Hsiao Kang's civil and military appointments, including his Cloud Canopy generalship, were for the most part third-grade offices, entitling him to a salary of two thousand piculs.

Hsiao Kang's command at Shih-t'ou ch'eng was a metropolitan post, but his duties here terminated within a year. On January 27, 510, the second day of the Chinese New Year, he was commissioned as Imperial Commissar holding the emblems of com-

mander and as military governor of the five littoral provinces
of North and South Yen, Ch'ing, Hsü, and Chi (extending from
modern southeast Shantung province through Kiangsu southward
to northeast Chekiang province); and as Propagating Fortitude
general and governor of South Yen province. This generalship
was a seventeenth-rank office and, like the governorship, a third-
grade appointment. There was a certain wishful thinking in
appointing commanders for some of these more northerly
regions. If they were not entirely under the control of the
hostile North, they were in any case only nominally under Liang
sovereignty. However, Hsiao Kang's governorship at South Yen
province was still within easy reach of the capital. The former
incumbent, Hsiao Kang's uncle, Hsiao Tan (478–522), was
transferred elsewhere, very likely to make way for the young
prince. One of Emperor Wu's close companions, Shen Yüeh,
composed the customary memorial of thanks for the appointment
on Hsiao Kang's behalf.[8]

In 511 and 512 some military action against the Northern Wei
occurred in the area under Hsiao Kang's nominal command,
but the seven- or eight-year-old boy would not have participated
in any decisive capacity. After three years in South Yen province,
in 513 he was brought back to the metropolitan area as Propagating Graciousness general, another seventeenth-rank generalship of the third grade, and prefect of Tan-yang, meriting an
official emolument of a discounted two thousand piculs, amount-
ing to perhaps sixty to eighty percent of the nominal figure.
Tan-yang lay south of the imperial city and included South
Lan-ling and Ch'ien-t'ang, where the Hsiao imperial mausolea
would be situated. All lay within the modern metropolitan
area of Nanking. The note of thanks was written by a proxy.[9]

Whether or not these posts were sinecures, the historians
dutifully report a measure of genuine effort, interest, and ability
on Hsiao Kang's part in dealing with such duties as were
allotted to him. "From the age of eleven [nine or ten in Western
count] he was already able to manage public affairs personally,
and he had frequently been tested in provincial administration,
during which he had gained a handsome reputation." His
biographer adds that later in his career "In judicial matters
he was gracious and merciful; in documentation and accounting

he could not be deceived in the smallest detail" (*LS* 4.8b–9a). However, apart from the example set by his tutor-companion Hsü Ch'ih and other associates like him, the boy could have seen little in provincial or court circles that would foster stern devotion to serious matters. "Could not be deceived" says much, as we shall see, about the corrupt activities of unscrupulous officers. A contemporary of Hsiao Kang, the great Liang observer and social critic Yen Chih-t'ui (529–591) describes the highborn youth of his day:

During the height of the Liang, the scions of the nobility were for the most part quite illiterate. . . . They would ride to the office, but not dismount from the carriage; that is how they performed their duty as *chu-tso*. Or else they would report sick; that is how they functioned as *mi-shu*. There was none but wore perfumed garments and shaved his face, which he then powdered and rouged. They would ride in long-tasselled palanquins; their shoes were high-heeled and tooth-patterned. They sat upon chess-square bolsters and reclined against cash-patterned cushions, spreading out their games and amusements to the right and left. Coming and going they were quite at ease; looking at them one would mistake them for fairies! . . . They hired others to sit the grading examinations in exegeses of the Classics in their stead, and in the literary tests, they submitted poetry composed by other men, in their own name. (*YSCH* 8)

In an amusing little vignette in verse, Hsiao Kang himself pillories the palace playboys entertained by his eighth brother, Hsiao Chi:

> The Courtiers of the Prince of Wu-ling
> Hair parted in twin-tufted crown,
> Long pins effect a bridal coiffure.
> Offering the wine-cup as if to pass it round,
> But hanging on if they think there's a drop left to drink!
> (*TFP* 1151)

Emperor Wu's leniency toward members of the nobility, for all that it was supposed to be an outcome of his Buddhist inclination toward clemency, did little to reform the general degeneracy of morale. In contrast with the harsh criminal code practiced upon the common people, crimes committed by members of the royalty and the high official families frequently went unpunished. Emperor Wu's attitude is typically described in records of the notorious behavior attributed to his nephew, Hsiao Cheng-te, a man who was to play a traitorous role in the collapse of the dynasty. During his youth, Hsiao Cheng-te is said to have assembled a gang of ruffians from among his noble peers and together they would rob and murder on the public roads. Pursued, they would take refuge in the mansion of some official, where they could demand complete sanctuary. The pursuers would not dare press charges, and Emperor Wu would merely shed a few tears and admonish these often brutal offenders with a lecture. There is too much similar evidence to discount entirely such reports, categorical and idealized as they may be; and it must be against such a background that Hsiao Kang's character and activities should be assessed.

Hsiao Kang's next appointment took him farther afield than before. On February 22, 514, within a fortnight of the Chinese New Year, Emperor Wu sent his son to be imperial commissar holding the emblems of commander and military governor of the seven provinces of Ching, Yung, Liang, North and South Ch'in, I, and Ning (corresponding roughly to modern east Ssuchuan, Hupei, and Honan provinces); garrison commander of the Southern Man tribes; governor of Ching province; and general as previously. He replaced another uncle, Hsiao Hui, who was transferred farther west to I province. A year went by and Hsiao Kang found himself on the move again; on March 28, 515 his uncle, Hsiao Tan, replaced him as governor of Ching province. It was not until June 12, however, that he received his own new commission. This time he was transferred to the military governorship of Chiang province (in modern Kiangsi, Chekiang, and north Fukien provinces). As previously, he was Cloud Canopy general; and governor of Chiang province, holding the emblems of commander.

In 518 Hsiao Kang was summoned to the capital to be major general of the West, in command of the garrison at Shih-t'ou ch'eng. Soon after, he once more became Propagating Graciousness general; prefect of Tan-yang; and received the additional title of Minister of the Chancellery. This last title was given to princes of the blood at the outset of their career.[10] His acknowledgement of this appointment is conventionally humble and is quite possibly from the pen of one of his staff. Yet it has a wistful air: the dream of an adolescent boy on the threshold of a great career, not daring to hope that he may become a legend, but at least aspiring to go down in history as a model administrator:

In the past Chang K'an of Yüeh[11] spread goodness and courage and thereby accumulated a handsome reputation. On the borders good government was broadcast and was in fact glorified in the folklore of the common people. I am still very young and of scant ability. I am not clear yet about the principles and way of government. A man of commonplace worth and shallowness, I have been placed in command of the defenses of the capital and the river. I fear that the "Five Trousers" folk song[12] will not be sung in reference to me, and that it will be hard to eulogize me in terms of the "Two Ears."[13] But my desire is to dispense benevolence and grace and to conduct myself in a way that may be taken as a model. ("Dictum on Being Reappointed Prefect of Tan-yang," *IWLC* 50; *YKC* 3000)

There still exists a poem reflecting Hsiao Kang's thoughts on winding up his affairs at Tan-yang (though the piece was not necessarily composed at this time). He considers the achievements and character of his administration there: he did not cheat the officials of their salaries, and his fair-minded legal practices left no cause for complaint:

My colleagues have long since been issued their grain;
And my old officials' cash has not been withheld;
The willows I planted are still there.
The shade of the apple tree: Why should you be sad?[14]
("On Parting from the Officials and People at the End of My Term at Tan-yang," *TFP* 1149)

Another tour of duty in the provinces, decreed on November 16, 520, was to take him to the military governorship of the seven provinces of I, Ning, Yung, Liang, North and South Ch'in, and Sha as imperial commissar holding the emblems of com-

mander, and governor of I province. This fourth-grade appointment would have meant virtual exile in the far western hinter-
land. However, his orders were changed and on January 28,
521, during the first week of the Chinese New Year, he was
directed to the offices of Cloud Canopy general and the governorship of South Hsü province, a few miles downstream from the
capital.

Between 523 and 526 Hsiao Kang served as imperial commissar
holding the emblems of commander, and military governor of
the four northern border provinces of Yung, Liang, and North
and South Ch'in, the Ching-ling prefecture of Ying province,
and the Sui prefecture of Ssu province (covering modern southeast Honan and east Hupei provinces); Pacifying the West
general (one of the four "pacifying" generalships, relating to
the four points of the compass), a high twentieth-rank, second-
grade appointment; garrison commander of the Ning and Man
tribes, an office set up by Emperor An (r. 397–418) of the
Eastern Chin which, like the command of the Southern Man
tribes set up by Emperor Wu (r. 265–289) of the Western
Chin, was traditionally associated with the Hsiang-yang district
of Yung province; and governor of Yung province. In this last
capacity he replaced his brother, Hsiao Hsü (fifth of Emperor
Wu's sons, and third by Lady Ting), who had taken the post
the previous year.

Hsiao Kang's term as governor of Yung province was an
important period in his youth inasmuch as this was the time
when his famous literary salon first came into prominence; many
of the associates who joined him here later followed him into
the East Palace. His court was established in the provincial
capital Hsiang-yang, which since Chin times had been an
important garrison town situated on the border between the
Chinese-occupied South and the hostile, barbarian North. Hsiao
Kang would have found here men who recalled Emperor Wu's
administration as garrison commander while Duke of Liang
under the Ch'i regime, and members of his mother's family,
whose native district this was. His route here from the capital
at Chien-k'ang would have followed the Yangtze as far as Ying
at the confluence of the Yangtze and Han rivers, and thence
have branched northward along the Han, passing by the town-

ship of I-ch'eng, famous for its bustling trade and good liquor.
A poem by Hsiao Kang describes scenes in Yung province:

> The Great Dyke
> At I-ch'eng we stop midway;
> En route we frequently linger here.
> Divorced women skilled in embroidery;
> Bewitching courtesans practiced in counting cash.
> Exotic dishes detain honored guests;
> Wine on credit, we pursue the gods.
> (*YT* 6.10–11; *TFP* 1106)

Some of his official correspondence dating from this period
still survives. It presents a stylized picture of a merciful and
incorruptible administration; but in all probability very little
of it was his own work. Even if he is credited with authorizing
these documents, it is doubtful whether he should be regarded
as anything more than a leisured nobleman acting out the role
of the humane, gentleman administrator of the Confucian ideal.
He occupied the highest offices of the realm; it was his administrative and ethical duty to censure the lower officials for the
corruptions by which they survived. His every material need
was satisfied; there is no hint of his having made any personal
sacrifice for the proposals made in his name.

In one item he advised that taxes in Yung province be
reduced. He pointed out that production increases were sufficient to meet national requirements and that the people therefore
should be released from additional expense:

I am sincerely prepared to cast myself into the breach in the dyke,
or to expose my body in the sun as a rain sacrifice. The Nine Attacks
[of the law] are widespread; the Three [directions of the] Chase[15]
are not held in abeyance. The distress of military conscription is the
worry of the military families. The expense of mobilizing armies
daily increases. Now the spring waters are rising, and our boats
urge forward. Grain transports pursue one after another; food supplies are not lacking. Righteousness survives in sympathy for the
anxious, and no further burden of expense should be imposed.
("Dictum by the Governor of Yung Province on Decreasing the
Taxes of the People," *IWLC* 50; *YKC* 3000)

Then there is an injunction against the avaricious and indolent officials holding office in Yung province. Again it was the plight of the common people that attracted Hsiao Kang's concern:

The young men are exhausted with the bearing of armor; the women are wearied at the loom. They suffer from hunger; their corpses lie in the ditches and valleys. The spring silkworm does not warm their winter skin; the winter harvest does not fill their summer stomachs. How can one be insensitive to all this? And exploit them even further! Punishments awarded the crimes of battery and robbery subsequently form ten percent of the revenue.[16] Gold is used for fines and this instead goes to embellish an estate. ("An Instruction by the Governor of Yung Province to Reform the Avarice and Indolence [of the Officials]," *IWLC* 50; *YKC* 3000)

Following long-standing Confucian precedent as an exhortation to his subordinates, Hsiao Kang decreed that the portraits of officials of ancient times, famed for their righteous way, be painted in the administrative offices.[17]

The basic problem facing these Liang administrators was that the dynasty had inherited all the social, economic, and fiscal ills that had plagued the preceding Southern courts. Following their flight from Loyang and the northern provinces after 317, the aristocratic families claimed the lands they had appropriated for their tax-exempt private use. Lower-class émigrés could exact no such privilege. Throughout the Southern Dynasties era, as at the beginning of the Liang, peasant refugees from the North as well as indigenous local farmers were shifted around under the so-called *t'u-tuan* system, whereby, in an attempt to rationalize census taking and tax collection, specified numbers of peasant households were assigned to a certain area of land. However, it continually proved impossible to legislate effectively against the nobility's encroachment upon the ever-diminishing reserves of public land that provided both subsistence for the peasantry and a tax base for government revenue. An endemic vicious circle ensued: diminishing areas of taxable land led to greater tax and corvée burdens on the peasants until they were forced to sell out to the big landowners. As "guest families" (in reality, serfs), they and the land they now tilled for the private landowner became tax-exempt, thus further adding to the burden on the surviving "free" peasant.

So harsh became the impositions of tax and labor, or of slavery and serfdom, upon the farmer that he frequently had no recourse but flight from his holding or patron. The census and land registers further fell into chaos as rapacious officials juggled figures to their own advantage. The problem of declining production as property was abandoned and became derelict became so acute that in the early years of his reign, in 518, Emperor Wu decreed an amnesty of three years' rent exemption to runaway taxpayers willing to return to the land. The destitute were allotted state land and housing. But the weight of privilege could not so easily be lifted—witness the great estates of the Hsiao clan themselves—and by 541 we find the emperor lamenting that most of the public land was in the hands of the powerful nobility. Indeed, throughout this period the number of peasant households on the tax registers showed no increase. Emperor Wu did attempt to prohibit the abuse, but the ineluctable exemptions for existing estates and tenants already controlled by the independent landowners vitiated the attempt.[18]

A chronic shortage of currency had also developed; in fact, during early Liang money was in circulation in only ten of the two dozen provinces, including the capital, the three metropolitan provinces, and Ching, Ying, Chiang, Hsiang, Liang, and I. In the majority of provinces and districts, including Yung province, mercantile activities were conducted through various forms of barter in grain and cloth. Such currency as did exist was of copper, gold, and silver—precious commodities which attracted hoarders, and which in bulk were lavished on religious icons, further aggravating the shortage. Emperor Wu attempted to solve the problem by minting iron currency in two denominations, called *wu-chu* (i.e., five fractions of a tael), so designated after its weight, and *nü-ch'ien* (women's cash), both of which were round coinage with a hole in the middle.

The populace, however, privately continued to deal in the old currency, valued at a hundred times the new iron coins. The ensuing confusion of currencies, values, and coinage weights provoked the emperor into prohibiting the circulation of anything but the new iron money, but this simply played into the hands of speculators.

During his administration in Yung province, Hsiao Kang was for the first recorded time involved in a military engagement with the enemy North. On January 30, 524, the tenth day of the Chinese New Year, he received the additional title of North Pacifying general. This was one of a series of eight generalships (differing from the series of four generalships which included Hsiao Kang's Pacifying the West generalship) relating to the four directions, right and left, front and rear, each held by a single incumbent. They were equal to the twenty-first of the twenty-four ranks, and corresponded to second-grade offices. Juxtaposed with this announcement in the dynastic histories is the notice that Hsiao Kang sent in a petition to the throne. The content of the petition is not specified, but the notice in the histories is immediately followed by the record that on February 8, 525, New Year's Day, Hsiao Kang was appointed director of an expedition against Wei.[19] There does survive a dispatch by Hsiao Kang arguing that the time was ripe for a campaign against the North. It concerns Jang-ch'eng city, a day or two's march from Hsiang-yang across the border in Northern Wei territory, a city that was to feature in Hsiao Kang's New Year's campaign. It is not certain that this is the actual petition mentioned in the histories, but it does come close to fitting the occasion. In this "Reply to the Dispatch on the Eternal Pacification of Jang-ch'eng City" (*YKC* 3003), Hsiao Kang elegantly alludes to the chaos of the Northern administration and to the refugees pouring south seeking sanctuary. He urges the emperor to mount an expedition to bring peace to the people.

Up to this time the Liang royalty, with the exception of Emperor Wu, had played a less than glorious role in Liang military history. Well might the young princes impress the emperor with their displays of martial prowess, but in an actual crisis, almost to a man they are represented as cravens. Bungling, inertia, superstition, cowardice, dereliction of duty, and outright treachery on the part of the Hsiao supreme command, and a demoralized rank and file, whipped into battle and chained together against desertion, aborted all of Emperor

Wu's campaigns against the North. If Hsiao Kang shows up well as a military commander on this one occasion, it was more likely thanks to his able factotum Hsü Ch'ih, who, it was said, was responsible for much of the drafting and issuing of the day-to-day orders. Hsiao Kang's large army, under the direction of an able general staff, advanced into Northern Wei territory. Within four days, by February 12, they had invested Nan-hsiang, Nan-yang, and Hsin-yeh prefectures, and had captured Chin-ch'eng, Ma-ch'uan, and Tiao-yang cities (in modern Honan province, to the southeast of Hsi-ch'uan district).

A curious anecdote relating to this campaign turns up in a list of examples of prodigious longevity. Jang-ch'eng city lay in the path of Hsiao Kang's forces. When the township fell, an inhabitant there was discovered to have reached the venerable age of 240 years. He could no longer eat but subsisted on the breast milk of his grandson's wife. Hsiao Kang ordered him to be cared for and sent him presents of cloth.

Information about Hsiao Kang's contribution to the war effort survives in a letter he wrote to Li Chih, governor of East Ching province in Wei, who commanded the garrison at An-ch'eng city during the campaign.[20] Li Chih was a Chinese official in the service of the non-Chinese rulers of the North. Counting on Li's pride in his Chinese blood, Hsiao Kang argued that Li should surrender on ethnic grounds. Li, he says, is of pure Chinese stock; his illustrious lineage had for centuries been stranded on the "wrong" side of the Yangtze, in lands long occupied by rude "mutton-reeking barbarians." Hsiao Kang continued with a threat of what would happen should Li ignore the offer of terms, and he described the "nature-confounding" might of his legions. Then, too, the usurping Wei dynasty under the domination of the "Hen" (the empress dowager of the Wei) is corrupt and not worth supporting, unlike the righteous Liang reign in whose court Li may expect a royal reception. He ends with another threat: make up your mind before it is too late!

Altogether, it is a very persuasive text, appealing to an ethic that one might expect would sway a Chinese of the Six Dynasties milieu. Li surrendered the thousand and more *li* of territory under his jurisdiction. One may not assume, of course, that Hsiao Kang's letter was the deciding factor, although Li was well treated and given posts at the capital. The outcome of Li's surrender is more problematic. We do not know if Hsiao Kang's deputies occupied the area nor if the Liang regime was able to exploit the political and economic resources of the territory. The most one can do is note this detail of the ever-shifting boundaries between the rival North and South.

Thus, Hsiao Kang's success in this campaign appears, typically, as a literary one; he would rather write than fight: "I'll not follow the arts of Sun and Wu; / Rather would I excel Chao and Li." In this poem, "Out Riding in the West Pavilion" (*TFP* 1134), he admits his preference for the accomplishments of the musician-poet Li Yen-nien and the dancer Chao Fei-yen of the Han dynasty over the martial arts of the generals of classical times, Sun Wu and Wu Ch'i. He sustains his image of the humane Confucian gentleman, saddened by the hardships of war rather than glorying in military honors:

> Light frost falls at night;
> Yellow leaves parted far from the branch.
> The cold is bitter; it's hard to think of spring;
> In a border town it's easy to be conscious of autumn.
> The wind urges; banners and standards snap;
> The road is interminable; armored horses flag.
> ("Magistrate of Yen-men," *TFP* 1096)

An item in parallel prose comments on the fallen in battle:

> Those who capitulated have been returned to their homes;
>   those who gave good service have been rewarded.
> Bounty has been distributed among the heroes of the State;
> Offenders have been reprieved out of Imperial mercy.
> The *chiao-wei* are steeped in glory;
>   the *shu-kuo* [*tu-wei*] are bestowed with honor.
> Alone I think of those souls that are cut short,
>   in eternal finality, turned to dust.
> At Kao-yüan stained by the sword;
>   their bones heaped up at Mai-ch'uan.
> In vain we learn that their mortal bodies are no more.
> How can we discern their names for posterity? (*YKC* 3031)

Nor does glory or honor feature even in a note of congratulation that Hsiao Kang composed commemorating a victory over Northern forces (the occasion is not identified), wistfully titled "Pacification of Loyang." Instead, moral law and order, the restoration of imperial suasion, and the relief of the common populace are his typical concerns.

Tolerable as Hsiao Kang's literary inclinations might have been in this insignificant little adventure, in the crucial defense of the dynasty a quarter of a century later there was no room for such gentlemanly pursuits. Even in this victory early in his career, he showed himself by nature to be ill-suited for the harsh responsibilities of high military command.

Whatever the future was to hold, in 526 Hsiao Kang was appointed military governor of the three provinces of Ching, I, and South Liang. Judging from a memorial he wrote on leaving Yung province, he would have us believe that he entertained a genuine affection for the people under his jurisdiction there:

Judging a case upon a single word was something only a sage of ancient times could accomplish.[21] Remaining unsaddened by responsibility was something heard only of wise men of the past.[22] Therefore, although a prison official be carved of wood, they could not bear to face it; although a prison be a mere drawing upon the ground they would not dare enter it.[23] Since I came to Yung province I have always been merciful and have spared the imposition of prison sentences. Fortunately there has occurred no drought or famine from heaven, nor have there appeared on earth abnormalities or pestilences. Now I am in my carriage upon the road, and my boats are prepared. Some of the willows I planted at the ferry stations are still there. . . . I grieve at this parting of the ways. It is fitting that I leave behind some kind of favor. ("An Instruction Concerning an Act of Grace at the Termination of My Service in Yung Province," *IWLC* 50; *YKC* 3000)

He passed on his experiences gained during his administration of Yung province in a note to his cousin Hsiao Kung, Marquis of Heng-shan (498–549), on the latter's appointment to the governorship of this province. The marquis is said to have been a firm friend of Hsiao Kang during their youth. We may indeed believe that Hsiao Kang was "opening his mind" on this occasion:

There the officials and literati are filthy and corrupt. They retain
something of the customs of the old metropolitan area. The common people of the district are obstructive; they give weight only to
the sword and treat death lightly. The subjugated tribesmen concern themselves only with avarice; the border savages know nothing
of etiquette or deference. In their minds black and white cannot be
distinguished, and the statutes of law cannot be employed in governing them. It is my wish to strengthen the border garrisons, and
that you do not constantly move them about. Your intelligence
sources should be far-reaching, and your granaries should be full.
Use long-range policies to control short-term expediency, and use
repose to control impetuosity. You have long favored me with your
affectionate consideration. I open my mind to you. ("A Personal
Commission to the Marquis of Heng-shan Kung," LS 22.14b; YKC
3000)

The marquis must at first have pleased Hsiao Kang; so eminent
were his official accomplishments in the province that the "populace petitioned that a stele be erected to honor his virtue." The
marquis gave permission, and the stone was to be called "Virtue
of Government." But the spirits apparently saw through his
real character. "That night, hundreds of voices were heard
calling the stone, and in the morning the stone was found
floating a foot in the air. The marquis had a huge tree trunk
placed on top and ordered several scores of strong men to hold
it down, but all to no avail. Sacrifices of wine and meat were
offered, and watchmen were set to guard it, but soon it rose in
the air by itself and disappeared from sight. The marquis was
furious when he heard about it" (LS 22.15a). It turned out that
Emperor Wu had stocked the granaries of the Yung border
garrisons with grain and produce from several other provinces
against emergency and that the marquis had embezzled these
stores for his own household use. Furthermore, he had exploited
his official prerogatives to fleece the common people. He was
impeached by the Prince of Lu-ling, Hsiao Hsü, and recalled.
Clothed in white he was brought before the emperor and censured. His name was struck from the registers and he never
held office again.

It should be mentioned that instatement of a man's name in
the court registers was vital to his status as an aristocrat. Demo-

tion to the rank of commoner was perhaps as serious as banishment or even a death sentence, and Emperor Wu quite often used this device, or the threat of doing so, as a deterrent to try to keep his family in order. Indeed, had he not been so free with his power of amnesty, he would have been more effective in his objectives and still have had little need for the death penalty, rarely employed during Liang, so preserving into the bargain his reputation for Buddhist compassion. Members of the "cold gate" (*han-men*) families—that is, educated but poor men, virtually no higher than commoners—would even forge pedigrees to obtain listing in the roster, thereby securing an office and so escaping their plight. In fact, this malpractice had by Liang times become so prevalent that Emperor Wu ordered the registers, dating back to Sung times, investigated and revised.

In spite or perhaps because of the evident corruption among the Hsiao and other noble families, not to mention the improper exactions of the lower officials and the misdeeds of a desperate peasantry, criminal reform was a topic of sustained concern during Liang, beginning at the outset of Emperor Wu's reign when, in 505, he appointed a university course in law. Hsiao Kang returned to the subject in a memorial presented during the decade 535–545. In correspondence with Emperor Wu he argued for an investigation into abuses of judicial power and submitted specific complaints about the inequitable imposition of penalties. These details are sufficient in themselves to give the document rare value. In broader terms, they are unique evidence of sincere efforts by the highest nobility to solve in a just manner a variety of problems of judicial organization. The memorial also contains clear evidence that petitions endorsed by low-grade officials were taken into account and even included in a high-level dispatch as support for the measures suggested. The validity of these petitions seems to bring the Liang high command and its subordinate officers into closer collaboration than might otherwise be believed:

During the Ta-t'ung era [535–545], the crown prince in the Spring Palace observed the situation and was saddened by what he saw. Thereupon he addressed a memorandum to the throne, saying: I submit that one is discriminating and circumspect in the Three

Statutes, and lenient and sparing in the Eight Punishments. The imperial mirror is forever merciful and this indeed is apparent in state announcements. At the time when your subject was favored with your imperial decree [I] was given charge of the various affairs of the capital. I observe that the keepers of the south and north solstice altars, the quartermaster, the grooms, the caterers, the *hsia-sheng*, the *tso-chuang*,[24] and other officers all present the following recommendation: Those sentenced to light imprisonment for four or five years or less should be employed in the capacity of assistants to indentured laborers. In order to achieve standards of equity in the punishment of crimes, the legal nomenclature should not be easily changed.

Yet one person is assigned to labor in the Mint and another is assigned to service at the solstice altars. However, at the three Mints labor is harsh, while at the six altars service is pleasant. Now, listening to the prison officials and taking their recommendations seriously will open up the way for specious litigation. Then hard will it be to encounter a just man; and the "streaming springs"[25] will readily show their teeth [i.e., wealthy men anxious to bribe their way will be quick to smile]. I fear that the severity or leniency of the jade code [of law] will become the sole preserve of the black cords; and the waiving or recourse to the golden documents [of the legal code] will be even more monopolized by the crimson brushes.[26] In my stupidity I say: It would be most fitting to establish[27] a detailed criminal code in order to achieve permanent equity. ("Memorandum on Employing Prison Inmates as Servants," *Sui shu* 25; *IWLC* 54; *TT* 170; *YKC* 3004)

Emperor Wu's rejoinder shows him unwilling to codify specific details of criminal law.[28] Proliferation of verbiage, he said, merely obscures an issue. Any surrejoinder by Hsiao Kang has not survived.

A long panegyric that Hsiao Kang composed in praise of Crown Prince Chao-ming reveals more about his humanitarian feelings. It was written after the crown prince's death, when Hsiao Kang was comfortably ensconced in the luxury of the East Palace. It is included in the surviving fragment of Hsiao Kang's "Preface to the Collected Works of the Crown Prince Chao-ming,"[29] which consists of a list of fifteen "virtues" Hsiao Kang considered his brother to have possessed. The sixth section eulogizes Crown Prince Chao-ming's care and mercy in judicial matters. Sections seven and eight continue the theme of Chao-ming's humanity. One alludes to his grace in providing coffins for the burial of the dead, whose corpses would otherwise lie rotting unattended. The other lauds his generosity in opening stores of grain to the poor in times of distress and contributing other relief. Such activities are recorded in Crown Prince Chao-ming's official biographies; writings such as Hsiao Kang's must have provided the dynastic historians with their material.

Thus far in his career Hsiao Kang had been honored with high third- and second-grade civil and military appointments commensurate with his status as a favored prince of the blood. However, in 526 he submitted a memorial[30] requesting release from his military governorship of Ching, I, and South Liang provinces on the grounds of ill health. The memorial reflects his weariness of provincial life and the hazards and difficulties of border governorships. He recounted how he left the comforts of court life at Chien-k'ang before he was twenty; now he would soon be thirty. He mentioned his untiring efforts to fulfill his responsibilities, but "opening his mind" once again, he admitted his dislike of being administrator to the "sly Chiang tribes." His self-disparagement seems genuine; he did not want to prevent others more qualified than he from occupying posts he had been assigned to fill.

The death of his mother, Lady Ting, on November 4, 526,[31] solved any problem of his release. As custom demanded, Hsiao Kang submitted an official request for compassionate release, and by imperial decree he was returned to the place of his original appointment. Presumably he went back to Yung province. The recording of his filial observance is a matter of course. The dynastic historians dutifully report that "his grief knew no bounds. Day and night he mourned ceaselessly until the very mat upon which he sat was quite spoiled by his tears" (*LS* 4.8b). One cannot assume the continence on his part that these filial observances demanded, but apart from his fourth and fifth sons, Hsiao Ta-lin (527–551) and Hsiao Ta-lien (527-551), both conceived before his bereavement, there is no record of a child born to him between his mother's death and the year 530, when his sixth son, Hsiao Ta-ch'un (d. 551) was born.

Hsiao Kang's first son, Hsiao Ta-ch'i (d. 551), later known as the Ill-fated Crown Prince, was born on June 10, 523, at the beginning of Hsiao Kang's tour of duty in Yung province. By this time Hsiao Kang was nineteen, but he had been married since the age of about eight to Wang Ling-pin (505–549). Ling-pin's father had been enfeoffed at the beginning of Emperor Wu's reign with an appanage of a thousand households; thus, she appears as an eligible daughter of an imperial favorite. The Wang were the most highly esteemed of the hereditary nobility and were in fact far superior in social status to the Hsiao clan. They had seen dynasties come and go. No doubt they could feel honored by Emperor Wu's choice of Ling-pin for Hsiao Kang's bride, but the marriage was no less a means of uniting the interests of this great family with those of the new ruling house.

Wang Ling-pin's scant and conventional biography in the dynastic histories describes her as "supple and bright, chaste and virtuous"; her uncle once remarked that "she is a model for our family. (LS 7.4b; NS 12.4b) Hsiao Kang's eldest son Ta-ch'i was her child, and she also bore his fifth boy, Ta-lien, and one of his daughters. Of course, she was by no means the only woman in Hsiao Kang's life. There are records, unfortunately little detailed, of ten other court ladies, mostly from the ranks of the highest nobility, whose only claim to notice was that they bore Hsiao Kang a son or sons. There are brief biographies of twenty sons; apart from a notice of a wedding, and an occasional anecdote, nothing is said about his daughters other than that there were at least eleven of them.[32] The third-generation Liang royalty was virtually wiped out during the rebel occupation of the capital between 549 and 552; hence the archivists' wry comment: "As for all the other offspring, we know not of them and do not record them" (NS 54.1a).[33]

In 529, while still in mourning for his mother, Lady Ting, Hsiao Kang was presented with a martial band. This accorded with precedent and was a signal honor, though by no means unique during Liang, awarded to members of the royal family and to officers of the fourth grade and above. The title and tone of Hsiao Kang's memorial imply that he refused the honor, but this was simply the conventional formality preceding humble acceptance:

Expansiveness is the greatest excellence; it may not be glossed by sound or brilliance. Achievement accomplished through imperial favor has never been enhanced by cymbal and fife. How may one perform the "Fragrant Tree" on the West River? Or sing the "Morning Birds" by the Blackwater? I do not fear the censure of others, but am ashamed of my own humble qualities.[34] ("Memorial Declining the Presentation of a Martial Band," *IWLC* 68; *YKC* 3002)

The West river and the Blackwater were in Yung province, confirming to some extent that his mourning retirement was spent in Yung.

The martial band itself, literally "drum and fife," was equated with "mounted fife players" and was organized into two divisions, parading before and after the carriages of the honored recipient. The complement varied according to the rank of the recipient, but typically numbered several hundred musicians. Its function was connected with ceremonial occasions and court entertainments, and could even be awarded posthumously, probably for the occasion of the deceased's interment. The titles of some eighteen "songs accompanied by drum, fife, and cymbal" dating from Han times have survived. These were originally composed to be performed on the march and to incite a fighting spirit among the troops. Early lyrics often embodied folk tales and satires of officials. But before the end of Han, they were already being played at court. The "Fragrant Tree" mentioned in Hsiao Kang's memorial was the eleventh of these songs, and just what he had in mind when drafting his text is revealed in his own version of the *yüeh-fu* song written to the tune of "Morning Birds":[35]

> The dawning sun lights upon the imperial demesne;
> The wilderness crossed by the spring fowl.
> A fleeting kite at times on a lofty crag;
> Or at Tu-ling suddenly wheeling aslant.
> Young men serve on distant campaigns;
> Resentful, their thoughts turn to desertion.
> Better follow a court profligate
> Where silken sleeves brush the robes of ministers.
> ("A Pheasant on His Morning Flight," *TFP* 1103)

Hsiao Kang was to hold only one more provincial appointment. Summoned out of mourning on February 14, 530, two days after the New Year, he became military governor of South Yang and South Hsü provinces, Daring Cavalry general, and governor of Yang province.[36] As governor of Yang province he would live at Chien-k'ang. His relief at receiving this first-grade metropolitan appointment with its ten-thousand-picul emolument is obvious in every line of his memorial acknowledging the appointment.[37] He gave a better picture, too, of what it meant to be promoted to the rank of Daring Cavalry general, highest of the twenty-four ranks, than is usually found in the lists of ranks recorded in the treatises on administrative organization. This rank, said Hsiao Kang, was the highest field rank and was prime among all the appointed offices. His concurrent appointment as governor of Yang province was the highest of the provincial offices and gave him control of the imperial demesne. He mentioned that he was now of the highest peerage, with special access to the throne, and was entitled to the crimson tally and the gold-mounted baton.[38] The memorial ended with a brief history of the Daring Cavalry general rank.

In spite of such official preferment, Hsiao Kang might well have lived out his days in such local administrative positions. However, the unexpected death of Hsiao T'ung shortly after this appointment brought him to the center of Liang politics and changed the entire course of his life.

CHAPTER 2

The Crown Prince

DURING Emperor Wu's fifty-year reign, a question of the heir-apparency to the Liang throne was raised twice: on the occasion of the birth of the emperor's first son, Hsiao T'ung (Crown Prince Chao-ming), and again at the time of Hsiao T'ung's death. A variety of circumstances were highlighted in the histories to account for Emperor Wu's choice of heir apparent, but it was generally agreed that his decision on each occasion was a major cause for the friction among the Hsiao princes that contributed to the collapse of the dynasty.[1]

Before the turn of the sixth century, Emperor Wu, then still an administrator in the service of the Ch'i dynasty, and his first wife, the jealous Hsi Hui, had produced no male progeny. And so, to ensure the continuity of his line, he had adopted his nephew, Hsiao Cheng-te (d. 549), one of Hsiao Hung's (473–526) sons. However, with the arrival of Lady Ting into his household, and the demise of Madam Hsi, Emperor Wu's fortunes changed. Lady Ting bore him his first son, Hsiao T'ung; shortly afterward Emperor Wu inaugurated the Liang dynasty, and a few months after that—in December 502—Hsiao T'ung was designated heir apparent, traditionally to be known as Crown Prince Chao-ming. The nephew, Hsiao Cheng-te, was sent back to his own family and enfeoffed as Marquis of Hsi-feng, with an appanage of five hundred households, a far cry from the power he had hoped to enjoy as heir apparent.

The grievances Hsiao Cheng-te and his family thenceforth cherished against the emperor were well-founded; Emperor Wu's contract of adoption should have been binding, and Hsiao Cheng-te by rights was entitled to seniority even over the emperor's own sons. But whatever injustice he may have suffered, his biographers could not condone his subsequent conduct. His boyhood, we are told, was spent in vicious crime, until in 522 he defected to the Wei court in the North, complaining of how he had been cheated of his claim to the heir-apparency, and claiming to be in danger of his life. An officer there, actually another member of the Hsiao clan, questioned Hsiao Cheng-te's integrity, concluding with the advice, "Best kill him." From then on, Hsiao Cheng-te was treated coldly by the Wei administration as well. To solve his dilemma, he killed a small child and pretended that it was his own son who had died. No one suspected his ruse when he requested permission to bury the body in his homeland, and in the following year he fled back to Liang.

Emperor Wu overlooked his treachery; but, safe again in the South, Hsiao Cheng-te assembled a gang of brigands and continued his plundering and murder. For a brief while he held a field commission in an expedition against the North led by Hsiao Tsung, Emperor Wu's second son, but he deserted his command and again made his way south. Emperor Wu reviewed his record of crime. His official rank was reduced, and he was banished to Lin-hai, but before the sentence was executed, a pardon was issued. Again his treacheries were overlooked, and after a tearful lecture the emperor restored him to his original fief.

There is no record of any dispute of Crown Prince Chaoming's claim to the heir-apparency, and affairs at the East Palace, the crown prince's official residence, appear to have continued peacefully for the next quarter of a century. Then, in 526, Chao-ming's mother, Lady Ting, died. The circumstances of her interment were seen by the historians as a major factor in the break in the succession.

The histories report that Crown Prince Chao-ming sent some men to secure an auspicious site for Lady Ting's tomb. A man with some land for sale offered a court eunuch a million cash (probably the iron *wu-shu* cash circulated after 523, when copper coinage was discontinued in the South) if the eunuch could obtain three million for its purchase.[2] The eunuch secretly informed the emperor that the crown prince's site was inauspicious toward the imperial person and that it did not compare with the land he himself had to offer. Emperor Wu, who was growing old and superstitious, sanctioned the purchase.

After the interment a Taoist priest declared that the site boded ill for the crown prince and that the evil aura must be dispelled if Crown Prince Chao-ming's life were to be prolonged. He fashioned a goose out of wax and buried it with other charms in the place reserved for the eldest son at Lady Ting's grave site.

Two officials, Pao Mao-chih and Wei Ya, had been in the crown prince's favor. Later, when Pao found himself neglected, he secretly reported to Emperor Wu that Wei Ya was conducting magic ceremonies for the crown prince. The emperor had the grave exhumed and found the waxen goose and the other charms. Greatly alarmed, he determined to get to the bottom of the matter, but at the insistence of one of his senior ministers the affair was dropped. The Taoist priest was made the scapegoat and was the only one to forfeit his life.

Pao Mao-chih's nephew was a Buddhist monk, and Emperor Wu was known for his Buddhist affiliations as well as for his anti-Taoist inclinations. Thus the Confucian historians make the point that the eventual collapse of the state was incurred through a court intrigue between Buddhist, Taoist, and eunuch elements. In passing, the mention of eunuchs here is curious. Eunuchs were not the prominent feature of court society in the South that they were during Han or would become in T'ang and later dynasties. It could be that this rare reference in Liang history is after all a slip, if not an invention, of the T'ang and Sung bureaucrat-historians, whose own status at court was much threatened by both eunuch influences and Buddhist power, if not by the Taoists.[3] In any case, the historians show that very real harm was done by this bizarre intrigue. They report that to the end of his life Crown Prince Chao-ming fretted in mortification and that at the time of his death five years later, Emperor Wu recalled the scandal and passed over Crown Prince Chao-ming's heirs in the succession.

Crown Prince Chao-ming died as the result of a foolish accident. Early in April 531 he was boating on a lake in the palace grounds. A palace girl rocked the craft and the crown prince fell overboard. He was rescued, but his leg was injured. Fearful that Emperor Wu would be angry, he nursed his injury in secret. He heard that the emperor was planning to visit him and he summoned his strength to pen a note to delay his father's visit. His condition worsened, and his courtiers would have notified the emperor. But the crown prince would not permit it: "How can I let His Majesty know how wicked I am!" (*NS* 53.5ab) The end came on May 7, 531. Emperor Wu was finally informed of his son's illness, but before he could arrive Crown Prince Chao-ming was dead. He was twenty-nine years old.[4]

Crown Prince Chao-ming's eldest son, Hsiao Huan (d. 541), was on the way to his post as governor of South Hsü province. Messengers were sent to summon him back to Chien-k'ang to be invested as heir apparent. But the promotion was not ratified. One source offers Crown Prince Chao-ming's involvement in the grave-purchase scandal as the reason. On June 21, the day on which Crown Prince Chao-ming was interred, Hsiao Huan was enfeoffed as Prince of Yü-chang and ordered back to his post in South Hsü province. A popular ditty was sung about the affair:

> A fawn opens the city gate;
> The city gate, the fawn opens.
> When it should be opened it remains unopened;
> I hesitate in my mind.
> All the young men in the city
> Go back to their sweethearts. ("A Song of the
> Liang Emperor Wu's Time," *NS* 53.6b; *TFP* 1598)

This little jingle was contrived from a series of topical jokes and puns so obscure that even the Chinese historians felt obliged to gloss them. *Lu-tzu k'ai* "the fawn opens" is a metathesis for *lai-tzu k'u*, meaning that the emperor wept for his dead son. Although Hsiao Huan was next in line for the succession, Emperor Wu felt that the dynasty was too new to be entrusted to so young a person. Furthermore, Emperor Wu "harbored some long-standing grudge, and favored the Prince of Chin-an [Hsiao Kang] for the position." *Huan* "go back" in the last line is a triple pun on Hsiao Huan's personal name, on his return to the provinces, and as a colloquialism meaning "the girl to whom one returns" or "sweetheart."[5]

The dynastic histories referred to this break in the succession in another context. Hsiao Ch'a, Crown Prince Chao-ming's third son, eventually became ruler of the Later Liang dynasty; and Emperor Wu's decision to nominate Hsiao Kang as heir apparent was cited to explain Hsiao Ch'a's defection to the enemy North.

In all events, Ting Ling-kuang was buried at Ning-ling, in her native Hsiang-yang area (modern Honan). Of interest to us is this evidence of land sales and prices during Liang. Clearly, real estate was a vendable commodity and was at a premium; even an imperial concubine's grave site could not have been all that extensive and was unlikely to have been a piece of prime agricultural or urban land, and three million cash, even Emperor Wu's iron cash, was an immense sum. Then again, if indeed Ning-ling was the disputed site, with such a price for this distant border provincial lot, one can imagine realty values for the metropolitan area!

Of course, public land could simply be requisitioned or allocated as imperial grants at the emperor's will, but on occasion even the nobility could be forced off their holdings. For example, Hsiao Kang's father-in-law, Wang Ch'ien, owned an old summer villa on more than eighty *ch'ing* (about thirteen hundred acres) of prime land next to the Ta-ai-ching temple that Emperor Wu had built in the Chung-shan hills, just to the northeast of the imperial palace complex. This land had been in the Wang family since its conferment in Chin times. Emperor Wu offered to purchase the property, planning to extend the temple grounds, but Wang refused, saying that he could not sell an imperial grant. This angered the emperor, who promptly assessed its value and forced Wang to accept. Wang was punished for his recalcitrance by being sent to serve for a while as prefect of Wu-hsing (not far from the capital though, in modern Chekiang province).

By the time these problems of the succession occurred, Emperor Wu's second son, Hsiao Tsung, was already dead. But even had he lived, like Hsiao Cheng-te he could never have been considered as Crown Prince Chao-ming's successor. Hsiao Tsung's had been a strange life, ending unnaturally, as did most of the Hsiao. His mother, the Virtuous Lady Wu, had previously enjoyed the special affections of Tung-hun Hou, who had succeeded to the throne as the sixth emperor of the Ch'i dynasty in 498. After the founding of the Liang dynasty, Emperor Wu took her, together with other ladies from the Ch'i court, into his own household, and soon she was found to be with child. Hsiao Tsung was born after a seven-month pregnancy, and the new Liang court speculated whether or not the child really was Emperor Wu's son. Precisely at this time, December 502, Hsiao T'ung was being invested as crown prince and his mother, Lady Ting, was pressing for instatement as empress. In these maneuverings for status and security in the new regime, Virtuous Lady Wu was defeated, and she and her son fell from favor.

The boy grew up to become a talented scholar, but, plagued by doubts as to his parentage and hurt by Emperor Wu's ignoring him, he developed eccentricities that would have distinguished him even among such a family as the Hsiao, whose hallmark was singular peculiarity of conduct. The histories give lusty details of his goings-on with his mother, of gory black magic ceremonies, of his scatological pranks and misbehavior at court, of his tyrannical provincial administration, and of his defection to the enemy North and his eventual death there, in 530, at the age of 29. In the end, however, out of consideration for their filial attitude toward the Ch'i ruler whom they had regarded as husband and father, Emperor Wu reinstated their names in the official registers and interred them honorably in the Hsiao mausolea.

Emperor Wu's fourth son, Hsiao Chi, had led an exemplary life, though even had he lived there is no indication that he might have been considered for the heir-apparency. But it is said that he never recovered from his grief at the death of his mother, Lady Tung, in 524; and five years later, on July 30, 529, he himself died at the age of twenty-four. Hsiao Kang wrote to Crown Prince Chao-ming mourning their half-brother. He probably addressed similar notices to other relatives, too; the Prince of Hsiang-tung at least replied, and his composition echoes some of the phrases Hsiao Kang had used in his correspondence with Crown Prince Chao-ming. Hsiao Chi's star had soon faded. However, his son, Hsiao Hui-li, would play a prominent role in the events surrounding the fall of the dynasty.[6]

To the objective onlooker, Emperor Wu's attitudes toward his sons and nephews must appear curious. On the one hand, those two troublesome scions, Hsiao Cheng-te and Hsiao Tsung, had been leniently used by the throne in spite of their paramount weaknesses, civil crimes, defections, and high treason. Hsiao Cheng-te had been rehabilitated as a high officer of state, and Hsiao Tsung had been reinstated in the roll of honor even during his attendance on the enemy court in the North. Their sons, too, had been honored and enfeoffed. And yet, on the other hand, the crown prince, Chao-ming, had remained alienated from his father's regard, ironically on an apparently false charge, and remained unforgiven to the end of his life. This coldness was also extended to Crown Prince Chao-ming's son, Hsiao Huan, who, by direct right of succession, should have been invested as heir apparent. But in the final analysis it was to be blood, not blood lineage, that was to determine the occupant of the dragon throne.

With his two elder brothers and next younger brother dead and the more eligible heirs to the throne disqualified, Hsiao Kang faced little competition from his four younger brothers. He was now the eldest son; furthermore, he was a full blood relative of the dead Crown Prince Chao-ming, and from all appearances he was Emperor Wu's favorite as well. Even Crown Prince Chao-ming seems to have sensed that Hsiao Kang would succeed him. In 531, just before the crown prince died, Hsiao Kang was summoned to court. Before he arrived, the crown prince remarked to his courtiers, "I dreamed that I was playing chess with the Prince of Chin-an [Hsiao Kang], and I presented him with a cash-patterned sword. When the prince returns, perhaps he will be conferred with additional honors." (*NS* 8.1a)

Emperor Wu's problem was public opinion. Time was running out for him; already the best part of two months had elapsed since the crown prince's death, and he had still reached no decision, apart from the problematic dismissal of Hsiao Huan. His urgency is sketched in the report that in the middle of the night he summoned a council of the dukes, including K'ung Hsiu-yüan (469–532), Ho Ching-jung (d. 540), and Hsieh Cheng (500–536), to the Banquet Hall to thresh out the question. Although the emperor had the power to nominate whomever he chose, it is clear that he was concerned with the opinions of his immediate court. The purpose of the council, it seems, was to lend an air of weighty decision on the part of high officers of the state to what was Emperor Wu's own foregone endorsement of his favorite, Hsiao Kang, as crown prince.

Just how one-sided Emperor Wu's council was becomes apparent when we consider the relation between the senior member, K'ung Hsiu-yüan, and Hsiao Kang. Emperor Wu had previously assigned him to Hsiao Kang's service during Hsiao Kang's term as Propagating Graciousness general in 513, and had enjoined him to watch over the nine-year-old prince. K'ung's manner of acceptance greatly pleased the emperor, who advised Hsiao Kang to emulate K'ung's handling of affairs, ceremonial usage, and manner of dealing with other men. K'ung supported his ward with exemplary administration and in turn received the boy's deep respect.[7]

Emperor Wu's troubled conscience comes out most clearly in his edict establishing Hsiao Kang as crown prince. The edict was promulgated on June 27, 531, within a week of Crown Prince Chao-ming's entombment.[8] It opens with references to classical precedents for his decision. It can be interpreted as an attempt to justify his decision on the grounds of Hsiao Kang's personal attributes rather than trying to prove that he had any actual claim to the position:

It is only through utmost impartiality that the empire may be controlled; it is only through immanent love that the Four Seas [the empire] may be ruled. That is why Yao abdicated in favor of Shun [over the head of his own son]; he would cede only to virtue. That is why King Wen overlooked [his eldest son] Po I-k'ao and established King Wu. Their fame pervaded heaven and earth, and illumined the Four Tribes. Now T'ai-tsung is distant; heaven's course is calamitous.[9] The pure ways [of antiquity] are still in depression and the common people are not yet at peace. If one is not recognized as most illustrious and most wise,[10] or if he is not accepted as both martial and cultured in civil matters, how can he be charged with the weightiness of the sacred vessels or inherit the dignity of the dragon charts? The Prince of Chin-an, Kang, in letters has innate knowledge and has a natural bent for filial respect. His dignity and gentleness are manifest externally; within, his virtuous conduct is diligent. The feudatory attribute him with fine qualities, and within our domains the people turn to him in their thoughts. Kang will be established as crown prince. Thus in the success and decline of a hundred years there may still flow the abundant blessings [of goodness accumulated].[11] Within a single generation goodness will prevail,[12] and forever will continue the occupation of the Chi river.[13] ("Proclamation on the Investment of the Prince of Chin-an Kang as Crown Prince," *IWLC* 16; *CHC* 10; *YKC* 2964)

The unanimous agreement of the council, prejudiced as it was, was of course little comfort. Emperor Wu's age was beginning to tell even upon his prodigious vitality—he was nearly seventy when Crown Prince Chao-ming died—and his sons were weakening in their allegiance to the throne and to the precedence among themselves. Soon they would cease to be transferred among provincial posts and would establish themselves in their own independent courts, some far removed from the authority of the capital. Protocol had already been fractured to accommodate Hsiao Kang. They now assumed themselves to be eligible for the throne could they muster the strength to seize it.

Emperor Wu fell back on his policy of appeasement. On July 14 he promoted Hsiao Huan to the rank of Prince of Yü-chang. Crown Prince Chao-ming's second son, Hsiao Yü, became Prince of Ho-tung. The third son, Hsiao Ch'a, became Prince of Yüeh-yang. On January 23, 532, New Year's Day, Hsiao Cheng-te was made Prince of Lin-ho.

By any standards, Hsiao Kang has had sympathetic treatment from his biographers. He has been universally described as modest, unassuming, and imperturbable. But in the maneuvering for the succession, we glimpse aspects of his character that are a little less than deferential. Hsiao Kang was no less endowed than his kinsmen with the Hsiao ambition for supreme power. He showed no qualms about stepping into his dead brother's shoes. Nor is there any suggestion that he was piqued at being less than first choice for Crown Prince Chao-ming's successor.

When Emperor Wu's edict appointing him crown prince was promulgated, Hsiao Kang's former registrar, Chou Hung-cheng (487–565), presented him with a memorial full of well-known references to classical precedents advising him to decline the honor.[14]

Chou Hung-cheng's motives were quite obvious. Though he had once been drafted into Hsiao Kang's service, he was closely associated with a rival literary faction and was in fact married to a daughter of the faction's leader, P'ei Tzu-yeh (469–530). P'ei Tzu-yeh was opposed to Hsiao Kang's policies and was worried enough by Hsiao Kang's growing influence to criticize the literary style practiced by Hsiao Kang and his salon. Significantly, P'ei's faction was initially based on the Prince of Hsiang-tung's salon! As for Chou Hung-cheng's memorial, the only thing Hsiao Kang did decline was Chou's advice.

The new crown prince's memorial of thanks for his nomination was as humble as etiquette demanded. But secure now in the metropolis, no longer faced with a lifetime of arduous traveling to hazardous outposts of the empire, he could resume his mild urbanity.

Humbly have I witnessed the text of your imperial edict establishing me crown prince. This mandate from heaven indeed astonishes this common audience. Vast fame and splendid ceremony are all concentrated upon so humble and shallow a person as I. Compared with the [responsibilities] of this position, even the lifting of a thousand *chün* is not a weighty matter; set beside this, even the ninety-thousand-*li* flight [of the Roc] is not far. I am by nature undistinguished and obtuse, and as a mere shadow of reality[15] am not worthy of selection. But I am raised up into the cloudy empyrean as heir apparent and, relying upon the sun, command the extreme reverence. My jade insignia will sound in the imperial palace,[16] and I shall direct the feudatory in the provinces. But I am still fearful of being unqualified and doubt that I can fulfill my duty. How much more so that I shall be required to supervise the military officers and to illumine the former classics with correct principles, to be respectful of civil institutions, and in right action make manifest the records of former ages. The crown prince occasioned the utmost in the death ceremony, and as second person in the state[17] he served with reverence. He nourished his vritue in the Northern Palace and attended to the tasks of the Eastern College. . . . I governed most clumsily in the Fan-Han region [as governor of Yung province in Hsiang-yang] and then received word to return to court [as governor of Yang province]. After that, though of the lowest capabilities, I became successor to the supreme. . . . ("Memorial of Thanks for Becoming Crown Prince," *IWLC* 60; *YKC* 3002)

Six weeks later, on August 5, Hsiao Kang underwent the ceremony of investiture. A general amnesty was declared. His memorial for this occasion merely rings the changes on the standard references to the heir-apparency:

I have heard that the sun adheres to the heavens, and that the roaming thunder lodges in *chen*.[18] One must necessarily be of splendid virtue[19] in inherent endowment, and in affairs one must be of sage insight. I am by nature empty and shallow, and my capacities are unworthy of selection. Already I have shamed the ambition of love of learning,[20] and furthermore lack an imposing presence [like Emperor Ming of Han]. Without merit I encounter your gracious encouragement, and this matter emerges from my mere timeserving.[21] I shall emulate [King Wen's] attendance at the bedchamber door and [his] inspection of the imperial fare. I shall examine the texts of memorials to be presented to the throne and promulgate the emperor's own stern and startling rescripts.[22] I shall emerge from the Dragon Tower respectful of the summons, and stop my carriage before the Imperial Highway. I shall attend the imperial chariot on its tours of inspection and expound the classics in the Hall of Confucius.[23] I shall walk on foot to the palace gates; elemental power of the position is close. Flying tumuli cast inverted shadows; the immortals' promotion is transcendental. How may I fulfill the duties of crown prince? Or accord with the responsibilities of guarding the vessels of state? ("Memorial of Gratitude at the Ceremony of Investiture of the Crown Prince," *IWLC* 56; *YKC* 3002)

Hsiao Kang's elevation was followed by a round of family enfeoffments. Fragments of three of his memorials to the throne on behalf of his sons Ta-ch'i, Ta-hsin, and Ta-k'uan survive (*IWLC* 51; *YKC* 3002) and remind us of the elaborate literary etiquette demanded in such situations. More comprehensible is the fatherly advice Hsiao Kang offered to Ta-hsin when in 535 the twelve-year-old boy became military commander and governor of Ying province. Mindful of his own youthful trials as a provincial officer, Hsiao Kang wrote: "The situation is very quiet and all has been put in your charge. Although you, Ta-hsin, will not personally conduct the affairs of the province, whatever you say should be according to reason. In this way you will astonish everyone into obedience" (*NS* 54.2b).

There still exist a few sentences of Hsiao Kang's memorial

on the promotion of Hsiao Hui-li, the fifteen-year-old son of
the deceased Hsiao Chi, to the governorship of Hsiang province
(*IWLC* 50; *YKC* 3003). Then there is the memorial Hsiao Kang
wrote on the promotion of the eighth brother, Hsiao Chi, Prince
of Wu-ling, to the coveted governorship of Yang province,[24]
which brought him to the capital from his governorship in
Chiang province. The promotion became effective on March 9,
532, the post having fallen vacant two days before under extraordinary circumstances. On January 25, 532, the third day of
the New Year, Hsiao Kang's sixth brother, Hsiao Lun, Prince
of Shao-ling, currently prefect of Tan-yang, was given the
governorship of Yang province. Hsiao Lun was on the archivists'
blacklist and hence was presented as a proud, arrogant man
quite unable to restrain his temper. He was a hated tyrant, and
a few years earlier he escaped the death penalty imposed by
his father only through the tearful and insistent intercession
of Crown Prince Chao-ming. He was entirely given over to
lustful desires and had accumulated vast stores of goods and
clothing. One day, soon after his promotion to Yang province,
he sent some men into the marketplace to buy several hundred
bolts of brocade and cloth on credit, intending to clothe his
courtiers in more magnificent style and to provide his womenfolk with draperies for their apartments. But the tradesmen
closed their shutters and refused to do business. One of Hsiao
Lun's retinue, Ho Chih-t'ung, informed Emperor Wu of this
evidence of popular dissent against Hsiao Lun's gubernatorial
mismanagement. Hsiao Lun was censured and returned to his
lodging.

Hsiao Lun's revenge upon the informer and his rearrest and
pardon are related with detailed and gory exuberance. Hsiao
Lun sent some men to seek out Ho Chih-t'ung. They cornered
him in a lane and speared him to death. The crime was perpetrated with gusto; the blades of their weapons protruded
through the victim's back. But before expiring, Ho Chih-t'ung
recognized one of the assassins. Dipping a finger in his own
blood he wrote the name Shao-ling (the district of Hsiao Lun's
enfeoffment) on the wall. Thus the murder came to light.
Emperor Wu offered a reward of a million cash for the appre-
hension of the criminals. An officer listed the names of the

men involved, and five hundred men were sent to surround Hsiao Lun's residence. The murderers were arrested in the women's apartments. One man escaped by leaping over a wall and breaking through the cordon, but Ho Chih-t'ung's son tracked him down. He was hauled out of the building in which he had hidden, engulfed in flames, and roasted. A cart filled with cash was put on display, salt and garlic were provided, and the local populace was exhorted to eat the corpse. For every slice consumed a reward of a thousand cash was given. All the man's followers and even his mother were similarly dispatched. Hsiao Lun was placed under close house arrest. He was reduced to the status of a commoner on March 7, but again, after some thirty days, he was released from confinement and his ranks were restored.

Hsiao Kang corroborated these reports of his brother's misdeeds in a piece he wrote, censuring him in the most direct terms:

The subject Lun is in his habits hardly different from a common night-prowler. He is unable to mend his evil ways. His inveterate criminal activities are widely known. Already he has received three convictions under the law. . . . We are close brothers, and I urge this injunction upon him. Let him look up and bear this devoted severity. Let his heart and countenance tremble in trepidation. ("Letter to the Prince of Shao-ling Apologizing for His Confinement," *IWLC* 54; *YKC* 3004)

Hsiao Lun's biographies list a number of his impeachments. The historians' sources are no longer known, but doubtless they included memorials like this one.

Literary evidence similarly confirms, at least in outline, reports of another court dispute which Hsiao Kang mediated. The details, for whatever their historical value, are that the Prince of Hsiang-tung's mother received imperial favor through the good offices of Hsiao Kang's own mother, Lady Ting. This, we are told, is why the Prince of Hsiang-tung was cordial to Hsiao Kang. He was friendly, too, with Lady Ting's third son, Hsiao Hsü, while they were boys; but after they had grown up the Prince of Hsiang-tung began to speak ill of him. When the Prince of Hsiang-tung was governor of Ching province he was

attracted to a personable girl in his entourage and brought
her with him when he returned to the capital; but because of
complaints made by Hsiao Hsü, presumably to the emperor,
the girl was forbidden entry. The Prince of Hsiang-tung pro-
tested to Hsiao Kang, but Hsiao Kang could do nothing, and
the Prince of Hsiang-tung sent the girl back to Ching province.
His sentiments are preserved in a poem called "A Concubine
Is Returned to the West" (that is, to Ching province), and
the incident appears to have been well known at the time.[25]

The historical records follow the estrangement of the Prince
of Hsiang-tung and Hsiao Hsü to the latter's death in 547
at the age of forty-four, while he was governor of Ching province. Hsiao Hsü, like his uncle Hsiao Hung, had been a secret
miser, and only when he was on the point of death was his
hoard revealed. His eldest son had suffered the death penalty
for his crimes, and his second son was an idiot. The denouement
of his feud with the Prince of Hsiang-tung has the prince, then
governor of the neighboring Chiang province, entering Hsiao
Hsü's office, dancing on his bier, and smashing it!

Another scandal involved the historians' choice as arch-
villain of Liang, Hsiao Cheng-te. His younger sister, the Ch'ang-lo
princess, was to be married to Hsieh Hsi, a member of Hsiao
Kang's court. Hsiao Cheng-te debauched her. He tied up one
of her slave girls, adorned the girl with gold and jewels, and
set the residence on fire. Then he spread the news that the
princess had been burned to death. The slave girl's corpse, still
wearing the ornaments, was discovered among the ruins and
was assumed to be that of the princess. Hsaio Cheng-te continued his incestuous liaison with his sister, introducing her
publicly as Madam Liu, and had a child by her. As time passed,
the crime became known.

Then one day Hsiao Cheng-te snatched a decoy pheasant
from an official named Chang Chun. Not long after, at a Buddhist
ceremony in the Ch'ung-yün Hall which was attended by the
imperial household and the lesser ranks, the man complained
for all to hear: "Chang Chun's decoy pheasant isn't the Ch'ang-lo
princess. How can he steal it!" Hsiao Kang feared that Emperor
Wu might hear of the remark, and he ordered Hsiao Chi to
resolve the affair. The decoy pheasant was returned to its

owner. The chroniclers commented that later the Liang dynasty tottered because of Hsiao Cheng-te. On hearing the name Lin-ho chün (Hsiao Cheng-te's enfeoffment), the common people would not wish to speak of it. A popular ditty was sung: "Better meet five tigers in town / Than chance on Lin-ho father and son!"

Hsiao Kang was by now the senior in his generation. It was his filial obligation to shield his father from the burden of family squabbles and misdemeanors, and it was his fraternal task to keep his brothers and cousins in order. We do not know how far he succeeded in the former duty—even in old age Emperor Wu appears to have been shrewd enough to surmise what occurred behind his back. In the latter obligation, however, Hsiao Kang failed. It would have taken a more forceful character than his to offset the weakness of his claim to the authority of the crown prince. As a precaution against his brothers, especially Hsiao Lun, who was now guarding the approaches to Chien-k'ang just downstream at Tan-yang, Hsiao Kang had a picked squadron of troops on constant watch in the East Palace.[26]

The correspondence between Hsiao Kang and Crown Prince Chao-ming had almost invariably been more cordial. For example, in 520 when Hsiao Kang was governor of South Hsü province, Crown Prince Chao-ming composed a set of twelve poems in the classical four-character line entitled "To My Young Brother, the Governor of Hsü Province," centering upon their fraternal relationship.[27] On the occasion of the spring purification rites, Hsiao Kang addressed two congratulatory poems, also in the four-character line and heavily allusive, to the crown prince. The preface to the first of these verses borrows freely from earlier compositions on the subject and is flattering in the extreme:[28]

The crown prince has innate knowledge and is of the highest virtue. His bright insight is inherent. His wisdom is profound [from whence spring forth] the magic pearls [of his literary composition]. His discourse is like the flow of the river. He rises beyond the splendid behavior of the Three Excellences and stirs the felicitous sounds of the Eight Districts [of the empire].[29] ("Preface to the Poems on the Serpentine on the Third Day of the Third Month," *ILWC* 4; *CHC* 4; *TPYL* 30; *YKC* 3016; *TFP* 1114)

Crown Prince Chao-ming's death inspired a number of encomiums from Hsiao Kang's brush. Particularly illustrative are the third section of his preface to the crown prince's *Collected Works* and the memorial accompanying the unofficial biography of Crown Prince Chao-ming that he compiled for presentation to the throne. The memorial describes the crown prince as having the disposition of a gracious sage and being endowed with inherent wisdom. The text continues, saying that he attained the very extremes of filial duty and veneration and that he was affable and respectful. In his youth he was a precocious writer, and as an adult he perfectly exemplified the virtues of a crown prince; he embraced the "three excellencies" and was extensive in the "four intelligences" (Legge, *Classics,* III, 41). There follows the inevitable list of apt references to the wisdom and virtue of princes of ancient times, and Hsiao Kang closes the memorial: "I regard former realities and ponder a means to extol the abundant path of his life, to propagate and record his virtuous reputation. I respectfully compile the "Unofficial Biography of Crown Prince Chao-ming" and his "Collected Works," and request that these be placed in the court library and deposited in the national archives, that they might forever display his lofty achievements and make manifest his vast excellence."[30] The third section of the preface says: "Giving down his brotherly affection, attached as we were as elder and younger brothers, he instructed me tirelessly in the ways of goodness [*Analects* 9.10], and in teaching others he never showed fatigue. He personally walked in the precepts of etiquette, and revealed himself as a model of behavior expected of a superior towards his inferior" (*YKC* 3016).

This evidence of fraternal regard is perhaps best supported by an incident involving the man who had triggered the grave-purchase scandal through which Crown Prince Chao-ming had fallen into disfavor. It happened that Hsiao Lun, then in Tan-yang commandery, reported a dispute over a girl between Pao Mao-chih (who had reported Wei Ya and Crown Prince Chao-ming to Emperor Wu) and a local inhabitant. Since the case involved Hsiao Lun, a royal prince, it was referred to Hsiao Kang, the crown prince. A cynical view would be that Hsiao Kang had been the chief beneficiary of Pao Mao-chih's earlier plot, which had left the way open for his appointment as crown prince. Pao Mao-chih's new misdemeanor—kidnaping—did not warrant capital punishment, but placing fraternal sentiment first and remembering how Crown Prince Chao-ming had been wronged, Hsiao Kang "brushed aside his tears and sentenced Pao to death." (*NS* 53.6b)

Hsiao Kang's predecessor had lived some twenty-five years in the East Palace.[31] Now these buildings were to be renovated. While repairs were in progress, the palace staff was dismissed, except for one of Hsiao Kang's former officers who was ordered to stay on, presumably in a supervisory capacity. Liu Hsing (487–536), during his sojourn in the unoccupied palace, worked on an annotation of one of Hsiao Kang's rhyme-prose compositions.[32] Apparently these texts were no more readily understood then than they are today!

Hsiao Kang lodged temporarily in the Tung-fu (East Commissariat). Finally, more than a year later, in October or November 532, he moved into the official residence of the crown prince.

CHAPTER 3

The Salon

F OR Hsiao Kang there now followed almost two decades of untrammeled leisure. Insurrections there were, and military skirmishes with the North on an increasingly urgent scale, but they were all distant, border affairs and could have had little if any material effect upon daily life in the southern capital at Chien-k'ang. Hsiao Kang listed some of the formal duties of the crown prince; in addition to these, as Emperor Wu was growing old, much of the government administration was delegated to the East Palace. On one occasion, from May 2–8, 544, Hsiao Kang was left in sole charge of the imperial city while Emperor Wu was away visiting the ancestral district of the Hsiao clan at Lan-ling. Hsiao Kang complained to the Prince of Hsiang-tung that there was "little room for amusement";[1] in another letter, to Hsü Ch'ih, he tried to arouse sympathy for the busy life forced upon him as a servant of the state, and seemed to answer charges of professional neglect. In justification he compared his own diligence with that of the timeserving officials he met at the imperial court:

Shan T'ao once said: "The sole concern of the East Palace is the fostering of virtue." But times today are different from the past. Now I am busy with the responsibilities of administration and cannot devote myself to the purging of faults and the advancement of merit. I assist but little in state legislation, or in calling attention to proprieties and improprieties, or in contributing to our holy government.[2] On this account I am deeply ashamed and at nightfall my mind is constantly beset with cares.[3] I exerted my best efforts in the Five Peaks, and for ten years I served among the barbarian Jung tribes where I experienced perils, difficulties, and hardships.[4] Regard then those timeserving ministers whose only interest is in self-preservation, those petty copyists[5] with no conception of the topog-

60

raphy of mountains and rivers, or of the labor of the common
soldier, or of the bitter existence of the peasantry, or of the cravings
of the common folk. They frequent the lofty palaces and crowd the
grounds at the tall gates [of the rich families at the capital]. They
feast upon the finest jadelike fare before the silken-gauze tapestries,
with yellow gold in their grasp. Fawning and flattering,[6] they follow
their heart's every desire. . . . If you show this letter to others they
will surely sigh long. ("Letter in Reply to Hsü Ch'ih," *IWLC* 26;
YKC 3010)

Hsiao Kang no doubt believed himself overworked in official
duties. But it was Hsü Ch'ih who was credited with most of
the practical affairs during Hsiao Kang's tours in the provinces,
and the historical sources tend to dwell on Hsiao Kang's leisure
pursuits: "[Hsiao Kang] liberally received literary scholars at
his court and never wearied of their company. They would
forever be engaged in discussions or in making compilations,
following up with literary compositions" (*LS* 4.9a).[7] And again:
"In the courts of the imperial princes the days passed in leisurely
gatherings and feasting. [Hsiao Kang,] together with his elder
brother Hsiao T'ung and his younger brother Hsiao I, competed
in the composition of most elegant and beautiful literature."[8]

After some years in the East Palace, Hsiao Kang's literary
associates, too, were relieved of unwelcome public responsibilities. In 539 Yin Pu-hai (505–589) was given an appointment
in the East Palace, and he and Yü Chien-wu, both of whom,
like Hsü, were from poor families, spent all day attending to
business. Yin Pu-hai is represented as an expert administrator
whose judgment was enhanced by deep learning in the classical
philosophies and who was much consulted in government circles.
Emperor Wu remarked to Yü Chien-wu: "You are a literary
scholar. Business affairs are not your strong point. Better let
Pu-hai handle things!" (*Ch'en shu* 32.2a). Such evidence suggests
that Hsiao Kang as crown prince, no longer burdened with
tiresome journeying on the southern roads and the administration
of sly, uncouth border tribes, could enjoy to the full his literary
predilections together with a congenial and settled company
of literati.

Since earliest times in Chinese society there existed the
tradition of noble patronage of men of distinction. *Hao-k'o,*

"delight in entertaining a clientele," was a term of praise commonly used of aristocrats in pre-Ch'in days. By the end of Han such gatherings had become predominantly literary in nature—witness the rival Ts'ao literary groups[9]—and began to be known by distinctive names; for example, the Seven Masters of Chien-an (members of Ts'ao P'ei's literary faction) and the Seven Sages of the Bamboo Grove. The trend continued through the Southern Dynasties and came to flower as never before or after during the Liang dynasty.

By early Liang a number of important salons, family associations, and literary schools emerged as distinguishable entities.[10] At the capital there were Emperor Wu and the survivors of the Eight Comrades from his provincial days. Then there was the select Orchid Terrace Association (Lan-t'ai-chü) where scholars "played at the dragon gates," centered upon Jen Fang (459–507), who was one of the Eight Comrades. Crown Prince Chao-ming held court in the East Palace. In the provinces Hsiao Kang, the Prince of Hsiang-tung, and Emperor Wu's younger brothers Hsiao Hsiu[11] and Hsiao Wei (476–533), the latter in his sumptuous estate, Fang-ling-yüan, established their own salons.

To gain entrée into the central court it was essential to have the recommendation of the imperial favorites. The biographies of a large number of personalities who received mention in the official Liang histories record the approval of Shen Yüeh, a minister of the old Ch'i dynasty, a renowned scholar and poet, and a member of the Eight Comrades. Other favorites were members of the arriviste class (hou-chin), which in Liang times referred to men who rose to eminence through imperial preferment rather than through family status. Particularly influential were Jen Fang and Ho Yin, and later Chu I (483–549). It would be far too ideal to say that literary skills were the only factor in gaining such recommendation.[12] However, other considerations of family status, personal relations, and "pull" being equal, literary excellence was an extremely important qualification. And so, to advance his career, a man without native literary ability would imitate a leading literary star of the day or subscribe to a vogue at one or another of the metropolitan salons.

In this climate, it was natural that personae non gratae at the capital, through personal shortcomings or as a result of some court intrigue, would be denied promotion and would be packed off to a provincial office. It was this milieu that gives significance to Hsiao Kang's complaints in his letter to Hsü Ch'ih. His remarks were undoubtedly colored by the discontents and resentments among his own rusticated officials, jealous of the timeserving ministers at the capital interested only in self-preservation; and of the petty copyists who spent their days in sycophantic attendance on the rich and influential members of the central court.

These literary courts were, of course, geographic entities and should not be confused with the literary clans or the literary theorists and their followers. For example, one or more of those "seventy members of the Liu clan who were skilled writers," and the Hsieh, and of course the Hsiao, were to be found in any of the court groups of the time. The family groups within a particular court setting—brothers, father-son associations—are another matter, indicating the tendency for offices and ranks to become hereditary.

The literary theorists, too, found their adherents in widely scattered localities, although men of like views would naturally tend to gravitate to a congenial situation. Thus the orthodox school (*cheng-t'i-p'ai*) was based upon Crown Prince Chao-ming's court, while the ancient school (*ku-t'i-p'ai*) and the Hsieh Ling-yün school were in their earlier stages associated with the Prince of Hsiang-tung's salon.

Hsiao Kang goes so far as to consider a moral virtue the inherent capability or personal character to attract great writers and honest officials into one's coterie. In his "Preface to the Collected Works of the Crown Prince Chao-ming," this virtue occurs as the fourth of fifteen sections, immediately after essential Confucian kinship obligations: filial piety toward one's father, love for one's mother, and fraternal affection.

There is another item by Hsiao Kang which has bearing on attracting literati into a salon. This is his "Ch'i-li" ("Seven Persuasions") (*YKC* 3014), the only extant example of his attempt at the "sevens" form. The "sevens" genre originated with a lengthy rhymeprose composition by the Han poet, Mei Sheng (second century B.C.), entitled "Ch'i-fa" ("Seven Stimuli"). Mei Sheng's composition consisted of a preface and seven parts, and took the form of a dialogue between the ailing heir apparent of Ch'u and a foreign visitor at his court. The visitor attempted to stir the prince out of his listlessness by describing the attractions of worldly delights. The prince recovered only after hearing of the seventh stimulus: intellectual pursuits in the company of great scholars. The composition conforms exactly to one of the prime functions of literature during the Han times—the moral regeneration of the ruler. Mei Sheng's moral could not be more obvious.

Eight centuries after Mei Sheng, Hsiao Kang might be permitted some variation in the incentives offered, though on the whole he remained faithful to the original model. What is significant, giving an excellent indication of the change of climate at court and the general function of literature, is that in Hsiao Kang's "sevens" the roles are reversed: it is the prince who importunes the "visitor." And instead of the moral regeneration of the sovereign, we have an attempt to attract a hermit-intellectual into a court salon.

The cornerstones of Hsiao Kang's own literary salon were laid early in his childhood. Yü Chien-wu at twenty was assigned to the service of the infant Prince of Chin-an. He continued in Hsiao Kang's employ, enjoying the flourishing literary activity in Yung province, and eventually followed his master into the East Palace. Next came the learned Hsü Ch'ih, who in 509 at the age of thirty-six became Attendant of Studies to the five-year-old Hsiao Kang at Shih-t'ou. Like Yü Chien-wu, he spent more than thirty years in Hsiao Kang's employ and ended his life in his master's service.

Chang Shuai (475–527) offended Emperor Wu by a cavalier attitude toward his official responsibilities, and in 509 he was transferred into Hsiao Kang's service. He stayed with Hsiao Kang for the subsequent decade, during which time he was "treated with the greatest courtesy and grace." Six years after this appointment, in 515, another distinguished scholar was added to the roll when Lu Ch'ui (470–526) joined Hsiao Kang's entourage. A prolific poet during Ch'i times, Yü Hsi ended his life early in Liang as a courtier of Hsiao Kang. And for a short period at the end of his life, around 518, the man who laid one of the cornerstones of Chinese literary criticism, Chung Hung, was appointed to Hsiao Kang's service in Tan-yang. This appointment had far-reaching consequences both on Hsiao Kang's personal views and on the course of the development of Chinese poetics.

Over the years the complement of Hsiao Kang's salon saw many changes. It would be interesting to know what, if any, recourse the princes in the provinces had to request the services of a particular man or to refuse anyone Emperor Wu saw fit to send them. But in any case, Hsiao Kang was a gregarious man, and his position in the realm brought him at least acquaintance with anyone of importance or ability. The most commonly cited list of personnel is in Yü Chien-wu's biography in the *Dynastic History of Liang*:

> When T'ai-tsung [Hsiao Kang] was in the provinces, he much enjoyed the company of the literary scholars. At the time, [Yü] Chien-wu, together with Hsü Ch'ih of Tung-hai, Lu Kao of Wu-chün, Liu Tsun of P'eng-ch'en, Liu Hsiao-i, and his younger brother Liu Hsiao-wei were all entertained with great hospitality. Then when [Hsiao Kang] was in residence in the East Palace, he opened up the palace to the Virtue of Literature and there set up his scholars, Chien-wu's son Yü Hsin, Hsü Ch'ih's son Hsü Ling, [Chang Shuai's son] Chang Ch'ang-kung of Wu-chün, the northern *mahassatva* Fu Hung, Pao Chih of Tung-hai, and others, all of whom enjoyed the fullest approbation of their patron. (*LS* 49.7ab)

Yü's biography in the *Dynastic History of the South* is more specific in identifying Yung province as the center of Hsiao Kang's provincial literary activities. It presents a rather different list of names, half of them otherwise unknown: "In Yung province, [Yü] was commissioned with Liu Hsiao-wei, Chiang Po-yao, K'ung Ching-t'ung, Shen Tzu-yüeh, Hsü Fang, Hsü Ch'ih, Wang Yu, K'ung Shuo, and Pao Chih, numbering ten persons in all, to transcribe and compile the literary repositories. They were lavishly entertained by their patron and were spoken of collectively as the Scholars of the Lofty Studio" (*NS* 50.11b).

Apart from these scholars, a Hsiao family group was also associated with Hsiao Kang in the East Palace. One of his cousins,

Hsiao Hua, was popular among the imperial family and was one of Hsiao Kang's special protégés. Hsiao Hua held private dinner parties with his brother Hsiao Ying and his cousins Hsiao Cheng-li (younger brother of Hsiao Cheng-te) and Hsiao T'ui (Hsiao Hsiu's son). They became known as the Four Comrades of the East Palace. Hsiao Kang would have them in his presence five or six times every day.

Another list of personnel, giving current appointment, age, and style, includes thirty-eight names of men associated with Hsiao Kang in a vast compilation of Buddhist materials. The list appears at the end of the Prince of Hsiang-tung's preface to the compilation.[13] The association of these men in this prolonged seminar cut across salon and factional interests. Contributions must have been delivered to Hsiao Kang at his court in Yung province from the several other metropolitan and provincial centers for the greater part of the duration of the project.

A tightly woven fabric of friendships and family interests can be fashioned from this list, serving to broaden our view of the new Liang nobility, which was frequently drawn from the arriviste scholars and the poorer families. Most important, it shows how official posts within the salons had become hereditary. Recruitment into government service was officially conducted under the old Han and Wei system known as the rectification of the nine grades (chiu-p'in chung-cheng). Theoretically, administrators graded the local population into nine ranks, according to moral and intellectual qualities. Recommendation was an important factor in the process. Thus, through their own recommendation, men already in court service ensured that their sons would gain employment. This nepotism preserved family influence and economic prosperity, and prevented the clan from retrogressing into poor family status. The son normally acquired the office and rank held by his father. Thus, after a generation or two the office and rank, de facto, became a hereditary privilege, the prerogative of a particular family or families considered to hold suitable status within the hierarchy of the nobility.

Intricate kinship relations also developed between sovereign and courtier. In time, members of the younger generation of Liang gentry became Hsiao Kang's in-laws, and naturally the granting of a royal bride or selection of a consort indicated that family's paramount status. Family status derived in part from the regional origins of its ancestry, in part from the precedence of emigration to the South, and in part from the hereditary ranks and offices held by members of the clan. The Wang, Hsieh, Yuan, and Hsiao were the oldest and most illustrious of the émigré families from the old Northern capital of Loyang. The native Southern gentry, considered inferior to the northern émigrés and frequently at odds with them, included the Chu and the Chang. Then there were other important families from various provincial districts.

In the matter of formal marriage, a girl from no less than the Wang clan was chosen for Hsiao Kang; but his properly numerous other womenfolk were drawn from the Hsieh, Ch'u, Ch'en, and Chu clans. One of his sisters was married to Chang Tsan, while Chang's son, Chang Hsi, and his nephew, Chang Kuan, were married to Hsiao Kang's daughters. Members of the Wang and Liu clans were also indirectly related by marriage to Hsiao Kang. Furthermore, these in-laws were all officers at Hsiao Kang's court.

Court protocol was naturally a concern of highest importance in the static, privilege-conscious society of these aristocrats, and many of the official biographies of Liang personalities are in large part taken up with researches and decisions on matters of precedent. The marriage of Hsiao Kang's fifth son, Ta-lien, to one of the Wang girls raised such a problem, and it was Hsü Ch'ih who was delegated to resolve the question. Hsü's biography reads:

The Duke of Lin-ch'eng [Ta-lien] married into the Wang clan; the girl was a niece of Hsiao Kang's wife, Wang Ling-pin. Since Chin and Sung times, it was the custom for the new bride to visit her parents-in-law and to be inspected by the assembled guests there. A precedent from the ritual of the Ch'un-ch'iu period [771–479 B.C.] states that on the *ting-ch'ou* day the bride arrives. On the *wu-yin* day [the next day] the husband sends the grand officers to pay their respects to the wife, hidden behind a veil. All former precedents agreed with this formula, and it was mooted that the tradition be continued. Hsiao Kang sought Hsü Ch'ih's opinion. Hsü said, "The *Book of Ritual* states, 'At dawn, the new bride is interviewed by her parents-in-law,' The *Various Records* also state, 'The wife meets the parents-in-law. Her brothers and sisters, standing in the hall below, formally announce that the bride is of an exogamous line. Her refinements and accomplishments have not yet been investigated, and the reason why she remains in attendance for three mornings is so that her seven virtues may be observed. Her father-in-law engages the exogamous guests; the mother-in-law leads the family visitors. The rites in the hall below are thereby completed in full ceremony. In recent times, if the bride is already related exogamously to her parents-in-law, no inspection takes place.' This girl is the niece of Madam Wang, and there are already connections through marriage. The ceremony of inspection may be curtailed." (*LS* 30.10ab; *NS* 62.14b–15a; *YKC* 3243)

Hsiao Kang accepted Hsü Ch'ih's recommendation and mercifully released the girl from her ordeal:

The ceremony of the crimson goose is the term given to the union of two surnames. A banquet is also held so that the relationship be not set asunder. Though only hazelnuts and spiced meats be served, a wedding breakfast must be offered. Though the headdress be of crosspins and jewels, a regalia must be prepared. That the ceremony of inspection be dispensed with is permitted only when kinsmen are lacking. Recently we sent gifts of sweet wine in token of respect, and have already complied with the marriage regulations. But offering the bowl, pouring water, and washing the hands is not performed in the case of high aristocracy. This is to appreciate that luxury and simplicity are not the same, and that substance and ornamentation belong to different worlds. The Duke of Lin-ch'eng's wife is the niece of my own spouse. This ceremony may be dispensed with.[14] (*YKC* 3000)

An example of the tendency for ranks and offices to become hereditary is provided by Hsiao Tzu-hsien (489–537) and his two sons, Hsiao Hsü (d. 549) and Hsiao K'ai (506–549), all of whom spent their lives with Hsiao Kang. There is an interesting notice in the dynastic histories referring to Hsiao K'ai and his father, giving more information about activities in Hsiao Kang's salon:

K'ai was famed for his scholarly abilities, and at the time people used to argue whether or not he was actually superior to his father. T'ai-tsung [Hsiao Kang] was prompt in welcoming him into the East Palace. Once ... K'ai ... was invited to a feast. ... During the proceedings, a poetry competition was held in which the contestants had to include the same fifteen difficult rhymes. K'ai was the first to finish, and furthermore he had produced a most beautiful composition. T'ai-tsung... said: "... Among the arrivistes there is Hsiao K'ai, who is most praiseworthy; I do believe he has great ability." (*LS* 35.9a)

Following this description of a salon literary game and evidence of the nobility's preoccupation with family status is a detail about Hsiao Kang's involvement in the lexicon known as the *Yü-p'ien*, compiled by the Liang classicist, historian, astronomer, geographer, painter, and specialist in the ancient script and philology, Ku Yeh-wang (512–574): "Ku Yeh-wang presented his compilation *Yü-p'ien*, commissioned under imperial auspices. T'ai-tsung rather suspected that there might be errors and omissions in the work. K'ai was particularly learned in philology and so [Hsiao Kang] appointed him, together with other scholars, to edit Ku's presentation" (*ibid.*). This work in thirty folios, completed in 543, was revised during T'ang and the original form was lost. Hsiao Kang's suspicions of its quality might have been based on criteria other than objective philology. In the first place, the Ku family was associated with rival salons, in particular with Hsiao Kang's bêtes noires, P'ei Tzu-yeh and Chu I. Furthermore, Ku Yeh-wang was of the native southern aristocracy, more or less an "out" group as far as the northerners were concerned.

Probably the most cogent of Hsiao Kang's objections related to dialect and pronunciation. The *Yü-p'ien* lexicon is arranged under a system of 542 radicals, based on the 540-radical arrangement of the great Han lexicon, *Shuo-wen chieh-tzu* (compiled by Hsü Shen in A.D. 121). The basis of such arrangement is of course graphic; however, by the mid–sixth century, especially through experience of translating foreign Buddhist materials, the tonal structure of the Chinese language was well understood; and phonology, and in particular its application in poetry, was at this time a subject of great interest. The *fan-yü*, or *fan-ch'ieh*, system of phonetics, by which the pronunciation of a graph is illustrated by splitting the pronunciation of two other graphs

respectively into initial and final and combining the two separate
elements, had been practiced at least since the second century
A.D. Within less than sixty years after Ku Yeh-wang's lexicon,
in A.D. 601, Lu Fa-yen compiled the *Ch'ieh-yün,* a dictionary
arranged by rhymes, based on the *fan-ch'ieh* system of phonetics,
which of course must have been developed from earlier proto-
types.

The pronunciation of the North, remembered from pre-émigré
times and reinforced to some extent by expeditions, embassies,
and trade exchanges, was regarded as orthodox in the Southern
courts and became a snobbish affectation among the learned
aristocracy, who ridiculed the lax speech habits of the poorly
educated members of their class and the various provincial dia-
lects of both northern and southern districts. Ku Yeh-wang's
native southern ancestry and his southern Wu accent would
have disqualified him in Hsiao Kang's mind for any such lexico-
graphic activity.

The Liang aristocrat, Yen Chih-t'ui (529–591), prided himself
on his exquisite Loyang diction and wrote much on this subject.
He cites specific occasions of wit and satire directed against
mispronunciation. He records how an intoxicated courtier mis-
read the name of Ying province as Yung province. Told of the
faux pas, Hsiao Kang remarked sarcastically, "He confuses the
place name Ying, where the Wu army entered on the *keng-ch'en*
day, with the *ssu-li.*" Hsiao Kang is showing off his classical
erudition and his discrimination of phonetic nicety: the references
are to the defeat of Ch'u state by the viscount of Wu, where-
upon on the *keng-ch'en* day (in the eleventh month of 505 B.C.)
Wu entered Ying (Ch'u territory); and to the Later Han *ssu-li
chiao-wei* officer, Pao Yung.[15]

Hsiao Kang, litterateur that he was, was indeed an adept
punster. Yen Chih-t'ui reports how he was never slow to make
fun of unlucky phrases and lines by his colleagues. For example,
a line by the Liang musician and essayist, Fei Ch'ang, reads,
"pu chih shih yeh fei" (I do not know whether this is right or
wrong); and another by Yin Yün reads, "yao yang yün mu chou"
(toss about in a mica boat). Hsiao Kang caught the chance of
punning on *yeh,* an interrogative particle, and *yeh* (father). He
split the term *yün mu* (mica) into its separate components, the

homophone *yün* for the poet's personal name, and *mu* (mother). He then combined the two lines as "Ch'ang does not know who his father is, and again Yün tosses his mother."[16]

As well as creative literary activities and philological interests, book collecting was a feature of the salon during the Southern Dynasties. The Liang era witnessed the founding of some very extensive libraries, and bibliographic compilation went on apace. Mere possession of a coveted text could enhance a man's status at court. For example, a distant scion of the Hsiao clan, Hsiao Chen, was serving in the provinces when he came upon an ancient text of a preface and biographical section of the *Dynastic History of the Han* in a monk's bottle-gourd. Hsiao Chen was convinced it was a genuine manuscript by the author himself, Pan Ku, and acquired it from the monk. The text differed considerably from those current during Liang times; the paper and ink were also ancient. The characters were "like dragons, neither the clerical *li* style nor the *chuan* seal script." (*LS* 26.8b) Hsiao Chen kept it to himself until he had deciphered it; then he presented it to his superior, Hsiao Fan, who in turn presented it to the crown prince. There was another instance where a noble family had fallen on hard times but retained a rare edition of the Han history. Having no breakfast to eat, the son suggested selling the manuscript, but the father replied that such a treasure could not be sold for mere sustenance. Actually, this concentration of manscripts, many of them rare even then, had disastrous consequences. Most of the great collections in the hands of the court nobility were destroyed or dispersed and lost during the swift attrition by which the Liang was brought to collapse.[17]

Hsiao Kang of course led the way in library building. A number of his writings discuss efforts to locate texts. In his "Seven Persuasions"—a prince's attempts to attract a hermit into court service—the subject of books comes up as the fifth incentive—the turning point in the hitherto abortive efforts. At the first mention of the court library, Hsiao Kang has the hermit show signs of being swayed. After the prince's long recital of famous stories and legends to be enjoyed in the histories and records—a long way from the utilitarian, didactic Confucian concepts of history and historiography—the hermit's "face lit up and he showed great interest." "Though I am only a rustic," he said,

"I am rather fond of the classical writings. But then, I've been carrying firewood and I'm rather weary. I cannot accept your invitation." Like the personal qualities that attract scholars into one's salon, Hsiao Kang considered devotion to book collecting a desirable virtue. In the list of Crown Prince Chao-ming's virtues, book-collecting is the thirteenth of fifteen sections. Hsiao Kang describes how "the schools of Punishments and Names, Mohists and Confucians" are all to be found in the crown prince's library, "each in its thick or thin wrapper of blue silk, including the most uncommon rarities," and how he "sought out surviving fragments, dispatched searchers, and rewarded bibliographic finds with gold" (*YKC* 3017). (Similar remarks were made in Liu Hsiao-cho's "Preface to a Collection of Crown Prince Chao-ming's Works" [*YKC* 3312].) Hsiao Kang lists the fourteenth of Chao-ming's fifteen virtues as his collation of ancient texts, lending ancient books to copy, and correction of graphic errors.

In these cultured circles, art was closely associated with literature. The Prince of Hsiang-tung had a good eye for painting and was himself an artist of the first order. Hsiao Kang does not appear to have had outstanding talent as a painter, though he no doubt tried his hand at it and was probably technically proficient. A work by Yü Chien-wu grades famous calligraphers of the past,[18] and there were a number of great calligraphers in Hsiao Kang's service at one time or another.[19] Both the formerly despised draft (*ts'ao*) script and the official script were highly appreciated at the time. Hsiao Kang, too, enjoyed fine calligraphy, and a fragment exists of a letter he wrote to the Prince of Hsiangtung thanking him for the gift of a scroll (*YKC* 3011).

Chess was another favorite pastime with Hsiao Kang and his friends. By the nature of the game, this must have occupied a great deal of their time. Literary discussions of chess were in vogue, indicating its wide appeal among the nobility. Judging from Hsiao Kang's contribution, he must have been a veritable grand master; two of his monographs on the subject, totaling six folios, were extant in T'ang,[20] but only a few lines of a preface have survived until now. However, even this fragment testifies to the associations with astronomy that characterized the Chinese version of the game in those times.[21]

All extant historical records combine in massive evidence that Hsiao Kang was surrounded with the companionship of men of great literary talent, sincerity, and high moral character. Nearly all are recorded as having been child prodigies in scholarship and literary composition; in fact, the rubber-stamp reiteration of the form and wording[22] of these eulogies does indeed grow wearisome to the reader. The formula usually includes a witty and epigrammatic nickname for the subject, said to have been uttered by a kinsman, or by a literary baron at the capital whose patronage was being enlisted. For his part, Hsiao Kang is cited for his genuine regard and generosity toward his friends and colleagues.

However, these testimonials occur in the very biographies of the men whose friendship with Hsiao Kang is being described. The tendentious nature of the report then becomes apparent: Hsiao Kang's interest and generosity, and especially his rank of crown prince, are cited only to illustrate the subjects' high standing in the realm. As supporters of the "legitimate" regime, these men are of "high moral character," and so on. Conversely, friends of "out" personages like Hsiao Lun and Hsiao Cheng-te become "ruffians," and what might otherwise be called a "salon" becomes a "gang." Hsiao Kang's own writings often coincide with historical opinion; but this too is uncertain evidence because the historical records are based on just such writings as these, with all their biases and prejudices. The literary abilities of Hsiao Kang's friends are nevertheless well attested to by the surviving works, and evidence of their close association with Hsiao Kang is apparent in the literary corpus surviving from that time.

For whatever purposes the records may have been compiled and preserved, Hsiao Kang's generous patronage is too widely attested to be seriously doubted. And in his own writings, formulaic as they may all too often be, his affection for the members of his entourage cannot be obscured.

One such piece is a letter he composed on the death of a special favorite.[23] This item is incidentally useful in throwing more light on the activities in court salons of the time, and it illustrates what was admired in personal qualities. The man had been filial and fraternal; he showed integrity and firmness and enjoyed a fine reputation among his colleagues. He was learned in letters and in the histories, and he was ambitious in his official duties. He conducted a fine provincial administration and commanded the respect of the common people even after he had been transferred elsewhere. He was humble, and never troubled himself with glory and riches. Never a day went by, says Hsiao Kang, when there were no meetings. "Wine parties ended up with ears growing warm; we expressed ourselves in poetry. We discussed men's characters . . . and debated the problems of belles lettres and history."[24]

In a society which demanded regular transfer of officials from one provincial post to another, farewells made up a large proportion of the literature of the period. Some are merely eulogies. Some dwell on season and the hardships of travel.[25] In one such piece Hsiao Kang reiterates his grumbles about official duties and asks for news:

Duties at one's office are troublesome; registers and records proliferate. . . . [Your] abilities in the carving of dragons [literary excellence] are inherent.[26] . . . You take some measure of ease in chapters and verses and find leisure in literary composition and reading. Recently, grasping your mace of office you set out westwards. You pass through cold and heat.[27] The morning river has not fallen; it brushes by the cassia craft as it presses onwards. The evening birds return to the thicket, but the lonely sail unfurled rests not. Enough to vex the heart frontier-bound, while thoughts of home turn ceaselessly.[28] But since we parted, we have long had no news of you. We are concerned for you, waking and sleeping. Please reply by return to comfort our thoughts of you. ("Letter to Liu Hsiao-cho," *IWLC* 30; *YKC* 3010)

Expressions of approval fill the pages of the standard histories and literary anthologies. But however congenial the atmosphere at Hsiao Kang's court, there appear hints of peccadilloes, quarrels, and disagreements inevitable among so distinguished a group of creative litterateurs. Hsiao Kang lost two important literati when Lu Ch'ui and Yü Yü-ling (Yü Chien-wu's brother) were cashiered for corrupt practices. The dismissal of his cousin Hsiao T'e (Hsiao Tzu-yün's son), a renowned calligrapher, from his retinue shows that while these aristocrats may have been above the law, they could not with impunity disregard the code of ethics of their peers.[29]

In court disputes Hsiao Kang usually comes out well as a tolerant man who relied upon his own observation in preference to rumored slander. This tolerance is exemplified by an incident at a feast attended by a kinsman, Hsiao Tzu-hsien. The histories state that Hsiao Tzu-hsien was "a stern, terse man, vigorous in his ways and unafraid even of ghouls and goblins." (*NS* 42.14b) Unfortunately, he tended to make an exhibition of his abilities and authority as a favorite of the court. Worse still, he ignored the various staff officers and guests at court and would not deign to speak to them. Instead, he would merely raise his fan and shake it. The court as a whole secretly detested him, but Hsiao Kang rather gave weight to his manly qualities. Hsiao Kang used to feast with his colleagues at the East Palace. On one such occasion, Tzu-hsien—an inveterate drinker—disregarded all ceremony and rose to "change his dress." To the seated company Hsiao Kang good-humoredly punned: "I once heard that from time to time an unusual man will 'emerge.' Today for the first time I realize that this refers to none other than the Minister Hsiao!" (*LS* 35.7b).

Some sort of feud is said to have existed between one of the Liu family and Hsü Ch'ih's son, Hsü Ling (507–583). Hsü Ling was dismissed on charges of corruption, but Hsiao Kang continued to respect his literary genius and invited Hsü to collaborate in a number of literary projects, the most important of which was the anthology *Yü-t'ai hsin-yung*.

The wealth of incidental detail in the dynastic histories provides rich description of salon life during Liang. In particular it permits further insight into Hsiao Kang's character, confirming the impression of him as a courteous, tolerant, independent-minded, and good-humored patron. It becomes clear too that even the highest royalty were personally associated with their entourage and were involved in the everyday issues and events at court. They were by no means the secluded, semi-mystical figures of later eras.

CHAPTER 4

Literary Theory

LIANG writings represent the apogee of the trend toward excessively ornamented composition which, already well established in the early fourth century, continued through Sung and Ch'i. In any discussion of this work we must keep in mind the court environment, in which interests were predominantly focused upon aesthetic pleasures to the virtual exclusion of other activities, government not excepted. Literary games and competition between rival court salons and factions resulted in a group literature largely devoid of individual characteristics. But these same conditions also led to heightened standards of critical insight. Literary theories evolved from the controversies that arose during the Ch'i and that culminated in the most highly developed canons of Chinese literary criticism and theory during early Liang.

In the sense that literary skill was a prime factor in gaining official and social advancement, and that one's literary views were important in gaining entrée to the various salons and factions, literature was a political activity. There is at least one instance of a courtier who pleased Emperor Wu by his skill at extempore verse being awarded official promotion on the spot. Naturally, men were attracted to literary activity in the hope of similar advancement; in fact, the fifty years of the Liang dynasty produced significantly more poets (according to extant works) than any of the Southern dynasties from Chin through Ch'en. In the same sense, an attack on a man's literary views and his work in an attempt to discredit him at court was a political attack. These political implications should not of course be overemphasized to the obfuscation of the genuine literary interests of the Liang nobility, but they should at least be borne in mind as one of the many crosscurrents in the factional bickering over literary theory.

Hsiao Kang's literary tastes were largely derived from his tutor, Hsü Ch'ih, and from Yü Chien-wu, both of whom remained in his service from his first years. His literary views, however, reflect the influence Chung Hung exerted on him, although Chung spent only a few months at his court. Hsiao Kang's own erudite and interested mind matured under Hsü Ch'ih's broad tutorage and in daily association with his literary friends. His writings cover a wide variety of subjects; he exploited most of the genres then available; and he appears in the van of the literary experimentation of the day.

Generally accurate textual references[1] throughout his work reveal a comprehensive training and grasp of the Confucian canon, the histories and the philosophies. As a philosophical writer himself, he lectured on the *I-ching* (*Changes*), the *Lao-tzu,* and the *Chuang-tzu,* and gave sermons on Buddhist doctrine. As a man of letters his predilection was for the *Shih-ching* (*Odes*) and the *Ch'u-tz'u* (*Songs of the South*). The *Songs of the South* in particular must have exemplified his ideal of the principle of "giving expression in song to one's feelings,"[2] as stated in the "Great Preface" to the *Odes* (although he vehemently refuted the utilitarian concepts expressed in the continuation of this line, "to condemn one's superiors"). On more than one occasion Hsiao Kang identified himself with the legendary figure Ch'ü Yüan (343?–290? B.C.), to whom the most important items of the *Songs of the South* are attributed.

He was much impressed, too, with the works of the Ts'ao royalty of the Wei dynasty (220–265), and from time to time with remarkable nicety he reiterated phrases from Ts'ao compositions. An introduction to Hsiao Kang's collected works by Chang P'u (1602–1641) indicates that such taste was commonly shared during Liang:

In the palace the days grew longer and the courts gave themselves over to parties and feasting. [Hsiao Kang] together with his elder brother, Crown Prince Chao-ming, and his younger brother, the Prince of Hsiang-tung, competed in the beauty of their literary composition. After the succession had been established, palace-style literature flourished. This style made a special feature of extravagant embellishment, while light and florid subject matter was not avoided.

Writers cherished Ts'ao P'ei's qualities, but their style was not the
antiquity of the Huang-ch'u era [220–226; Ts'ao P'ei's year-title].
That too was surely the influence of their times![3]

Yen Chih-t'ui observes that Hsiao Kang also "had a ... taste for
the works of T'ao Yüan-ming [T'ao Ch'ien (365–427)]."[4] Hsiao
Kang's attitudes indeed confirm his distaste, exemplified by T'ao,
for the vulgar world and for official cares.

Throughout his life (first as a provincial governor and then as
crown prince) the leader of an important literary court salon
and patron of an influential faction whose literary practice remained in the vanguard of literary trends, Hsiao Kang confronted
one and all of the rival factions of the 520s and early 530s. Emperor Wu's salon was of course the most powerful of these
various factions and was attended by the highest and most
favored ministers of state, and by his Eight Comrades from his
own provincial days, among whom were the great literary barons
Shen Yüeh, Jen Fang and Chiang Yen—men who controlled
recommendations into metropolitan court circles. Both Shen
Yüeh and Jen Fang held their own courts; entrée into Jen
Fang's Orchid Terrace Association was particularly coveted.
Also at the capital was Crown Prince Chao-ming's orthodox
school, served by one of the foremost Chinese literary critics,
Liu Hsieh. In the provinces, the Prince of Hsiang-tung held
court at Chiang-ling, the bastion of the ancient school led by
P'ei Tzu-yeh, and the haven of the Hsieh Ling-yün school.

These several factions came to similar conclusions in their
analyses of current literature. They all understood the problem
of imitation. Uncritical imitation defeated its own object; the
writer failed to achieve the excellence of his model and lost
his own individual quality. They all complained of the concentration on ornament, generally at the expense of content, that
at best only obscured the writer's meaning. Acrimony arose
from the strong political overtones that attended acceptance
or rejection of their respective solutions to these problems. A
basic conflict arose, with especially serious political consequences,
over their understanding of what constituted literature. In this
conflict they all turned to similar sources, in particular the
"Great Preface" ("Ta-hsü") to the *Odes*, for the interpretation

of the origins and function of literature that best supported their respective views.

Hsiao Kang saw the purpose of literature as giving expression in song to one's feelings, unfettered by borrowings and imitations of style and content. The "Airs of the States" ("Kuo-feng") of the *Odes* and the "Lament" ("Sao") of the *Songs of the South* were to Hsiao Kang the epitome of poetic expression. Ch'u Yüan, to whom the "Lament" was attributed, and whose expression of personal sentiment remained unrivaled for its breadth, profundity, and elegance, was a hero with whom Hsiao Kang repeatedly identified. Hsiao Kang's ideas were in essence a rudimentary theory of pure literature; the expression of these ideas is strongly reminiscent of the "Rhymeprose on Literature" ("Wen fu") by Lu Chi (261–303) and of the *Classification of Poetry* (*Shih-p'in*) by Chung Hung (d. 518).

Crown Prince Chao-ming was conscious of the ennobling influence of literature. With Liu Hsieh he emphasized the classics as models for composition to ensure the gravity and authority which could not otherwise be attained. P'ei Tzu-yeh, too, quoted the "Great Preface" to the *Odes*; but where the litterateur Hsiao Kang was concerned with the free voicing of sentiment in the *Odes,* untrammeled by artificial rhetoric, P'ei Tzu-yeh the historian recalled the statement in the "Great Preface" that the purpose of the *Odes* was to "condemn one's superiors," and thus reaffirmed the Han Confucian concept of the political function of poetry.

Hsiao Kang presented no single, systematic statement of his literary views. These must be gleaned from surviving items of correspondence and from prefaces. It is as much for this reason as for any other that Hsiao Kang's important contribution as a rare critic of the orthodox Chinese concept of literature has largely been overlooked, in contrast with that of his rival contemporaries and colleagues Shen Yüeh, Crown Prince Chao-ming (*Wen-hsüan*), the Prince of Hsiang-tung (*Chin-lou-tzu*), Liu Hsieh (*Wen-hsin tiao-lung*), Chung Hung (*Shih-p'in*), Hsü Ling (*Yü-t'ai hsin-yung*), and Yen Chih-t'ui (*Yen-shih chia-hsün*). The most sustained of Hsiao Kang's writings on literary criticism is a communication he addressed to the Prince of Hsiang-tung soon after Hsiao Kang became crown prince. For the most part, the item is a complaint about current literary practice and was not intended as an exegesis on principles of literary theory such as Liu Hsieh and Chung Hung had formulated. But subjective and topical as these complaints are, the letter gives a comprehensive picture of the literary scene in the Southern courts of mid-sixth-century China.

We too have no place for amusements.[5] All we may do is spread our books and read. I am by nature inclined toward literary pursuits and from time to time compose short verses. They are but a commonplace sound,[6] but I cannot lay down my pen and am ashamed of the endemic impulse to show off what I can do.

When I regard the literary styles at the capital, so utterly uninspired, with writers competing in shallowness and superficiality and contending in the refinement of drawn-out intonation, though I stay awake deep into the winter evenings, I cannot fathom why this should be so. Their works are quite devoid of the principles of metaphor [pi] and allegory [hsing], and are diametrically opposed to the tradition of gentle remonstrance [feng] and lament [sao]. There are occasions when the "Six Statutes"[7] and the "Three Canons of Etiquette"[8] may be applied: in the event of good or bad fortune and in social intercourse,[9] there is an apt usage for them. But I have never heard of anyone giving expression in song to his feelings[10] turning around and copying the style of the "Rules for Women";[11] and how much less would anyone taking up his pen to describe some notion[12] imitate the "Injunction against Drunkenness"![13] "As the spring days lengthen,"[14] they imitate the "Kuei-tsang."[15] "On, on the river's waters roll,"[16] yet they simulate the "Great Treatise."[17]

I am rather a clumsy writer myself, and dare not lightly make specific and individual criticisms.[18] But contemporary works are without exception imitations of the great writers of former times: in the distant past, Yang [Hsiung], [Ssu]-ma [Hsiang-ju], Ts'ao [Chih], and Wang [Ts'an]; and more recently, P'an [Yüeh], Lu [Chi], Yen [Yen-chih], and Hsieh [Ling-yün]. But when I observe [contemporary] use of words and functioning of mind,[19] these bear no comparison with these former writers. If one subscribes to the literary practices of today, then one must oppose those of antiquity; if one acknowledges the praiseworthiness of the earlier literary giants, then one has to reject present-day styles. I cannot allow that one can contribute to both sides at once.[20]

Then again, there are those today who imitate the work of Hsieh K'ang-lo and the Grand Nuncio [hung-lu] P'ei [Tzu-yeh]. I have my doubts about this, too. Why so? Hsieh K'o[21] gushed forth words that were heaven-sent; his origins were in natural spontaneity.[22] But sometimes he was just too unrestricted, and what he wrote at such times was no more than dregs. Now P'ei for his part excelled at historical writing, but his work lacks the beauty of the *Odes*.[23] And so, by copying Hsieh one does not attain his vitality or his vividness. All one achieves is his verbosity.[24] In taking P'ei as one's model one never captures his merits, only his shortcomings. Hsieh's art is beyond reach; P'ei's unadorned writing should not be admired.

Hence those people, full of fanciful preconceptions,[25] the sort who care only for empty name, ignoring reality,[26] imitate the virtuous beast in its sharing its prey,[27] or mimic the Han-tan stroll.[28] Having entered the fish market, they become accustomed to its stench and no longer notice it.[29] Imitation more than anything else leads to calamity.[30] In breaking a feather with Master Hsieh, how can those writers equal one of the three thousand?[31] They prostrate themselves before Master P'ei, fearful lest the two T'ang should not be recorded.[32]

Thus it is that silken jade thongs and golden bow mounts are objects of derision in ignorant eyes.[33] Rustic jingles have more appeal to the people of Ying. The "Yang-ch'un" was lofty music and difficult to accompany.[34] Now its wondrous melody is lost and is heard no more. In the end, those writers do not vigorously investigate all the finest details,[35] nor do they balance embellishment and content. They differ from the artistic mind[36] and are after all put to shame by the true master. That is why the scholar clasped his jade[37] and, looking toward Cheng, realized that he must retire; and the wearer of the ceremonial cap and kingfisher shoe gazed toward the Man territories and sighed.[38] Poetry having come to this, prose, too, follows suit. Only the inkstick cannot complain and must suffer the abuse of its stain. Paper and tablet have no feelings and must endure shaking and pleating. A serious matter indeed, that literature should have deviated to this extent.

As for contemporary writings, the poetry of Hsieh T'iao and Shen Yüeh and the prose of Jen Fang and Lu Ch'ui are indeed the crown of belles-lettres and the models for documentary writing. The rhymeprose compositions of Chang Shih-chien and the dialectics [*pien*] of Chou Shen-i are also masterworks.[39] It will not be easy to meet with such men as these again. If belles-lettres are not to degenerate, someone of outstanding ability will have to come to the rescue to lead it by the sleeve. If you are not the man to do it, then who is?

Whenever I think of discussing the matter, there is no one with whom I can do so. I think of my Tzu-chien[40] and of talking things over together, discriminating between the clear and the muddy, just like the Ch'ing and Wei rivers.[41] We would practice "first of the month" criticisms as did the [Hsü brothers of] Ju-nan.[42] And when the scarlet and cinnabar have been decided,[43] and we shall know where to apply the ink eradicator,[44] then we shall have disgraced the ratsellers[45] and shamed the flautist.[46] [We shall cause these writers to be like] Yüan Shao, who was afraid to face Tzu-chiang;[47] and [to be like] the ox thief, who was embarrassed that Wang Lieh, though living far away, should have heard of his crime.[48]

I long to see you again and am constantly concerned for you. ("Letter to the Prince of Hsiang-tung," *LS* 49.7b–9b; *YKC* 3011)

The text of the letter appears in Yü Chien-wu's biography in the "Biographies of Distinguished Litterateurs" section of the dynastic histories. The placement here is appropriate. Other men, like Hsü Ch'ih, could similarly claim to have had a lifetime association with Hsiao Kang and to have influenced his thinking. But Hsü's biography, for example, is situated in a section of the histories devoted to antiquarian scholars, where literary debate would be out of place.

The historians' introduction states categorically that the letter was an outcome of Hsiao Kang's concern for the degeneration of literature at the capital:

During the Yung-ming era of Ch'i [483–493], the literati Wang Jung, Hsieh T'iao, and Shen Yüeh first employed the four tones in their composition. This was considered an innovation. Thenceforth [composition] became trammeled in tonality and tended toward a gorgeous degeneracy far exceeding that of former times. At the time, the crown prince [Hsiao Kang] wrote to the Prince of Hsiang-tung discussing it. (*LS* 49.7b)

The historians clearly define "degeneration" as the use of tonality in poetry, and they locate the innovation of tonal euphony in verse at the end of the fifth century. Early in the sixth century Chung Hung completed his *Shih-p'in* and left on record his jeers at Shen Yüeh's attempts to rationalize tonality in formal terms.[49] Hsiao Kang in some ways subscribed to the general tenets of Chung's position, which expressed aversion to artificial restrictions upon instinctive taste. But two decades later, in the 530s, although it was still a crucial literary issue, tonality had been established as an acceptable literary device. Hsiao Kang experimented with tonality in his own verse. In his letter to the Prince of Hsiang-tung he praised the innovators Hsieh T'iao and Shen Yüeh in the highest terms (although, as will be seen, this may have been as much for political reasons as any other). Perhaps he did indeed feel that their innovations in tonality served to enhance rather than hinder their natural expression. It is curious that no mention of so sustained a controversy appears in Hsiao Kang's work. In the entire corpus of his surviving writings there is only one casual and undeveloped reference to the literary term *yün* (rhyme, or consonance);[50] and his criticisms of metropolitan composition in his letter to the Prince of Hsiang-tung include but a single term, having only general connotations of smooth, drawn-out, deliberately retarded musical qualities. If the historians' statement quoted above is pertinent, then it must be assumed that misuse of tonality is implied in Hsiao Kang's strictures against other literary abuses.[51]

Whether Hsiao Kang's motives were political or purely literary, it was not without good reason that he addressed his remarks to the Prince of Hsiang-tung. The prince had been served during his provincial administration by the leaders of the factions that Hsiao Kang criticized in his letter, notably P'ei Tzu-yeh and Wang Chi, and the Prince of Hsiang-tung was known to subscribe to the views they represented. He was a first-class writer himself, and now that Hsiao Kang was at the capital as crown prince, the Prince of Hsiang-tung was the leader of the most important provincial salon. Hsiao Kang called him "my Tzu-chien." Tzu-chien (Ts'ao Chih) was one of the greatest poets in Chinese history and was much admired during Liang. Hsiao Kang thus paid great homage to the Prince of Hsiang-tung's literary talents. But the compliment might have been a backhanded one. Ts'ao Chih had been doomed to political exile after his elder brother, Ts'ao P'ei (186–226), became crown prince. The parallel relationship between the Ts'ao brothers and Hsiao Kang and the Prince of Hsiang-tung is striking and could hardly have escaped notice in Liang times. (There was a prince of Hsiang-tung named Hsiao Tzu-chien, the twenty-first son of

Emperor Wu of Ch'i. He was murdered at the age of thirteen.
Hsiao Kang must have been aware of this family history.) Hsiao
Kang added that whenever he wished to discuss literature there
was no one with whom he could do so, and that only the Prince
of Hsiang-tung's example could reform current literary practices.
Again, it would seem that Hsiao Kang was paying the prince
high praise. But these remarks, too, become more sinister if
their reference were political. In this case, Hsiao Kang's complaint of having no one to talk to would not refer to convivial
literary discussion in his own salon, but would imply that the
most prominent Liang litterateurs who could have challenged
his views—Shen Yüeh, Jen Fang, Chiang Yen, Liu Hsieh, Crown
Prince Chao-ming, P'ei Tzu-yeh—were by now already dead.
He exerted his authority as crown prince and summoned the
Prince of Hsiang-tung to rescue literature from degeneration
and "lead it by the sleeve"; in other words, to silence remaining
opinions contrary to those Hsiao Kang advocated. There is some
support for this latter interpretation in that no literary faction
arose to challenge Hsiao Kang after his accession to the heir-
apparency.

In his opening attack, Hsiao Kang expressed perplexity at the
vogue for pedantic trivialities in the literature of the metropolitan salons. If his perplexity were not mere rhetoric, it
could confirm that the provincial salons were largely out of
touch with day-by-day developments in metropolitan literature.
More likely it is a criticism of the powerful literary barons
who had dominated the central stage. Hsiao Kang had come to
the capital in 529 as governor of Yang province, but, being on
equal terms with other provincial administrators and an outsider
in terms of the metropolitan courts, he could not have expressed
such criticism. Only after he became heir apparent in the
summer of 531 dared he voice his opinions. If the "deep winter
evenings" during which he pondered these literary problems
were the first he spent as crown prince, then he lost no time
in laying his charges!

His theme is the indiscriminate imitation by his contemporaries of the work of leading writers of former times and the
abuse of style and recondite textual references and allusion
unsuited to the subject matter of a composition. He is a just—or

a cunning—critic in that he never condemns outright the object of his attack, and is selective even in tilting at both imitators and their imitations. Hsieh Ling-yün (385–433) and P'ei Tzu-yeh, who were his central targets, are first applauded for their good qualities. These qualities attracted a following; but the trouble arose, said Hsiao Kang, when both the good and bad qualities of such writers were blindly copied by lesser men.

Culprits were never identified. In Hsiao Kang's day, overt mention of their names would have been clumsy overstatement, and in so doing Hsiao Kang might also have risked offending his father, whose friends he was attacking. He did, however, name men—Shen Yüeh, Jen Fang, and Hsieh T'iao (464–499) among others—who warranted his approval. But since these men were all members of Emperor Wu's group, this may again have been an attempt to direct his thrusts away from the throne. Shen Yüeh and Hsieh T'iao, he said, were the "crown of belles-lettres," while Jen Fang and Lu Ch'ui (470–526) were models for prose composition. Indeed, poems by Shen Yüeh and his colleagues appear in the *Yü-t'ai hsin-yung* anthology which Hsiao Kang sponsored, suggesting that he was genuinely impressed by their work. His assessment followed popular opinion, cited in Chung Hung's *Shih-p'in* and in the dynastic histories, which paired "Shen's poetry and Jen's prose."[52] Chung Hung placed these men in the second grade of his categories of poets, as high as he rated any contemporary poet. But he extenuated his commendations. Hsieh T'iao, he said, lacked vigor; Chiang Yen's (444–505) talent was exhausted, and so Shen Yüeh faced no competition for the status he enjoyed.[53]

With the possible exception of Shen Yüeh, the Eight Comrades did in fact only distinguish themselves as arriviste scholars through Emperor Wu's rise to power. By the time they had established their hegemony over the metropolitan literary, and hence political, scene they were already old men. Historical records suggest that they had lost their literary creativity and that, as a substitute for fresh and spontaneous poetic thought, they turned to pedantic scholarship:

[Jen Fang] became known for his literary ability, and at the time people used to say, "Jen's prose, Shen's verse." Jen was much upset by this and in his later years turned to writing poetry to compete with Shen and reverse the judgment. But his work was too full of references and his phraseology never gained fluency. However, writers at the capital all greatly admired his work and went in for burrowing and boring. From this arose the phrase "exhausted talent." (NS 59.9a)

The "burrowing and boring" for references and allusions must be a fair description of Chiang Yen's literary efforts toward the end of his life and of the activity in Jen Fang's Orchid Terrace Association, attended by such men as Liu Hsiao-ch'o (481–539) and Chang Shuai (475–527). These arrivistes were imitated by lesser men hoping for advancement. In particular, Liu Hsiao-ch'o "was the cynosure of the arrivistes, and the whole world gave weight to his work. If he completed a piece in the morning, by evening everyone knew of it. *Au courant* scholars memorized it and copied it out and it was heard throughout the empire." Then there was Wang Hsün (511–536), a favorite of Emperor Wu's court, whose beautiful writings "led the arrivistes by the sleeve." All this must be what Hsiao Kang had in mind when, commending Chang Shuai's rhymeprose and Chou She's dialectics as "masterworks"—a popular opinion during Liang—he cautions that "their like will be hard to meet again."

Another member of the Orchid Terrace Association was Tao Kai (478–549). He had been appointed by Emperor Wu as tutor to the Prince of Hsiang-tung and the prince had been enjoined to take Tao Kai as his model. Like Liu Hsiao-ch'o and Chang Shuai, Tao Kai was known for his association with Crown Prince Chao-ming's orthodox school. No conflict of loyalty or interests arose here, for the reason that by the time the orthodox school was flourishing in the 520s the leaders of the Orchid Terrace Association were dead. The individual could not maintain his status as a member of the literati outside one or another of the salons. It was natural, then, that members of the defunct Orchid Terrace Association should find entrée into another important salon at the capital.

The orthodox school was characterized by the theory that the classics should be the model for literary composition. In the early stages of the school, Liu Hsieh was its principal exponent. He enjoined that just as a heavy bell produces only the most solemn tones, so too the classics impart profound authority to composition modeled after them. Liu Hsieh subscribed to the orthodox Confucian concept of the didactic function of literature; hence, in his view all composition was enhanced by a classical model.[54] Hsiao Kang accepted Liu Hsieh's theory in part but denied its categorical application. For example, he warmly approved of Crown Prince Chao-ming's orthodoxy:

When it came to ascending high ground[55] or descriptive writing [*t'i-wu*][56] he [Crown Prince Chao-ming] developed poetry [*shih*] to express his thoughts in words.[57] The content was as profound as "Yellow Bamboo";[58] the embellishment [*wen*] crowned the "Green Locust Tree." His quotations exemplified the lament [*sao*]; his work encompassed the principles of metaphor [*pi*] and allegory [*hsing*]. He wrote inscriptions [*ming*] even on basins and bowls, and his appreciations [*tsan*] appear on every portrait and image. His "sevens" surpass the purpose of curing ailment,[59] while his memorials [*piao*] were especially forceful. His epitaphs [*pei*] attained the very limits of classical orthodoxy. . . . His discussions [*i*] never strayed from the argument. . . .[60] The correspondence between his literary composition and his emotion was profound; his words attended the very changes of his hand. [How] beautiful [his work]! Yet it avoided licentiousness. ("Preface to the Collected Works of Prince Chao-ming," *YKC* 3017)

Crown Prince Chao-ming, he said, had the ability to handle classical styles. Like tonality in Shen Yüeh's poetry, this orthodoxy enhances the crown prince's natural expression of thought and sentiment and preserves his embellishment from the charge of licentiousness.

What Hsiao Kang consistently condemns in his letter to the Prince of Hsiang-tung is the dull, superficial classicism in metropolitan writings. These writings lacked Crown Prince Chao-ming's profound taste and insight; they were devoid of the orthodox didactic principles of "metaphor" (*pi*) and "allegory" (*hsing*) and of "gentle remonstrance" (*feng*) and "lament" (*sao*).[61] Yet these ancient principles are claimed as the rationale for modeling composition upon the classics. Hsiao Kang was scornful of the insensitivity of writers in suiting style to subject matter. He agreed that the ancient texts had their place, but he ridiculed those writers who quote Confucian canons of uncompromising morality and cosmological mysticsm to express light, personal sentiments. The crown prince's achievement was too hard to emulate; the writings of the so-called classicists fell short of the models they professed to follow. One must choose, said Hsiao Kang, between the products of the current orthodoxy or the orthodox texts themselves. The two were incompatible.

In looking to the ancient classics for models of literary style, the ancient school (*ku-t'i p'ai*) of P'ei Tzu-yeh lay fairly close to the "orthodoxy" of the Crown Prince Chao-ming—Liu Hsieh school, but, like Hsiao Kang, P'ei Tzu-yeh demonstrated his dismay at the overburdening reference in metropolitan verse. P'ei Tzu-yeh had fallen foul of Jen Fang and the city poets early in his career and had spent many years in provincial service, largely with the Prince of Hsiang-tung. He eventually earned redemption and was recalled to the capital for the last ten years of his life. Just before he died, he published an essay entitled "On Insect Carving," in which he discussed current literary practices from the standpoint of the principles of this ancient school.[62]

In practice P'ei Tzu-yeh, and of course his imitators, went far beyond anything Liu Hsieh and the orthodox school envisaged:

Tzu-yeh's style of composition was of a stern, classical air, and swift-written.[63] He gave no value to beautiful and degenerate phraseology. Sentence structure was largely modeled on ancient writings and was completely different from contemporary styles. Some men of his day disparaged him, but toward the end of his life they came to admire him. Someone asked him why his work was so swift-written, and he replied, "Everyone else accomplishes in the hand. I alone accomplish in the mind. Though my work may be disparaged in some quarters, it cannot be edited or improved in any respect." (*LS* 30.4b–5a)

Had P'ei Tzu-yeh restricted his literary activity to writing history, Hsiao Kang would probably have had no complaint to make of him. Indeed, Hsiao Kang readily admitted P'ei's unusual historical ability. P'ei's *Concise History of the Sung Dynasty* (*Sung Lüeh*), based on Shen Yüeh's own history of the Sung, brought him acclaim from Shen himself. Chou She, whose dialectics Hsiao Kang so admired, commended the compilation. P'ei's associates were all historians and bibliographers known for their antiquarian interests, and Emperor Wu conferred immense prestige upon P'ei by approving the work produced by the ancient school.[64] But then P'ei stepped outside of his recognized area of competence and posed as a literary critic—and attacked Hsiao Kang's concept of literature emancipated from all utilitarian functions.

Although there is no direct evidence that Hsiao Kang's letter to the Prince of Hsiang-tung was a specific rebuttal of P'ei Tzu-yeh's essay "On Insect Carving," the chronological juxtaposition of the two items suggests that Hsiao Kang's letter may have been a counterattack, penned as soon as Hsiao Kang had attained a position powerful enough for him to defend himself against possible reprisals. What is important is that after P'ei Tzu-yeh's death in 530, Hsiao Kang immediately set about undermining the support for P'ei's views at the capital and in the provinces. Thus we read that the Prince of Hsiang-tung, who had entertained P'ei in his court salon and had hitherto supported literary classicism, now joined Hsiao Kang "in the vanguard of novel and licentious composition" (*Sui shu* 76.1b, Palace ed.).

Hsiao Kang disparaged P'ei's work for "lacking the beauty of the *Odes*."[65] This cryptic piece of descriptive and comparative criticism, leading into the morass of literary aesthetics, is all the more baffling for lack of clarification from other sources. Hsiao Kang's praise of Crown Prince Chao-ming's epitaph compositions, for example, showed that he recognized that classicism had its place in literary composition. Hsiao Kang demonstrated frequently enough in his own prose writings that allusion and reference could be employed to artistic advantage, though in his verse he eschewed such devices and aimed for the natural spontaneity of the folk song. But nothing could be further from the style of the *Odes* than Hsiao Kang's own poetry! His poetic output was prolific and obviously must demonstrate his poetic values. Occasionally he quoted from other men's

work lines that pleased or offended him, but he made little
objective commentary on these quotations.[66] The most outstanding anomaly is the inclusion of P'ei Tzu-yeh's poetry in the
Yü-t'ai hsin-yung anthology, which exemplifies Hsiao Kang's
"taste for the beautiful and degenerate."

P'ei Tzu-yeh had offended Hsiao Kang on a number of counts.
He advocated archaic syntax and an unadorned, historical style
as a general theory of creative writing. He derided the thesis
proposed by Chung Hung and Hsiao Kang that literature could
and must be emancipated from utilitarian functions. Moreover,
he had been influential. Hsiao Kang's letter was most scathing,
then, in meeting the charges P'ei listed in his "On Insect Carving"
essay, and in defending Hsiao Kang's own literary ideology.
"Having entered the fish market [of imitation]," Hsiao Kang
sneered, P'ei Tzu-yeh's imitators "become accustomed to its
stench"—they lose their independent judgment. Like ignorant
rustics they are incapable of appreciating the refinement of
elegant embellishment—which characterized Hsiao Kang's
composition. The "true master"—Hsiao Kang identified with
Ch'ü Yüan—cannot hope to reform the barbarian taste (at the
capital) for crude doggerel. Like Ch'ü Yüan, he must "sigh"
and "retire" into his own lofty sophistication.

Hsiao Kang, however, was not prepared to "retire." Still
ridiculing imitation, he turned to another school popular enough
to cause him concern. Just as he had denigrated P'ei Tzu-yeh
for being too unmannered, so he denounced Hsieh Ling-yün's
work for its occasional verbosity and lack of discipline. If P'ei
Tzu-yeh's writing was "unadorned" (chih), Hsieh Ling-yün's
work was "artful" (ch'iao).[67] It was not only for prosodic balance that the space allotted to the Hsieh Ling-yün school in
Hsiao Kang's letter equaled that given to P'ei. Hsieh Ling-yün's
landscape tradition (shan-shui) was fundamental to Liang composition, but it posed problems for less able writers. The object
of Hsiao Kang's attack was no secret. In fact, the most ardent
admirer of Hsieh Ling-yün's landscape verse was the subject
of a popular joke: it was said that Wang Chi was merely
another name for Hsieh Ling-yün. "Chi was fond of literature
and had great ability. In writing verse he admired Hsieh
Ling-yün. His [writings] came so close to [Hsieh's style] that

[Hsieh himself] would not have been ashamed of them. At the time, everyone said, 'Wang Chi is to K'ang-lo what Ch'iu-ming was to Chung-ni, or what Yen-chou was to Lao-tan' "[68] (*NS* 21.12a). Wang Chi had been in the Prince of Hsiang-tung's service. He attracted Jen Fang's notice and received invitations to Shen Yüeh's literary meetings, circumstances that brought his work wide acclaim. To his credit, he did take genuine delight in natural scenery, however much he may have copied Hsieh Ling-yün's poetic style. Hsiao Kang was a stern critic of imitation, but even he, who knew a good poem when he saw one, was impressed with some of Wang Chi's verse. Wang Chi's most famous piece, "At Jo-yeh Brook," one of his two surviving poems, was said to transcend the bounds of literary invention. Hsiao Kang "repeated it constantly and could not put it out of his mind."[69]

An older contemporary of Wang Chi was Hsieh T'iao, one of the Eight Comrades. He shared the love of natural scenery enjoyed by Hsieh Ling-yün. Perhaps because Hsieh T'iao's poetry was a free expression of his own sentiments inspired by landscape themes, Hsiao Kang was able to pair Hsieh T'iao's verse with that of Shen Yüeh as the "crown of belles-lettres." So too, Hsiao Kang could praise the work of his brother, Crown Prince Chao-ming, who was a byword for his love of nature. The unpopular Hsiao Tzu-hsien was another "ardent writer on landscape themes," which he "exploited to show off his abilities and to express his mind" (*NS* 42.14b).

The work of each poet in Chung Hung's *Shih-p'in* was seen as deriving from that of an earlier poet or work. Within this format Hsieh Ling-yün's work was derived from Ts'ao Chih (*ch'u yü* Ts'ao Chih) and to a lesser extent from Chang Hsieh (third century).[70] The terminology of Chung Hung's criticism of Hsieh Ling-yün—"artful . . . unrestrained"—suggests that Hsiao Kang's analysis of Hsieh Ling-yün in his letter to the Prince of Hsiang-tung might not have been entirely original. However, Hsiao Kang's derivation went only so far as to say that Hsieh Ling-yün's work was "derived from natural spontaneity" (*ch'u yü tzu-jan*). Hsieh's diction, said Hsiao Kang, was "heaven-inspired" (*t'ien-pa*). Hsiao Kang must have been deeply intrigued by Hsieh's work himself; he developed his criticisms of Hsieh into a three-folio exegesis.[71] Thus, while he well appreciated and gave unstinting praise to fine original work, Hsiao Kang could not nor would not forgive untalented hangers-on at court who, in their fiddling imitations captured nothing more than Hsieh Ling-yün's dregs.

Hsiao Kang's views of the origins and evolution of poetry were on occasion orthodox enough. For example, in what must have been a schoolboy exercise, Hsiao Kang traced traditional concepts from the *Documents,* through Confucius, the "Great Preface" to the *Odes,* and Han utilitariansm, as indeed Liu Hsieh did more thoroughly in his dissertation on poetry.[72] Hsiao Kang says: "Poetry is thought and its expression in words. When deliberation takes place in the mind, that is called thought. Words reveal one's sentiments. That which embraces them, expressed in words, is poetry; expressed in music, is song. The roots are one. Hence it is said, 'I admonish him with this song'."[73] This syllogistic gloss on the "Airs of the States" illustrates Hsiao Kang's concept of "gentle remonstrance." It is a categorical statement on the political function of poetry, and is in complete agreement with P'ei Tzu-yeh's quotation from the "Great Preface."

Similar ideas are expressed in Hsiao Kang's "Preface to the Collected Works of Crown Prince Chao-ming": "Refined writings [*wen-chi*] came into being; documentary records [*shu-chih*] were produced. Recitation and song [*yung-ko*] arose, and rhymeprose and eulogy [*fu-sung*] flourished. These perfected the sentiments of filial duty and respect in human relationships, and transferred moral common custom into royal government.[74] ... This is called human refinement [*jen-wen,* civilization]" (*YKC* 3016). Solid support for traditional Confucian concepts of literature also appears in one of Hsiao Kang's memorials to the throne.[75] But in this item, a hint of Hsiao Kang's true feelings come through in his condemnation of the Han "old-text school" (*ku-wen*) exegesists, Ma Yung, and Cheng Hsüan.

Criticism of Han utilitarianism is overtly stated in a letter Hsiao Kang addressed to Chang Tsan (499–549).[76] Chang Tsan was a noted adherent of P'ei Tzu-yeh's ancient school. In this letter Hsiao Kang referred to the famous Han writer, Yang Hsiung (53 B.C.–A.D.18), who regretted "wasting his youth on rhymeprose composition." Hsiao Kang complained that later in life Yang Hsiung turned from these purely literary writings to moral didacticism.[77] Ts'ao Chih, too, said Hsiao Kang, found inspiration for verse in his frustrated political ambitions. This exploitation of literature for didactic and political objectives was anathema to Hsiao Kang's view of pure literature, and for this he considered Yang Hsiung and Ts'ao Chih unforgivable. Yang Hsiung and Ts'ao Chih were cited for different reasons in Hsiao Kang's letter to the Prince of Hsiang-tung. Here they were placed in historical perspective and included in a list of "great writers of the distant past." These were the writers, said Hsiao Kang, who were so unsuccessfully imitated by metropolitan litterateurs.

Following his criticism of Yang Hsiung and Ts'ao Chih in the letter to Chang Tsan were several lines of landscape description. According to Hsiao Kang, these were composed by humming over short verse and patching together commonplace sounds, expressing the sentiments of homesickness and of heroic resentment through what met the eye and through factual realities. Liu Hsieh took such realities to be outside the realm of literary composition, although he admitted that since Han times these realities had been increasingly exploited in literature. Chung Hung, too, complained of the abuse of factual reality in literature and gave this as the reason why Jen Fang's poetry lacked freshness and spontaneity. Hsiao Kang was no less critical and, by way of humble deference in his letter to the Prince of Hsiang-tung, described his own work as "short verse" and "commonplace sound."[78]

Essentially, Hsiao Kang was a practical poet-critic, rather than a theoretician. His descriptive criticism covered a relatively small area and was confined to immediate contemporary and local problems. This limited scope was balanced by his specific, detailed analyses. He less often restricted his remarks to the ellipsis and epithet that marked Chinese descriptive criticism. His prescriptive and cautionary advice concerning what a writer should or should not do to improve his verse was addressed to fellow poets. Technique, he said, required a balance between embellishment and a certain "use of the mind" (*yung-hsin*) and "artistic mind" (*ch'iao-hsin*).[79] These requirements were specified as lacking in the imitations of Hsieh Ling-yün and P'ei Tzu-yeh, and in metropolitan literature in general. The "Airs of the States" and the "Lament" were his ideal of poetry. Spontaneous inspiration was the basis of creative writing; the inspiration of the audience was the test of a true work of art. Utilitarian objectives served only to curb this spontaneity. He named writers who could be taken as models by would-be poets, but warned that poets like Hsieh Ling-yün were too elusive for such purposes.

Hsiao Kang's critical writings were calculated to reform tastes toward an appreciation of his own work. In the literary-political atmosphere of the day, such appreciation would be support for his own literary hegemony. He expected a writer to be a discerning reader as well; the "true master" must recognize as well as be recognized for expertise and elegant literary sophistication. Even his genuine interest in literary aesthetics assumed political overtones in his condemnation of influential factions.

The practical rather than the theoretical nature of his criticism was apparent in his use of fundamental principles of Chinese literary theory as tools. He saw no need to define his terms as Liu Hsieh had done. Even when he touched upon genre and writers he thought best exemplified a genre, as in his letter to the Prince of Hsiang-tung, his opinion was usually borrowed and incidental to his main argument. The list of genres in his "Preface to the Collected Works of Crown Prince Chao-ming"[80] is natural enough in its context, but it is stereotyped and uninformative and is no improvement on Ts'ao P'ei's pioneer effort three centuries before,[81] let alone an advance on the genre studies of Liu Hsieh and Crown Prince Chao-ming.

The arrangement of this list of genres, and the list in the letter to the Prince of Hsiang-tung, was, however, by no means arbitrary. Poetry came first. As Hsiao Kang said, "By the age of seven I had an overwhelming fondness for poetry, for which I never weary even as an adult" (LS 4.9a). Much the same sentiments were expressed in his letter to the Prince of Hsiang-tung and in his letter to Chang Tsan, in which the more general term "rhymed writing" (wen) took the place of the specific "poetry." Ability to compose poetry ensured a man the highest respect. Even Jen Fang, secure in Emperor Wu's circle as one of the two most powerful literary figures of the first decade of Liang, was dissatisfied with his reputation as a prose (pi) writer, and he attempted to "move up" into poetic composition. (Chung Hung coupled him with his rival, Shen Yüeh, among the second-rank poets in the *Shih-p'in.*) Hsiao Kang was proud of his own poetic genius and, as he admitted to the Prince of Hsiang-tung, he had an "endemic impulse to show off what he could do."

The rhetorical antitheses of the generic terms Hsiao Kang used are particularly informative. In his letter to the Prince of Hsiang-tung, Hsiao Kang paired poetry (*shih*) with unrhymed prose (*pi*). This antithesis was more precise than the current rhymed writing/unrhymed prose (*wen-pi*). Then the antithetical term "poetry/unrhymed prose" was matched with paired literary and discursive prose forms, "rhymeprose/discourse" (*fu-pien*). To Hsiao Kang all writing, including documentation, properly belonged to literature. He defined poetry (*shih*) as "rhymed writing" (*wen*) or belles-lettres (*wen-chang*); and distinguished this from unrhymed prose (*pi*), which he defined as narrative prose (*shu-tso*).

Hsiao Kang's most controversial item of prescriptive criticism is his letter to his son, Hsiao Ta-hsin, written shortly after 532.[82] Brief as it is, it suggests a startling theory of literary creation, quite unprecedented for its unbridled license:

You are still young and what you lack is study. Indeed, there is nothing other than scholarship that increases with perseverance. K'ung Ch'iu [Confucius] said: "I once went a whole day without food and a whole night without sleep, so lost in thought was I. But all to no avail. It would have been better to have studied."[83] To stand facing a wall[84] or be no more than a monkey wearing a crown[85] is not what I would choose.

The principles underlying development of personal character and those governing literary composition are quite different. One establishes oneself first by being circumspect and serious. Literature, on the other hand, should be the uninhibited expression of sentiment. ("Exhortatory Letter to the Duke of Tang-yang, Ta-hsin," *IWLC* 25; *YKC* 3010)

The first half of this letter is a restatement of the Confucian virtue of scholarship, with two references to the *Analects*, one quoted in full. To Hsiao Kang scholarship was of paramount importance. He further eulogized scholarship as the twelfth of

Crown Prince Chao-ming's virtues in his "Preface to the Collected Works of Crown Prince Chao-ming." However, Hsiao Kang was aware that lack of formal education could be matched at the other extreme by an empty parade of erudition. His advice to his son, then, should be considered in the context of his criticisms of metropolitan scholar-poets.

The second part of the letter adumbrates a unique antithesis between personal conduct and literary practice. The behavior he recommends to his son echoes the advice he had given in another communication,[86] and would merit a universal parental nod of approval. Perhaps Hsiao Kang had in mind the wild and even criminal irresponsibility of much of the noble-born youth of Liang.[87]

In this antithesis Hsiao Kang once and for all dissociated literature from any utilitarian function. Liu Hsieh agreed up to a point that "in literary composition, the purpose is to express feeling which has been repressed; therefore, it is necessary that a writer be able to give free vent to his feelings in a happy and spontaneous manner."[88] But Hsiao Kang's theory, expressed in the two characters for abandoned and dissolute (*fang-tang*),[89] far more extreme than the relatively restrained "giving expression to the feelings in song," was flamboyant to the point of deriding persisting ideals of literature as a moral force.

Attempts have been made to explain in psychological terms the paradox between Hsiao Kang's circumspect conduct and his literary license. He was a man of profound sensibility, and it is suggested that his literary license rendered the necessary release from the rigid etiquette he imposed upon himself as a scholar-official.[90] Others see his theories as a reflection of the decadence of the Ch'i and Liang courts.[91] These explanations move away from the field of literary discussion, and in any case they fail to explain his unique reaction to a situation universal at least during the Six Dynasties period.

Essentially, Hsiao Kang's "licentious" theories were an extreme expression of his consistent complaint against the uninspired imitations and the patching together of allusions and references which were passed off as creative poetry. To Hsiao Kang, creative literature meant artistry achieved only through the natural, untrammeled expression of emotion, elegantly conveyed. This view went against deeply rooted concepts of literature and its functions, and obscured the fact that in most other respects Hsiao Kang was very orthodox. None of his opponents would have argued against him that content determines the form and that form determines the style, and that hence all writing comes under the general scope of literature. Hsiao Kang met eventual disaster in divorcing poetry from its traditional political and didactic utilitarianism, and so it is overlooked that in his formal prose compositions he paid full service to orthodox concepts of literature. He assumed an aggressive role in the literary debates of his day, and on occasion he crushed his literary adversaries with his very cruel pen. However, he freely admired any work which demonstrated artistic achievement, regardless of the author's theoretical commitments.

CHAPTER 5

Literary Practice

THE literary practice of Hsiao Kang and his group was known as palace-style (*kung-t'i*). Hsiao Kang was closely associated with the origins of the style and was the most influential, most prolific, and by general agreement the most accomplished of palace-style writers. Thus, although it is not the aim here to furnish a description or a definition much less a history of palace-style writing, in evaluating Hsiao Kang's palace-style compositions some incidental trespass on those larger areas of interest is inevitable.

If Chung Hung influenced Hsiao Kang's literary theories, then Hsü Ch'ih molded his literary tastes. Hsü Ch'ih's biography in the dynastic histories states categorically that Hsü was the innovator of palace-style:

As a youth, Ch'ih had been fond of study. By the time he had grown up he had read the *Classics* and *Histories* in their entirety. In literary composition he went in for innovation and did not restrict himself to the old forms. . . . His style of composition was very individual. The entire Spring District [East Palace] was captivated by it and strove to emulate it. Such writing was contemporaneously designated "palace-style." Kao-tsu [Emperor Wu] was not impressed by the reports that reached him. Angrily he issued a summons intending to censure Hsü, but during the audience he found the man perceptive and intelligent in his responses and highly articulate. Kao-tsu's mind was set at rest, and he continued to question him on the meaning of the Five Classics, then the Histories through the ages, the Hundred Philosophies, and miscellaneous records. At the end, the discussion moved on to Buddhist doctrines. Hsü went into the very length and breadth of the subject and gave pertinent answers to all the problems the emperor posed. Kao-tsu sighed [in admiration of Hsü Ch'ih, whom Emperor Wu had hitherto dis-

98

missed as a mere bureaucrat scholar-pedant with no appreciation of religious metaphysics]. (*LS* 30.8b; 9ab; *TCTC* 4810, Hu San-sheng's commentary)

These statements are corroborated in the official biography of Yü Hsin (512–581). Here it is seen that before the literary style of Hsiao Kang's salon in the East Palace acquired the name palace-style, it was known by the names of its two most prominent exponents and their sons: "The literary composition [of Hsü Ch'ih and his son Hsü Ling, and of Yü Chien-wu and his son Yü Hsin] was ornately beautiful in the extreme and was popularly known as the 'Hsü Yü' style" (*Pei shih* 83.17ab). Hsiao Kang's official biographers agree with these descriptions of the nature of palace-style and on the currency of the term. "[Hsiao Kang's] composition suffered the fault of being frivolous and degenerate and was referred to at the time as 'palace-style'" (*LS* 4.9a; *NS* 8.4a). Independent sources contain similar statements: "Emperor Chien-wen [Hsiao Kang] and Yü Chien-wu of Liang and their group were the first to write in a frivolous, licentious, highly ornate and degenerate style, which was called 'palace-style.' Writers later followed and imitated the trend and indulged in this bewitching form."[1]

As the name indicates, palace-style was both a product of the palace and a reflection of palace life. Critics have been most assiduous in classifying the subject matter of these court poets; Hsiao Kang's works provide examples of all the categories that have been devised. There are the landscape themes of court pleasures—boating on the rivers; views from some high vantage; strolls in gardens, parks, or woods; country rambles and picnics—still-life description (*yung-wu*), and categories of palace women—the court favorite, dancing girls, now-neglected former favorites, courtesans, deserted wives, beauties of former times, girls awaiting the return of conscript husbands.

As a product of the palace, palace-style composition reflected the salon society of the day. Salon conditions tended to enforce a uniform group-style literature that effectively swamped the individuality of all but those content to remain virtual outcasts.[2] It is nearly impossible to distinguish the work of any one writer who engaged in the court activities of the day. The authorship of not a few compositions of the time is indeed in dispute, and the same poems are attributed to different writers. And instead of expressing thought and genuine feeling, as the works of men like Ch'ü Yüan, Ts'ao Chih, T'ao Ch'ien, or Pao Chao had done, literature now degenerated into a mere after-dinner entertainment. Poetry became a matter of expertise. In admitting his constant urge to display his skill, Hsiao Kang himself unconsciously testified to the premium on ready wit rather than on profound deliberation.

Salon members derived entertainment from a wide range of literary games that had developed since Han times or were new to Liang. These games, too, have engaged the attention of later scholars, who have been equally assiduous in classifying the various forms and their complexities.[3] A common game was the "matching" of verse; this perhaps above all else was responsible for the lack of individuality in the poetry of the day. Extant examples of matching verse include in their titles such words as "matching" (ho or feng-ho), "similar" (t'ung), "imitating" (ni), "by order of a superior" (ying-ling), "ordered" (feng-ming), and "on behalf of" (wei). Doubtful attributions and massive losses from this period preclude accurate statistics, but roughly fifteen percent of Hsiao Kang's extant poetry falls into this category. Conversely, many of his own poems were imitated, especially by members of his own salon. Besides these specified correspondences, much common ground was covered in the titles and subject matter of Hsiao Kang's and other Liang poetry. The "music bureau" (yüeh-fu) titles and themes inherited from the Han and subsequent regimes were of course in the public domain.

By Liang times, "linked verse" (lien-chü) had already had a long history, dating at least from early Han, but in the hands of the Liang literati the genre developed hitherto undreamed-of elaborations. Various forms of palindrome, and verses in which one or more words were reiterated, were also popular literary games. These were signaled by titles bearing the words "parting and meeting" (li-ho)—i.e., anagram poetry—"palindrome" (hui-wen), and new to Liang, "great words" (ta-yen) and "little words" (hsi-yen).

Hsiao Kang wrote three poems called "Song of Chiang-nan"

which correspond to compositions by Emperor Wu.[4] In these correspondences, Emperor Wu's title "Song of Chiang-nan"[5] is subtitled "Matching the words of the 'Spring Road'; / With graceful charms she comes forth from the light silk." Hsiao Kang's subtitle reads, "Matching the words of 'While on Spring Road,' / Have a beautiful maid come over." Similarly, Emperor Wu's "Song of the Dragon Flute" is subtitled "Matching the words of the 'Sounds of Chiang-nan,' / One singing is worth a thousand gold"; and Hsiao Kang's subtitle reads, "Matching the words of 'Song of Chiang-nan' / Will surely bring down the soaring phoenix." And Emperor Wu's "Plucking Lotus Song"[6] is subtitled "Matching the words of the 'Plucking-Lotus Islet,'/ The elegant, refined and beautiful dancing-girl." Hsiao Kang's subtitle reads, "Matching the words of the 'Plucking Lotus and Returning,' / Splashing waters soak our robes" (*TFP* 1112). Each of these poems consists of three lines of seven characters, followed by four lines of three characters. The first three-character line repeats the last characters of the third seven-character line (aaa/abca):

> Spring has returned among the branches and upon the river;
> The long willow sweeps the ground and peach blossoms fly.
> A romantic breeze blows upon her, and the sunshine lights
>   her dress.
> The sunshine lights her dress;
> Dusk is drawing nigh.
> We throw down yellow gold,
> To stay an honored guest. (*TFP* 1111)

The word "presented" (*fu, fu-te*, or *fu . . . te*) in a title indicated that the poem had been extemporized on a given title. The term originated in Liang, although the practice was already current in the preceding dynasties; in Sung and Ch'i the word *yung* ("on the subject of") in a title indicated that the poem was composed on a set theme.[7] Examples of this transition are Hsiao Kang's two poems on a red rose, 'Fu-te ch'iang-wei" and "Yung ch'iang-wei" (*TFP* 1147; 1152), and, even more clearly, his "Fu-yung Wu-yin shih chih" (*TFP* 1144). Thirteen poems with the word *fu* in the title and thirty-six with *yung* are attributed to Hsiao Kang, but many other verses are clearly extempore poems from whose titles *fu . . . te* or *yung* have been omitted. One effect of impromptu composition was that verses inevitably became shorter, and indeed the majority of still-life poems do not exceed four lines.[8] Hsiao Kang was a master of extemporization, and this gives more point to his claim to enjoying writing "short verse" in his letter to the Prince of Hsiang-tung.

Fu-te verse was more complicated than its forerunners in that, as well as covering subject matter previously treated, it now exploited whole lines from earlier poems as elements of a title. A new poem would be written on the theme and imagined circumstances of the original model, using the original vocabulary. Though less often attempted, the treatment of lines, in dealing with concepts rather than objects, led to more abstract thought, greater skill, and more precise conventions than the purely objective description of still-life (*yung-wu*) poetry. Sometimes, as a variation, even rhyme-words of an earlier poem would be selected as the subject for a composition. This was indicated by the term *fu-yün* (presented rhyme). Even at the time, such poetry was not considered a writer's best work, and it less often found its way into the *Yü-t'ai hsin-yung* anthology.

The members of the salons were saturated in their literary heritage. Styles of composition changed little after Han times; it was possible for Hsiao Kang's "Serving Wine" (*TFP* 1101)[9] to be attributed to Lu Chi, who lived more than two centuries earlier. Any deviation from conformity attracted attention. Hsü Ch'ih was criticized for his "innovations unrestricted by old forms." However, the terms "innovation" and "unrestricted" were not peculiar to the palace-style writing of Hsiao Kang's salon. In his letter to the Prince of Hsiang-tung, Hsiao Kang criticized Hsieh Ling-yün for being unrestricted. Hsü Ch'ih displeased Emperor Wu for his innovations, but the term "innovation" was also applied to the writings of Emperor Wu's favorites, Shen Yüeh, Wang Jung, and Hsieh T'iao. However, by the time Emperor Wu noticed Hsü Ch'ih, in the 530s, Shen Yüeh had been dead nearly twenty years. Perhaps Hsü Ch'ih's innovations differed from Shen Yüeh's in their tendency to freedom from formal restrictions rather than in their use of tonal formulas.

Hsiao Kang's innovations were of course no more than a

development of current literary trends. Palace-style was to a large extent an aristocratic refinement of the romantic "Songs of Wu" ("Wu-ko") and of the "western melodies" ("hsi-ch'ü") native to the largely non-Chinese South of pre–Six Dynasties times. These folk songs were adapted to the Chinese poetic tradition and were embellished with elegant courtly diction. Tonal refinements added to their transformation. Palace-style verse owed as much to the form of these folk songs as it did to their subject matter. Examples of the seven-character-line quatrain common in the folk songs but rare in Chinese poetry of the time are found in Hsiao Kang's palace-style poems. His poetry also includes an example of the twelve five-character-line verse that was new to Ch'i and Liang. This form antecedes the twelve five-character-line, varied as six five-character-line, "regulated verse" (*lü-shih*) of the T'ang.[10] Then there was the eight five-character-line "regulated verse" form in one of Hsiao Kang's verses on a Han *yüeh-fu* title[11]—A very new bottle under a very old label! "Regulated verse" of seven-character lines was seldom tried before the seventh century, and Hsiao Kang's "Spring Feelings"[12] is one of the few examples that survives. The first six lines are in seven characters, and the last couplet is in five.

Palace-style writing was by no means restricted to verse. Most of the literary prose genres, notably rhymeprose, sevens, and the various inscription forms, had evolved as vehicles for still-life *yung-wu* description. The distinction between these prose forms and poetry was further diminished by the literary prose style known as parallel prose. This style predominated during the Six Dynasties period and by Liang exhibited all its variations of parallelism:[13] simple or interrupted, graphic, semantic and grammatical, with occasional or regular rhymes and growing attention to tonality. Han rhymeprose compositions generally consisted of many hundreds of characters. The southern dynasties continued this tradition but also developed a short, lyrical rhymeprose form. Almost without exception both the long and short rhymeprose of mid-Liang fell within the palace-style, still-life, and landscape conventions.

Hsiao Kang's twenty-three surviving rhymeprose compositions illustrate all these features, and he was, as might be expected, in the van of Liang innovations in rhymeprose writing.[14] He exploited the short/long interrupted parallelism in rhymeprose that had already been tried during Sung in the opening four lines of his "Rhymeprose on a Lute" (four/eight; four/eight) (*YKC* 2996). Four/six simple parallelism was the most common structure in Ch'i and Liang rhymeprose, and only at the end of Liang did interrupted four/six parallelism appear. In Hsiao Kang's "Rhymeprose on Plucking Lotus" (*YKC* 2998), four consecutive lines four/six//four/six occur. Five-character line and seven-character line rhymeprose had also been known as early as the Han, but these forms, too, were given more attention from the end of Liang, as in Hsiao Kang's "Rhymeprose on Facing the Candle" (*YKC* 2997). Of the thirty-two lines here, eight are in five characters and ten are in seven characters. In "Rhymeprose on Repentance" (*YKC* 2995) there are two pairs of seven-character lines and the last eight lines are of seven characters each. Inscriptions (*ming*) are in regular lines of four characters, with end rhyme. Thus there is virtually no difference between this form and the five-character-line still-life poem. As in poetry games, Hsiao Kang used the inscription very aptly as the form for a palindrome (e.g., "Inscription on a Circular Fan," *YKC* 3025).

During the late Six Dynasties period there was a keen interest in precise historico-geographical detail. Hsiao Kang occasionally did some research himself.[15] Buddhist elements feature largely in the landscape literature of the time. Three of Hsiao Kang's fourteen extant inscriptions were dedicated to mountains. Their massive Buddhist content befits a description of the idyllic mountain retreats favored by monastic communities. Hsiao Kang dedicated six inscriptions to temple images of Buddhist deities. One inscription appeared beneath the spire of the Ta-ai-ching Monastery. Though designated a *ming*, there is little difference between this and the stone inscriptions (*pei*), nine of which survive, that he composed for other halls and temples. The grave inscription, or epitaph (*mu-chih-ming*), offered Hsiao Kang the chance to display his skill in portraying grief. They are of course an extension of the tradition of discussing men's characters and of the palace-style theme of parting.

A category of still-life prose much indulged in by the salon members was the letter of thanks. These usually come under the generic term memorial (*ch'i*); less often as memorial to the throne (*piao*), which acknowledges the conferment of an honor or rank, or which accompanies a presentation to the throne; or as letter (*shu*). Hsiao Kang's extant prose compositions include some two hundred items. At least a fifth of these are letters of thanks (although their bulk does not correspond with this proportion). Items range from "Memorial of Thanks for Being Elevated to the Position of Crown Prince" to "Letter of Thanks for a Gift from the Throne of a Silk and Bamboo Lantern" or "Letter of Thanks for Permission to Accompany the Emperor to the Temple" (*YKC* 3002, 3005, 3006). Letters of thanks to Hsiao Kang reveal him as a liberal-handed patron. There are three letters from the Liu brothers thanking him for a gift of wine (*YKC* 3311, 3316). He also sent them cakes and confectionery, venison, charcoal, arrowroot, and oranges "from beside the city wall." To Liu Hsiao-i he gave a silver-mounted silk sash, while Liu Hsiao-wei received a gift of money when he married, and some shrimp paste (*YKC* 3317, 3318, 3319, 3316). To Yü Chien-wu he gave a house, antiques, and betel nuts, chestnuts, rice, and apples. Yü's wife received a new spring robe (*YKC* 3341, 3343). For family presents Hsiao Kang favored livestock: to the Prince of Hsiang-tung he gave some fine horses (*YKC* 3046); to his father, Emperor Wu, he gave a white rabbit "that it might play in the sovereign's garden" (*YKC* 3003).

Considering the overpowering eloquence of these epistles, far exceeding the demands of the occasion, the gift itself becomes a test of erudition of donor and recipient. Hsiao Kang was never at a loss to draft a perfectly balanced literary gem.

Throughout Chinese literary history a basic element of poetry was rhyme. Rhyme is appreciated in China, as in the West, as an identity of sound between words, and is exploited for that quality. In Hsiao Kang's day end-rhyme was obligatory. Rhyme schemes rarely deviated from the *abcbdbeb* formula. Demands of formal parallelism—tonal, graphic, grammatical, semantic—had to be met. Verse was composed extempore in salon competition or under the conditions imposed by a salon game where the rhyme word or words were given. A study of Hsiao Kang's artistry in manipulating these conditions goes far in revealing his poetic technique.

Hsiao Kang was a prolific poet. "The histories mention the 'Collected Works of Emperor Chien-wen of Liang' in 100 folios; and 600 folios of miscellaneous writings. From ancient times no member of an imperial family has equaled such a quantity of literary production."[16] Included in this vast corpus, there survive some three hundred poems. Given the relatively limited phonetic variation of the language, it was inevitable that his rhymes should occasionally be stereotyped. His most frequently used rhymes include the soft, languorous -*ang*, -*uang*, or the sonorous -*ung* sounds. These sounds occur in such emotive words as *ch'uang* (couch), *chuang* (make-up, cosmetics), *hsiang* (perfume), *fang* (fragrance), *kuang* (sun or moonlight), *kung* (palace), *feng* (breeze), *k'ung* (empty, in vain). In the two dozen verses in which these sounds are exploited, Hsiao Kang employs perhaps less than a score of words. If only out of convention, he must have been well aware of the poetic possibilities of such combinations of romantic sound and meaning and would have no difficulty in adopting these rhymes in versifying the sensuous luxury of the palace and its ladies. He found the same rhymes appropriate to add sonority to court congratulations or gloom to a battle scene and to lonely traveling; and to suggest spacious landscape seen from a high vantage or to the drowsiness of sultry summer weather. In the palace-women themes, these rhymes are used both to support the description of the sumptuous surroundings of the court favorite or dancing-girl and also to enhance the contrastive poignancy of the rich decor in the themes of the neglected wife.

Occasionally he turned to shorter sounds to express bitter grief. Such sounds combine with equally emotive meanings: *li-chih* (beautiful disposition), *tzu* (charms), *ch'i* (appointed time), *mei* (eyebrows), *se* (complexion), *ssu* (silk), *yi* (suspicion), *pei* (turn the back on), *ch'ih* (delay), *chüeh* (cut short). The first rhyme in "A Matching Poem on Exchanging a Concubine for a Horse," *li* (parting), sets both the phonetic and the semantic scene (*YT* 7.26b; *TFP* 1104).

The modern Western critic demands that rhyme justify the attention it attracts by enhancing the imagery of the context or in some way give point to the thought expressed. In so doing, it must avoid any sense of forced arrangement. Whether or not these demands were made in Hsiao Kang's day, his "Extemporization on a K'ung-hou Lute"[17] more than meets these criteria:

> The plectrum hesitates on the first notes of the song;
> As the tempo quickens, the dance urges faster.
> Armlets tinkle to the cry of the strings;
> Skirts swirl, half obscuring the pillars.
> If you must know what so disturbs my heart,
> Then watch her inked brows meet![18] (*YT* 7.17b;
> *WYYH* 1317; *TFP* 1146)

The first rhyme-word *wu* (dance) highlights the subject of the poem and culminates in the description of the accelerating tempo of the dance itself. The next rhyme *chu* (pillar) serves as a pivot. It is the technical term for the bridge of a stringed instrument and is used here to set the palace scene where the dance is performed. Thus, as in the first couplet, both instrument and dance are portrayed with a single rhyme word. The dancers' skirts partially hide the pillars, introducing the little mystery of the question in the last couplet. The final rhyme-word *chü* (meet), the focal point of the poem, is beyond anticipation and yet is a witty and logical answer to the question posed in the previous line. Furthermore, the "meeting" of the strong black ink-line of the dancer's eyebrows recalls both the strength and support of her beauty and the firm line of the pillar or the bridge of her lute. But in the end it is not the instrument or the dance that hold the attention but an acutely observed expression on the dancer's face.

Nothing so sustained as these rhymes could be accidental. Hsiao Kang demonstrated that he fully appreciated the effects for which rhyme could be exploited.

Shortcomings in his rhyme technique usually reflect the conditions under which he was writing; nevertheless, the majority of rhymes in his three hundred extant poems are competent, and many are inspired. Of course there is more to a good poem than simply good rhyme; but good rhyme complements and enhances other aspects of a poem, and it demonstrates poetic sensibility. From this point of view alone, then, Hsiao Kang deserves his reputation as one of the finest poets of the period.

In the competitive atmosphere of the salons, poetry was a game. The urgency of poetic composition was not a compulsion to express one's mind but a social obligation to display one's wit. These conditions were not conducive to contemplative verse. By mid-Liang very little within the relatively narrow palace environment had escaped poetic scrutiny, whether it be the reflection of a moonbeam on a pool or the folds of a courtesan's robe. The richest, most ornately embellished diction was accorded to the most insignificant trivia. Little other than expertise was required to dress up some overrefined fragility, and any inconsequential novelty of perception would initiate a spate of imitative or matching poems. This salon still-life verse, sensuous to the degree that it was, sustained only the flimsiest thought. Having little subjective experience to convey, for all their glitter, said one eminent Chinese critic, these palace-style poems fail to inspire the reader as do the brilliant *Songs of the South*.[19]

The concern with sensuous word-pictures hindered the development of a continuous line of thought. Lines appear to be contrived as individual entities, and outside the formal framework of rhyme and parallel prosody there was little reason for the particular order of lines within a poem, or for the inclusion of a line in one poem rather than in another, or for its inclusion at all. However immaculate the verbal antitheses may be, and however colorful the imagery, the reader is not compelled by any cohesive and vitalizing thought to proceed from one line to another. These verses too often fail as poetry because they are not a poetic expression of a whole, preconceived, and experienced thought. Again, no matter how acute the poet's observation or how unusual his glimpse of the subject, the poem lacks that warmth of personal impression and greater philosophical insight that might elevate the glossy surface into a meaningful exposition of human experience.

Where Hsiao Kang did introduce human reaction to his word-pictures, this reaction was too often expressed in the form of a conceit, a pun, or a joke. Furthermore, although his intention was to sum up or round off what had been said, the discrete nature of each line tends to reduce the relevance of the remark, or the very triteness of the thought weakens whatever tenuous relation there may have been. Indeed, it becomes all too clear that the context was contrived merely to allow a punch line; that the poet's problem was to satisfy some extempore demand of a competition.

While puns and jokes or local topical references abound, Hsiao Kang's subject matter and treatment are too concrete and too objective, his diction too exotic, and his thought too simple and direct to allow those hidden levels of meaning that accompany more serious, personal, and reflective writing. Even the all-pervading landscape elements share little of that close identification with Buddho-Taoist principles of nature that characterized the poetry of men like Hsieh Ling-yün.[20] The philosophical, anchorite view of the profound massif, mystical to the men of the fifth century, had in general become an empty conceit, a mere challenge to delicate, sensitive, objective observation and wit.

> Ascending a knoll one's thought turn to Chien-ko;
> Roaming by a stream one thinks of Ch'en-yang.
> A flying cascade like frozen rain,
> The night moon like autumn frost.
> Fireflies turn, struggling for late warmth;
> Insects mind the autumn cool drawing in.
> Tinkling ripples approach obstructing stones;
> Shadowed grasses part from orchid fragrance
> ("Enjoying the Cool in the Park of Mysteries,"[21] *TFP* 1140)

More rugged scenery simply becomes a palace-style opulence of cliffs and crags, piled up much in the same way as the sumptuous riches of a courtesan's boudoir are heaped up before one's eyes:

> [One character missing] coming by the serried mountains
>   and rivers,
> This place is nought but twists and turns.
> A hundred summits, winding, obscure each other,
> A thousand precipices all obstruct the sky.
> Overhanging peaks now block the river,
> Or sheer embankments give access to the stream.
> Looking back you lose your sense of direction,
> Pressing on, you doubt you are going forward.
> The evening waves reflect the orphan moon,

And mountain branches toy with nocturnal mists.
At this time melancholy grows intense,
[Two characters missing] the spirit goes through its
    nine changes.
("Passing by Pipa Gorge," *IWLC* 27; *WYYH* 983; *TFP* 1119)

Personal reflection is evident at the end of this poem. However, the thought is not very profound; furthermore, a long tradition of expressing homesickness (*ssu-hsiang*) in such terms stemmed directly from the *Odes*.[22] Hsiao Kang best exploited this emotion and the sentiments of heroism (*hsiung-hsin, pien-hsin*) in his *yüeh-fu* describing the hardships of the soldier on active service on the inhospitable western borders.[23]

In general, it is apparent that Hsiao Kang conformed to his literary principles in eschewing the pedantic scholasticisms he criticized in the poems of his contemporaries. His *yüeh-fu* in particular were considered successful in preserving the flavor of their folk-song models.[24] But much as he may have striven for a more colloquial flavor, he never entirely freed his work from the concepts and language of the nobleman. His "Boatgirl's Song" starts in the spirit of vernacular poetry, except perhaps for its setting on the Hsiang River, with its classical romantic associations. Then aristocratic taste takes over. The imagery no longer evokes the robust fatigue of the common boatgirl, long inured to the dampness of river life, but dallies among the rich delicacy more familiar to the soft, idle hands of the poet. Silks and brocades, surely foreign to the river folk of his day, are muddied and refreshed in the stream. Names of the rich, powerful, and beautiful in court tradition intrude, even though the implication is that their accomplishments are inferior to the boatgirl's. Hsiao Kang's boatgirl, improbably, wears make-up, and the honest spray on her powder becomes an erotic image in being likened to fine perspiration.[25]

Other boating songs, reflections of the river society of the South, in the same way no longer represent the ferryman's labor but are the occasion of court outings. The boats are without exception of exotic woods and rich decor. Of all the flora and fauna of the rivers and lakes, characteristically it is the lush melilotus and lily that attract the poet's eye.

> Oars of cassia late against the turning tide.
> Frail boards knock against the passing bank.
> Hooked carp borne upon purple lotus;
> Short-stemmed lilies set in silver baskets. (*TFP* 1101)

Images of time passing also reflect this aristocratic environment. The perennial cycle of life, the rhythm of peasant labor are entirely alien to Hsiao Kang's thought. Here seasons come and go to the flowering of plum and peach, wisteria and orange, and the migration of mated geese and swallows. Springtime does not represent the vital energy of sowing and rebirth but becomes a time of languid dalliance. Nor does autumn signify the joy of bountiful harvest, but brings relief from the heat of a southern palace and, less happily, the cooling of summer passion, when leaves turn yellow at the first touch of frost and when beauty begins to fade. For the well-fed nobleman clad in his furs, harsh winter snows become fluttering butterflies, flying brine, or floating petals; and for the faded beauty, the icy chastity of neglect. More intimately, time passes as the sun inches across the lattice of a lady's boudoir and a golden clepsydra drips out her lonely night. Orchid candles and incense braziers burn out and are relit as she lies sleepless in her grief and resentment. In palace-style poetry, time, like grand natural landscape, has lost its philosophical implications and instead takes on a more negative melancholy where physical beauty must inevitably fade.

Any symbolism apparent in Hsiao Kang's treatment of still-life themes might not always have been entirely intentional. But whatever the subject, be it hunting or cockfighting or a description of a tree or a plant, Hsiao Kang's thoughts tended inexorably toward women.[26]

> The first peach, beautiful in its new blush.
> Lustrous, exuding fragrance.
> Raveling swallows within its branches;
> Among its leaves exuding light perfume.
> Blossom borne aloft enters a dew-filled spring;
> Fronds entwining brush a painted chamber.
> Like sunlight on a willow before the casement;
> One fancies a complexion powdered and rouged.
> ("The First Peach," *TFP* 1141)

Women were a favorite subject. Their every smile and gesture is recorded; no detail of their dress and cosmetics, bedchamber furnishings and accessories, sighs and resentment is missed. Treatment is uniformly sumptuous, but differs in various ways to suit tears or laughter. Conversely, similar treatment is applied for different effects, as when, for example, descriptions of luxurious surroundings either enhance the favor with which a lady is graced or add poignancy to the loneliness of a former favorite now neglected. The common factor is feminine charms. Herein lies the difference between Hsiao Kang's palace-style verse and the innocent love expressed in the *Odes*, where the emphasis is on feminine virtue. While there is no more suitable theme for genuine poetic expression than love, the great fault in Hsiao Kang's verse, and in palace-style verse as a whole, lies in the concept of woman not as a partner sharing an emotional experience but as a chattel and an object of still-life scrutiny. With the possible exception of the best of the abandoned-wife themes, it lacks that profoundly moving spirit that immortalizes the *Odes*.[27] One poem even includes a suggested price for the lady!

> Her crimson robe in disarray;
> Jade hairpins now come awry.
> Delightful! Incomparable!
> Surely worth a thousand gold pieces!
> ("Glimpsed from Afar," *YT* 10.20; *TFP* 1150)

Descriptions of dancing-girls afford a writer great scope for this still-life observation, since the movement of the dance and the color of the scene could be portrayed within the refinements of phraseology. Much of Hsiao Kang's verse was written on this theme, and he is obviously much at home when conjuring up the breathless whirl of the dance, the flushed disarray of the girls, and the mounting excitement of the audience.

The most successful of Hsiao Kang's palace-style poetry, as indeed of all the verse in this genre, is probably that which is written, like its model the *Songs of the South*, overtly or to be understood in the first person. Characteristically, such poems are expressed from the woman's point of view, and usually the subject of the poem is from one of the more unfortunate categories of women. As a rule, less emphasis is placed on objective descriptions of luxury or external beauty. There may be inherent hypocrisy in such verse; after all, it is the poet himself and his class who are responsible for the predicament of which the girl is complaining, and the poet may only observe or guess at the feelings he writes about. Yet the delicacy with which personal sorrow is delineated is seen as one of the great accomplishments of palace-style writing.[28]

> The Northern Dipper lies across the sky.
> Night after night my lonely heart grieves,
> Moonbeams slant across my pillow,
> And my bed, half shadowed in the lamplight.
> ("Night after Night,"[29] *YT* 10.19a; *TFP* 1108)

> Your sad one, lonely, pines away her evenings.
> Snuffing the candle, she retires to her orchid boudoir
> Fearful only that the thrilling moon
> May shine upon her couch.
> ("Night after Night," *YT* 10.26a)

The earliest extant criticism of Hsiao Kang's work is by his brother, Crown Prince Chao-ming. This is a letter of thanks for a poem and a covering note that Hsiao Kang had sent him (*YKC* 3064). It is entirely congratulatory. Hsiao Kang, said his brother, was endowed with natural ability. His composition was well formed and pure in style and could be considered fine work. Another letter of thanks by Crown Prince Chao-ming reiterates his praises and compliments Hsiao Kang on phrases that the crown prince found especially pleasing:

I have received your letter, together with the eulogy you composed and recited. From beginning to end it is certainly worth reading. It is a most unusual and fine work. The phraseology has a classical air and the embellishment is most beautiful, both warm and elegant. Indeed it is meaningful, too, not a mere showy polish. It may be said to be lofty beyond any common throng. I read it over and over again and find it really good enough to cure an illness. As for the "twin trees" and the "Eight Arguments," you have the attainments of a Buddhist teacher. In your phrases "silver'd grasses" and "gilded clouds," you particularly bring out the visual beauties of the natural scene. I am extremely pleased by the basic intent. I will write again in more detail; I cannot exhaust all I have to say here.[30] ("Dictum in Reply to the Memorandum on the Recital in the Hsüan-fu Garden," KHMC 20; YKC 3060)

Crown Prince Chao-ming's criticism was, of course, of the work Hsiao Kang completed before he came to the East Palace as heir apparent and before palace-style composition was so designated. A quarter of a century later, the rebel general Hou Ching had a very different opinion to express. Hsiao Kang's literary composition, he said, did not rise above the libertine ideas expressed in the poem "Sang-chung" ("Among the Mulberries").[31] Since Liang times, Hou Ching's opinions, rather than Crown Prince Chao-ming's, have prevailed. Hsiao Kang's best poetry may not have survived; however, as a modern critic complains, there is still too much that is unacceptable to even the most tolerant reader.[32] A poem like "The Catamite" (YT 7.20a; TFP 1126), almost blatantly homosexual in its treatment of the charms of a young boy, must have scandalized men schooled in the tradition of poetry as the fount of morality. "Not for gentlemen," said Hsiao Kang's official biographers (LS 4.9b).[33]

Hsiao Kang himself became dissatisfied with the way palace-style poetry was developing. Crown Prince Chao-ming had compiled his Wen-hsüan anthology to exemplify the theories of the orthodox school and to demonstrate the superiority of classical over contemporary styles of writing. An eighth-century source suggested that Hsiao Kang resorted to the same method:

Originally, Emperor Chien-wen [Hsiao Kang] of Liang as crown prince enjoyed writing beautiful poetry, and all within the boundaries of the empire were transformed by it. It spread until it became common custom, and was called palace-style. In later years Emperor Chien-wen made attempts to rectify the situation, but it was too late. So he ordered Hsü Ling to compile the Yü-t'ai anthology to elevate the genre.[34]

The Wen-hsüan and the Yü-t'ai hsin-yung, one the compilation of the best of pre-Liang writings, the other including the best of contemporary lyric verse, are indeed the "crystallization of the tastes of the age."[35]

Of the 841 items in the *Yü-t'ai hsin-yung*, Hsiao Kang's is by far the largest contribution.[36] Hsü Ling, however, made no great claims for the material he was ordered to compile: "One has here recorded love songs enough to make ten scrolls. They are not fit to put alongside the *Odes* and hymns, nor are they the overflow from the bards; it is rather like the waters of the Ching and Wei."[37] He declined to include a single piece of Hsü Ch'ih's verse, despite his father's paramount importance in setting the trend. Of his own work, he selected two *yüeh-fu* compositions and four other verses, all of which were matching poems or were commissioned by Hsiao Kang.[38]

Hsiao Kang's efforts were perhaps not without results. In any case, palace-style verse continued into the succeeding Ch'en dynasty, captivated the North, and, after a temporary setback under Emperor Wen of the Sui, swept into the T'ang era as the prevailing literary taste. But the style was a spent force. Although major poets like the Four Masters of Early T'ang[39] brought new glow to its setting sun, other critics attacked its degenerate influence:

[T'ang] T'ai-tsung said to his courtiers, "I find great entertainment in composing ornately beautiful poetry." Yü Shih-nan rebuked him, "Although Your Majesty may be adept at such versifying, the style is not pristine. What the sovereign on high delights in, those below will follow. Should this writing maintain its popularity, I fear it will lead to the degeneration of manners, both now and in the future. I beg Your Majesty will heed this advice." T'ai-tsung replied, "Since you dare speak so frankly, I will respect your opinion. If all my ministers were like you the empire would never need fear disorder." Thereupon he presented Shih-nan with fifty bolts of silk. Originally, Emperor Chien-wen of Liang as crown prince enjoyed writing beautiful poetry . . . and ordered Hsü Ling to compile the *Yü-t'ai* anthology to elevate the genre. Yung-hsing's [i.e., Shih-nan] rebuke stemmed largely from this situation of the past. (*Ta-T'ang hsin-yü*)

P'ei Tzu-yeh, in "On Insect Carving," had had the disadvantage of pitting his arguments against the appeal of innovation. Later critics attacked from the strength of hindsight. All could point to governments that fell because of the taste for palace-style literature and the life it reflected.

When Chien-wen of Liang was at the East Palace, he too was fond of the *Odes*. His pure phraseology and artistic blending stopped at the sleeping mat [*Classics* IV, 89]. [His composition] was cut and polished, winding and flowery. His thought penetrated the deepest interior of the ladies' apartments. Later there appeared an *au courant* following, who indulged [in this style] to excess, until it flourished throughout the land. It was called "palace-style." Its dissoluteness spread unchecked and ended in catastrophe. (*Sui shu* 35.14b–15a [Palace ed.])

After the Ta-t'ung period [535–546] of the Liang dynasty, the ways of pristine elegance were drowned out. Composition became increasingly overloaded with allusion, and writers contended in their haste for the novel and artful. Chien-wen and Hsiang-tung were in the van of this licentiousness; Hsü Ling and Yü Hsin were the spearhead of this divergent trend. Shallow and flowery in content, their writings were obscure and overembellished. They valued frivolous and startling phraseology and were overly concerned with sentimental and melancholy thoughts. If judgment be made by the standards of Yen-ling, then this [poetry] would surely be the sound of a state in collapse![40] (*Sui shu* 76)

Many traditional Chinese writers felt that there was inherent immorality in palace-style writing. Richly embellished composition seen in the rhymeprose tradition stemming from the *Songs of the South* and the personal sentiments and love themes of the *Odes* were commendable. But even men of the open, tolerant Ming morality could complain that "Emperor Chien-wen's poetry is too concerned with women. Reading it, one seems to become half-intoxicated, sated, and bored."[41] One critic suggested that Hsiao Kang's writings were tabooed on account of his ill fate![42] Today the literature of the latter half of the sixth century is frequently ignored, glossed over, or trounced as a "poetic disgrace," "a crime," and "a black spot" in Chinese literary history.[43] Hsiao Kang's extreme views violated the cherished ideal of the Middle Way. His pursuit of artistic beauty overstepped the bounds of excess. Literature in Liang was the preserve of the aristocracy and was a political activity insofar as it was an important means of obtaining office and of advancing in rank. But the "politics" required of the highest ministers of state were literary parlor games and made mockery of the deep-rooted concepts of literature as both the tool and the critic of government.

Yet while his critics have been united in chorus against his style and subject matter, no one denies Hsiao Kang's impeccable technique.[44] Later writers may have scorned to choose his palace-style writing consciously, but it was less easy to escape the more subtle influences that Hsiao Kang's work exerted. Even when one consults comprehensive source books like the *P'ei-wen-yün-fu* for usage of an unusual term, more often than not it is Hsiao Kang's own line that meets the eye. Again, in the aids to composition and in major anthologies compiled in T'ang and thereafter, Hsiao Kang's pieces appear with noticeable frequency as the model of a genre on a particular theme.[45]

CHAPTER 6

Philosophy and Religion

THE cultured gentleman of the Six Dynasties period was expected to be learned in the Confucian tradition, to be adept in Taoist-oriented metaphysical discourse, and, especially during Liang times, to be au courant with trends in Buddhist scholarship and a patron of Buddhist art and literature. Hsiao Kang's erudition and lifelong interest in these three teachings is exemplified in his prolific writings on these subjects. His biography says that he "read ten lines at a glance and was versed in the Nine Schools and the Hundred Philosophies. He remembered everything that passed before his eyes. He had a wide understanding of Confucian writings and at the same time excelled in discourse on [Taoist] metaphysics" (*LS* 4.8b).

His contemporary, Yen Chih-t'ui, made particular reference to Hsiao Kang's Taoist activities: "Coming into the Liang era, the [Taoist] metaphysics of Chuang, Lao, and the *Chou Changes*, known as the Three Mysteries, again became fashionable. Emperor Wu and Chien-wen [Hsiao Kang] lectured and discoursed in person."[1] Bibliographies of Hsiao Kang's works in the official histories list exegeses of Confucian and Taoist canons totaling many folios.

Hsiao Kang's formal education was necessarily strictly Confucian. However, in literati-official circles of the Southern courts, Taoist ideas were an everyday topic of discussion. The popularity of Taoism waned somewhat as Emperor Wu became more deeply attracted to the Buddhist cause, and early in his reign he decreed the abolition of Taoist shrines and the return of Taoist priests to the laity. Characteristically, Taoist practitioners like the renowned T'ao Hung-ching (451–536) chose an anchorite existence in the southern mountains, and, despite repeated requests from the throne to take an active part in the government,

118

they remained aloof from court circles. Sometime between 521 and 523, while Hsiao Kang was governor of South Hsü province, he made T'ao Hung-ching's acquaintance. The elderly recluse is said to have attended the audience dressed in the simple garb of a hermit, but nevertheless Hsiao Kang received him with the deepest courtesy. They spent several days in discussion, which suggests that they found stimulation in each other's conversation. T'ao Hung-ching was a noted chess player. One imagines the ancient sage and the youthful prince engaged in abstruse Taoist philosophies over a chessboard. Nearly two decades later, when T'ao Hung-ching died, Hsiao Kang composed an elegant epitaph. This was only one of a number of obituaries written by men of the time to mourn T'ao's passing. But Hsiao Kang's extraordinary elaborations suggest his genuine regard; those few days' talk sixteen years before probably were not the sum of their association (*YKC* 3027).

Articulate presentation of ideas in extempore debate (as opposed to prepared oratory) was highly esteemed among the nobility. Regard for this accomplishment dated from pre-Han times and flourished particularly during the Chin and Sung eras. A man could establish a formidable reputation on the strength of his ready wit alone. These conversations, known as "pure-talk" and "analysis of principles" (*ch'ing-t'an ming-li*), were still popular in the late Six Dynasties period, but by that time they had acquired a more formal function in official society. From Ch'i through Liang, and until T'ang, oral examinations testing a candidate's prowess were a condition of entry into official employment. An item by Hsiao Kang in praise of his brother, Crown Prince Chao-ming, testifies to the popularity of this practice during Liang and to the high status enjoyed by an expert.[2]

These philosophical discussions were frequently held in the Hsüan-fu garden of the East Palace. In this idyllic setting, Hsiao Kang lectured on the Taoist mystic writings of Chuang-tzu and Lao-tzu. Here too, lectures and recitations were given by other members of the royal family and by favored ministers. Chou Hung-cheng, an officer who had opposed Hsiao Kang's selection as crown prince, had since boyhood been a leading figure in Three Mysteries studies; and one of Emperor Wu's closest associates, Chu I, had for years attracted large audiences to his expositions of the classics. In 540, after a decade in the East Palace, Hsiao Kang sponsored Chu I in the presentation of an exegesis of the *Changes* in the Hsüan-fu garden (*YKC* 3003). Chu I was a member of a faction hostile to Hsiao Kang, and the power of Hsiao Kang's pen eventually led to Chu I's death; but at this time, perhaps to flatter Emperor Wu, Hsiao Kang had only compliments for the minister. Hsiao Kang was equally famed for his oratory. Not to be outdone by the lesser nobility, he once recited an exegesis of the Five Classics, composed by Emperor Wu. On this occasion the entire court and everyone from the surrounding district flocked to the Hsüan-fu garden to listen.

The Liang era represents the terminal stage of what is termed the "period of domestication" of Buddhism in China. Buddhism was introduced into China at about the time the Christian era began, and by the turn of the fourth century was becoming absorbed into Chinese patterns of civilization. The two centuries of the Chin, Sung, and Ch'i eras were characterized by Chinese attempts to comprehend Indian Buddhist ideas. Efforts were made to secure authentic texts and to improve translations. Exegesis went on apace. By Liang times, readier communications between the clerical establishments proliferating in both the North and the South and the general availability of texts and new translations, together with the secure patronage of the aristocracy, gave added impetus to these efforts. New ideas evolved from constant discussion, which in turn developed interest in comparative studies and attempts to relate doctrines to particular systems of Buddhist thought. Scriptures and treatises were selected for special study and propounded by experts. Herein lay the origin of the schools of Buddhism which came to flower in Sui and T'ang times.[3]

The Liang intellectuals were primarily attracted to the study of the Mahāyāna (Great Vehicle) *Nirvānasutra*, which taught that all sentient beings would in the future attain Buddahood; and the so-considered Hīnayāna (Lesser Vehicle) *Satyasiddhiśastra* (Essay on the Perfection of Truth), which taught the dual categories of mortal and transcendental truth, and Hīnayāna concepts of analysis of individual beings. Under Emperor Wu attention began to shift away from these theories in favor of the *San-lun* (Three Treatises) Mādhyamika (Middle Path) system developed by such famed foreign clerics as Seng-lang and his disciples Seng-ch'üan and Fa-lang (507–581), a trend that continued into T'ang times under Fa-lang's great disciple, Chi-tsang (549–623). More popular was the *Vimalakīrtisūtra,* the story of the rich, lay patron of Buddhism, Vimalakīrti, which provided a model with whom the Liang nobility could identify.

In terms of scholarly interest on the part of the literati-aristocracy and the lavish material support ensured by the throne's lead in making donations, the half-century duration of the Liang dynasty was a heyday of Buddhism in China. However, the dynastic historians of the Confucian T'ang era preferred to ignore, if not deliberately suppress, records of the Buddhist affiliations professed by officials and ruling members of the imperial family as being outside the scope and interests of exemplar, Confucian history, unless those affiliations so far intruded upon their official functions in the Confucian state as to provoke censure—a prime example being the religious eccentricities of Emperor Wu himself. (On several occasions Emperor Wu voluntarily entered Buddhist establishments as a slave, requiring a ransom of millions of cash from the nobility for his restoration to the imperial court.) Thus, other than a list of his works on Buddhist topics, interspersed among the titles of his other writings, no mention is made in Hsiao Kang's official biography of any Buddhist activity on his part.

It was quite usual, however, for the nobility to take lay vows. For Hsiao Kang, growing up in a household and court environment dominated by his father's religious fervor, this would have been obligatory. Lay ordination took place at the age of twenty, at which age Hsiao Kang was governor of South Hsü province, or had begun his tour of duty in Yung province. He returned to the capital to make his vows in the P'ing-teng temple under the eye of his father. His letter to the Prince of Hsiang-tung contains a vivid description of the ceremonies he underwent and records his emotions. Informal as the letter is, it may well be unique as a subjective depiction of a Buddhist ceremony of the Liang period.

Apart from the Buddhist content, there are incidental points of interest. At this time Hsiao Kang had not yet lost his youthful enthusiasm in the decadence of provincial court life, and he writes that he was not overly irked by official responsibilities. There is further confirmation of the literary life he enjoyed with his friends, including Hsü Ch'ih and Yü Chien-wu who accompanied him on this visit to the capital.

During the evening of the eighteenth, in the outer apartment of the Hua-lin Hall, I received your letter of the first day of the ninth month. This did much to alleviate my worries about you. Autumn is chill and clear; we are having seasonal weather. My appointment in the provinces is not overly tiresome. I have time for pleasant reflection just as before. I enjoy myself to the full and from time to time there are happy occasions. My literary colleagues and guests chat together and enjoy good conversation, and we keep company to the end of the feast. What is like recent times? Your commentary on the *History of the Han* proceeds in sequence. I have a great hunger to see this work.

I have received the Boddhissatva precepts and have accepted the Māhāssatva office. This was on the twelfth. Then I made my private confession in the East City. Early in the morning of the seventeenth I entered the Pao-yün [Jeweled Cloud (Hall)]. The walls and doors were sunlit. Bronze dragons belched forth a fog [of incense]. Reddened fountains enclosed shadows; blue lotus exuded fragrance. The clergy congregated in crowds; the "golden mountain" was fully occupied.

My body and mind were elated; I experienced a miracle. Yesterday morning, after being in the congregation of monks at the P'ing-teng Temple, my ordination was conducted without impediment. The emperor himself assisted in the ceremony, and his pure countenance personally bore witness. Although I made many prostrations I was not aware of fatigue. And when [the small patch on] my head was shaved, I attained ecstasy. My mind and mouth made the responses automatically; my lusts were shorn away.... [The abbot] Seng Chin's classic sermon differed in no way from ancient days. All day I questioned him, just like Tzu-lu [the disciple of Confucius who was intent on perfecting each precept, fearful that he would hear another before he had perfected the one].... The emperor affixed his seal of approval; now I have undertaken the rules of [lay Buddhist] conduct. Yesterday evening I returned to my lodgings. Hsü Ch'ih and Yü Chien-wu were in constant attendance, day and night.... [There follows news about mutual acquaintances.] But since I arrived at the capital my mind has been agitated. I may open my mouth to laugh, but I am not truly happy. It is two hundred days since I drank any wine.[4] (*KHMC* 27; *YKC* 3011)

Although the official histories say nothing of Hsiao Kang's Buddhism, there is a column of incidental detail in a study of the monk Pao Ch'ang; typically it has to do with Hsiao Kang's literary endeavors: "When [Hsiao] Kang occupied the Spring District [East Palace], he was devoted to the inner teachings [of Buddhism]. He compiled the *Fa-pao lien-pi* [a work of] more than two hundred folios and commissioned the monk Pao Ch'ang to edit and revise the work."[5]

Hsiao Kang wrote many hundreds of folios on Buddhist themes, a quantity far exceeding his poetry, official writings, and Taoist exegeses. Subject matter consisted of letters and epitaphs for clergymen, sermons and vows, letters relating to temple visits and donations, palace-style descriptions of Buddhist retreats, stele inscriptions, essays, hagiography, and massive compendia of Buddhist lore. These items vary from a few words to several thousand. Some of this writing has been preserved in anthologies of Buddhist texts, but his major dissertations, including the monumental *Fa-pao lien-pi,* are lost. It is ironic that had any of these survived, Hsiao Kang might be remembered above all as a great Buddhist writer. It has been suggested, on the other hand, that he had no more to say in a million words than in a hundred, and that we have been spared the bulk of his commonplace labors. His work is never mentioned in discussions of Buddhism in China; his contribution to the religion has been overlooked in the maze of his rhetoric or has been dismissed as superficial literary dazzle. But if he was guilty of mere display of erudition (a charge laid against Emperor Wu), at least he was well-enough versed in the Buddhist tradition to assimilate its terminology and canons smoothly into native Chinese idiom and bring a high degree of literary elegance to Chinese composition on Buddhist subjects.[6]

The literary quality of Hsiao Kang's Buddhist work is well exemplified in a story about floating stone Buddhas. One version of the story, told by a monk of the early Liang dynasty, is a bald account in less than two hundred characters. The "facts" were stated briefly, in plain narrative style: "These [two stone images] had been found [in 313] toward the end of the Western Chin dynasty, floating in the Hu-tu estuary of the Wu-sung River. Fishermen thought they were marine deities."[7] Hsiao Kang developed the tale into an epic of some thousand characters. After a preamble containing a series of allusions to similar phenomena in Chinese history, the text continues:

In the first year of the Chien-hsing period of the Chin, the *kuei-yu* year [313], the estuary of the Sung River within the Lou district of Wu prefecture was called Hu-tu. The region was inhabited, and the populace made their living by fishing.
Suspending their abundant lines, they do not pot the small *chieh*;
Spreading their ninefold dragnets, long they await the six giant turtles.
Gazing out to sea they observed what appeared to be two human forms.
Seen in the light of day, half-submerged [the stone images] resembled ephemeral water-spray;
By night they emitted a radiance, suddenly like submarine fire.
And thus they were called marine deities.[8]
"Inscription on the Stone Images of Wu-chün," (*IWLC* 77; *Su-chou fu chih*; *YKC* 3031)

After adding new detail to the narrative, Hsiao Kang leads up to an inscription in sixteen four-character-line couplets.

Such is the range, variety, and exuberance of Hsiao Kang's allusion in this and other pieces that his mastery of the Chinese and Buddhist texts available in the South is indisputable. A contribution so creative and appreciative is more than enough to expect of a man in his position. Rather than seeking profound analysis of Buddhist doctrine in Hsiao Kang's work, the modern reader might better enjoy the valuable literary descriptions he furnishes of Buddhist life as practiced by the lay nobility at the capital.

The Buddhist writings of the lay nobility, as might be expected, contain little theological analysis, but they do nevertheless provide clues to the degree to which the nobility even at this relatively late date still confused Buddhist concepts with native Chinese tradition. In some instances this confusion arose from ordinary misunderstanding, but frequently the author saw no need to distinguish the traditions and drew upon either source for apt reference. A text that illustrates this characteristic is Hsiao Kang's "Absolution for the Six Senses." This long oration enjoined the congregation to repent with sincere heart the deeds of the senses of sight, hearing, smell, taste, touch, and mind which obstruct the attainment of the Buddha state (*YKC* 3032).

Throughout the piece the important Indian Buddhist distinction between *ken* "indriyam" (sense organ) and *shih* "vijnana" (perception of the sense organ) is ignored and the two words are freely interchanged. In the first vow, to excise the mortal eyes and blink the eyes of Buddha, the phrase "vermillion and purple" used to describe the ignorance of the sight *indriyam* is foreign to Buddhist rhetoric. Its classical location is the Confucian *Analects,* and a long tradition existed in China of red, a primary color, representing orthodoxy, while purple, a secondary or impure color, represented deviance. The aural sense, said Hsiao Kang, is obtuse, seeding the many hosts of evils. It delights in the taints of strings and songs. Hearing the meritorious voice of the Dharma one is dimly conscious and drowsy, but listening to the "licentious strains of Cheng and Wei" one sits up and bends the ear. Here again the *Analects* provided Hsiao Kang with his rhetoric. The Taoist *Chuang-tzu* provided a reference in the section on the olfactory sense, wherein the crow unwittingly craves loathsome vermin.[9]

The Indian tradition differentiated the taste function of the tongue *indriyam* from its function as a speech organ. The excesses of speech occur in a different context. The Chinese, however, tended to fuse both functions. Thus, having listed exotic Chinese delicacies which inevitably pall the gourmet palate—turtle broth, mutton stew, stomach of the *pao* bird, belly of the deer, phoenix wings, and dragon's womb, served upon napkins of gauze and in tripods and rhinocerus-horn utensils—Hsiao Kang referred to the Confucian canons to illustrate the consequences of the slander of a "three-inch tongue," a description commonly found in the Chinese classics. And having deviated thus far from the Indian notion, he stressed his point further by referring to Indian stories—the scolding of Ananda when he was begging for milk, and the silence maintained by Vimalakīrti—neither of which had to do with the taste function of tongue *indriyam*.[10]

A similar misconception existed with regard to the body

indriyam. The Indian concept limited this sense organ to the physical body. Hsiao Kang, however, included the "person" within the scope of the body. And so, after expatiating on physical indulgences—elephant-bamboo matting, fresh and sleek for the summer quarters; double-lined white fox fur, warm and cozy in the winter apartments; the four-in-harness; the spacious mansions—he trespassed upon consideration of the "real self."

The litterateur Hsiao Kang was of course more concerned with rhetoric than with theological niceties; the juxtaposition of Chinese and Indian references brilliantly served the demands of parallel prosody and misconceptions or misrepresentations of dogma could not diminish the literary effect. In this exhibition of scriptural erudition there was no place, nor desire on the part of author and audience, for intellectual contribution to Buddhist learning. Within these limitations, though, Hsiao Kang characteristically excelled his contemporaries in the scope and perfection of his work and in his easy familiarity with the contemporary Buddhist canons.

The ritual aspects of Buddhism and the rules of lay conduct were important to the protocol-minded Liang court. Clerics specializing in Vinaya (discipline) studies found an honored place with the royal family. Such a man was the eminent metropolitan monk Shih Seng-yu, a colleague of the literary critic, Liu Hsieh. So immense was his prestige that he had access to the women's apartments, where he supervised the undertaking of the lay precepts by the imperial wives, including Hsiao Kang's mother, Ting Ling-kuang. One of Seng-yu's disciples was Pao Ch'ang, whose literary merit earned him the invitation to edit Hsiao Kang's massive *Fa-pao lien-pi* compilation.

The canonical and intellectual aspects of Vinaya, of course, were of less concern to the nobility than everyday "good form." There survives a curious item by Hsiao Kang listing the penalties for various breaches of discipline or etiquette during a lay (*upāsaka*) ceremony. This too is a rare description of lay practice:

Dozing, falling asleep, and failing to answer the roll call: penalty, twenty prostrations and attendance of a recital of three *sutras* at the incense burner. (1)

Leaving without permission: penalty, ten prostrations. (2)

Leaving and failing to return for [the space of] three *sutras*: penalty, ten prostrations. (3)

Those seated at the sides who doze off and fail to speak upon the arrival of a proctor: penalty, ten prostrations. (4)

Those seated at the sides who fall asleep, hide their faces, and fail to speak to the proctor: penalty, ten prostrations. (5)

A proctor who, not diligent in following [the ceremony], commits a breach of the rules, fails to ask punishment, and is discovered by the assembly, that proctor shall be penalized by twenty prostrations and attendance of a recital of three *sutras* at the incense burner. (6)

Clerical and lay proctors will conduct mutual disciplinary investigations. If there be laxity in vigilance: penalty, twenty prostrations. (7)

Those who fail to chant "amen" at the end of a *sutra*: penalty, ten prostrations. (8)

Asking leave out of turn: penalty, ten prostrations. (9)

Clerical and lay proctors who mistakenly grant leave: penalty, ten prostrations. (10)
("Preface to the Ceremony of the Eight Abstentions," *KHMC* 28; *YKC* 3018)

In reality, *upāsaka* ceremonies during Liang times became little more than an extension of literary salon activity. The Buddhist calendar provided frequent occasions for palace-style sermons and prayers. Hsiao Kang's surviving work provides plentiful illustration of these, the most notable items being the "Prayer for those ordained on the eighth day of the fourth month [Buddha's birthday]," "Absolution for the Six Senses," and "On Repenting of Arrogance." The tedious liturgy of these items gives meaning to Hsiao Kang's strictures against somnolence! (*YKC* 3034, 3032).

Buddhism, for the nobility, was more for enjoyment than for reverence. Visits to temples in idyllic garden and mountain settings were often organized. There exists considerable correspondence between Hsiao Kang and his father that illustrates the frequent trips between the court and various monasteries to

view newly erected spires and *stupas* and to attend sermons
and orations on the sutras. On occasion, these excursions were
formal family outings. One of Hsiao Kang's pieces is "A Memorial
Requesting a Visit to the Ch'ung-yün Temple to Attend a
Sermon." This and the two subsequent repetitions of the request
open with the petitioners' names—the three princes Hsiao Lun,
Hsiao Chi, and Hsiao Kang. Letters of thanks provided opportunity for palace-style descriptions of sumptuous temple furnishings and natural landscape (*YKC* 3005, 3006). Among the best
of this genre is a poem by Hsiao Kang, "On Viewing the T'ung-
t'ai Temple Spire":

> Seen from afar, the monastery spire
> Is girdled with jade and hung with pearls.
> Candle-bright silver o'erleaps the Han and Ju;
> Jewelled bell clappers o'erdistance the Kun and Wu.
> In the dawning aura, emitting bright scintilla;
> In a murmuring breeze, distinct the pentatones.
> Ever full the catchments in the falling dew;
> *T'ung* trees grow there; the phoenix never depart.
> Fluttering pennants commingle in evening iridescence;
> Painted birds join the morning geese. (*TFP* 1120)

In addition to these outings, vast Buddhist convocations were
held from time to time. A letter from Hsiao Kang to the Prince
of Hsiang-tung described the enormous scale and the protracted
duration of one such gathering. Hsiao Kang talks of the clergy
and laity congregating together, coming from near and far.
"Every day the assembly of white-robed laity and black-garbed
clergy numbered some twenty or thirty thousand." But just at
this time, in the spring, Hsiao Kang was ill. More than half
the letter describes his sufferings. Yet he was quite as unhappy
at missing the proceedings as he was over his physical discom-
fort. However, by the "thirteenth day" he was well enough to
put in an appearance (*YKC* 3011).

A letter Hsiao Kang wrote to one of his clergy friends, the
dharma-master Hui Yen, tells of a Buddhist convocation to be
held in the "northern hills" (*YKC* 3013). Again it was springtime, and again the occasion must have been a grand one with
the "gathering of the imperial sages." Hsiao Kang was impatiently

awaiting the time, and while anticipating the event "one day seemed like three years." The mood of the letter points to a casual intimacy between the correspondents. Hsiao Kang ingratiates himself as a devout Buddhist by complaining of the distractions of his lay duties and of his fatigue in mundane cares. He regularly refers to himself as "disciple" (*ti-tzu*) here and in his formal Buddhist essays. The old controversy over the respect to be shown by the clergy toward the throne had long been settled; in a regime during which the emperor himself entered the church as a slave, it was not remarkable for a prince to humble himself before a cleric. The formulaistic "obeisance to the South" at the end of the letter—obeisance to the land of the Buddha rather than to the Chinese emperor (which required the subject to face north)—emphasizes the thorough domestication of Buddhism in China by mid-Liang times.[11]

One such convocation became the cover for an attempted coup d'état. Hsiao Hung, Emperor Wu's brother and father of Hsiao Cheng-te, was having an incestuous relationship with his niece, Emperor Wu's daughter by Madam Hsi, Hsiao Kang's half-sister, the Yung-hsing princess. Hsiao Hung promised the princess that if she helped him kill Emperor Wu, and he himself could usurp the throne, he would make her his empress. They chose for their coup the occasion of a vegetarian ceremony convened by Emperor Wu, at which the entire royal family was to be in attendance. The princess armed two of her men with swords and disguised them in women's clothing as maids-in-waiting. However, as one of them crossed the threshold into the hall of ceremony, he dropped a slipper. A palace guard noticed this highly improbable little mishap and reported his suspicions to the noble consort, Lady Ting. Lady Ting would have informed the emperor, but was afraid he would not believe her. Instead, she had the palace guard station eight palace coachmen dressed in livery behind an arras. After the ceremony had concluded and the congregation had dispersed, sure enough the princess begged a private audience with the emperor. Permission was granted, and as the princess advanced up the steps her two men sprang forward. Just then, Lady Ting's eight coachmen jumped out from behind the arras and seized them. The emperor was so startled he fell back into the screens behind his throne. The princess's men were searched and their swords discovered, and they admitted they were under Hsiao Hung's orders. Emperor Wu exacted a fiendish revenge: he kept the information to himself, killed the two men and sent the princess into banishment in a black-lacquered coach. She died soon after of rage and resentment; nor did the emperor deign to visit her deathbed. Hsiao Hung was left in ignorance of the outcome of his plot, and by April or May 526, he too was on his deathbed. Seven times the emperor made formal state visits to his mortally sick brother, but without ever revealing his knowledge of Hsiao Hung's complicity, until finally, on May 14, at the age of fifty-three, the terror-stricken Hsiao Hung died (NS 51.18ab).

Emperor Wu's religious compulsions ensured the lavish support of the metropolitan temples, some of which, like the famed T'ung-t'ai temple built to the memory of Lady Ting, were established by his personal decree. More than once the aristocracy were obliged to pay ransoms totaling millions of cash to redeem him from his voluntary bondage; and conforming to his example, much of their private wealth was funneled off in lavish donations. The embellishment of these temples imposed huge demands on the precious-metal resources of the state. As mentioned in Chapter One, an immediate result was the shortage and debasement of gold and copper coinage and the introduction of iron coinage to alleviate the critical fiscal situation. Lack of a stable currency forced recourse to barter in some provincial areas and a general decline in trade.

More than half a dozen letters that Hsiao Kang addressed to Emperor Wu elaborated on particular donations. There is specific reference to the donation of one hundred thousand cash to the King Asoka temple; memorials thanking Emperor Wu for the gift of two hundred thousand cash and ten *chin* each of white sandalwood and fragrant incense for the erection of a spire and a gift of ten thousand *chin* of copper, and for the gift of thirteen thousand *chin* of copper for casting the "spirit-pan" on the *stupa* of the Shan-chüeh temple; and a series of correspondence on the erection of spires for the Shan-chüeh and T'ung-t'ai temples. In addition, Hsiao Kang composed elegant vows to undertake charitable offices himself. These bore such titles as "Vow to Establish a Thousand Buddhas," "Vow to

Create an Eighteen-feet High Lacquer and Gilt Image for Mankind," and "On Building Temples for Mankind."[12] A typically elaborate item is the "Vow to be Donor to All Temples." In terms of Buddhist dogma, this is a solidly Mahayanan text; although typical of Liang court Buddhists, Hsiao Kang was far less aware or concerned with the subtleties of Buddhist sectarianism than he was with the oratorical brilliance of his text:

> I, the disciple Hsiao Kang, who have taken the Boddhisattva precepts, take refuge in the entire Buddahood of the Ten Quarters, including all the realms of space; I take refuge in the entire worshipful *dharma* of the Ten Quarters, including all the realms of space; I take refuge in the entire holy *sangha* of the Ten Quarters, including all the realms of space. . . . I make this vow: I, this day, on behalf of the T'ai-p'ing temple of Mount Wu-tang, and the Wang-ch'u, Pai-t'a, T'ung-an, Hsi-shan, Yen-ming, T'ou-t'o, Shang Feng-lin, Hsia Feng-lin, Kuang-yen, and other temples of this city, vow that so long as I may live, I will forever be donor to them. . . . With this merit I plead for blessings upon the emperor and the Spring Palace, and that within the imperial domains and without, all may share in this excellence. Then all will be recipients of this blessing to the very eight classes [which begin with] heaven and the *nagas*, the six paths [of transmigration], and the four forms of birth.[13] (*KHMC* 28; *YKC* 3034)

A description par excellence of the fabulous decor of the richly endowed temples at the capital is contained in Hsiao Kang's "Eulogy on the Boddhi Tree," although as at least one commentator observes, "It is not always easy to disentangle literary flights from description."[14]

More practical and perceptive aspects of Hsiao Kang's piety are revealed in another unusual item. Here he charged monastic communities with laxity in their temple responsibilities and with lazy acceptance of empty form in religious practice. His eloquent plea was for deeper understanding of the significance of the gorgeous icons and ritual in metropolitan Buddhist life. Although there is none of the anguished concern of a Tao-an or a Hui Yüan over the concept of icons and the necessity of visualizing Buddha through mental concentration, Hsiao Kang showed characteristically sensitive appreciation of the purpose of religious paraphernalia. His remarks are reminiscent of his "Preface to the Ceremony of the Eight Abstentions," where, concerned with the problem of "controlling the serpent of the mind and expelling the drunken elephant," he recommended that one's "eyes be on the Golden Countenance, and ears feast upon the jade tones"—that focusing one's gaze on an icon and concentrating on the music will help blot out mundane distractions and bring the whole mind to dwell on pure Buddhist teachings.

The temples and *stupas* in this region proliferate. Despite their numbers, however, they are splendidly embellished and fully equipped with ceremonial vessels. Externally they certainly appear glorious and lavish; but the underlying intent is not in fact so noble. Why is this? The object here of casting metal, carving jade, chasing lacquer, and painting pottery is to revere and proclaim the Incarnate Person and to concentrate attention upon Divine Enlightenment. . . . Therefore, worshiping the spirits as if they were present is the most exalted way of honoring them; the sages being so remote [in time] is the most profound reason for cherishing them.[15]

The substance of Hsiao Kang's complaint is that the objects of veneration, which he felt should be on permanent display, were exhibited only infrequently and were otherwise stored in boxes:

Without exception, the temples of this district exhibit their images only briefly, on the day of the nativity. After that, [these images] are sealed in cases, and even the clothing is stripped from their bodies and the flame aureoles detached from their heads. Sometimes five or ten saints are placed together in a single shrine, or bodhissatvas and buddhas are packed away in the same cabinet. In truth it may be said that the heart contradicts the fact; that appearances are right though the intentions are wrong. There is much desire for glory, but little interest in spiritual advancement. The red coffers in the pagodas of ancient times preserved only holy relics. The white canopy on the head of the image [or elephant?] was not a reference to the whole body. Painted images were used for commemorative purposes, and they furthermore taught the lower officials and the common people a sense of reverence. The map molded in metal kept the ruler of Yüeh forever mindful. It is just as the [swords] Lung [ch'üan and T'ai]-a were able to leap from their scabbards; and just like the tiger and the rhinoceros that were spoken of "as escaped from their cages."[16] How much more so should this be true of the Almighty, the Completely Merciful, the Peerless Aggregation of Goodness, whose name when heard dispels care, and whose form when seen enters one upon the Way. Yet they would screen this carven fragrance, and pile up the sandalwood, bind and hoard the jade hair, and seal up the gold palms. It is a different situation from the time at Rājagṛha when for so long [Buddha] entered the four heavens; and again there is a difference from [the practice] at Jetavana of closing the doors for three months. The jeweled halls [of the metropolitan temples] are vacant, and the magnificent staircases are empty. The closed curtains are never opened—but not because of [Tung] Chung-shu's perverse teachings. The red walls are forever locked in, as though they were Pin-ch'ing's sanctuary from his enemies.[17] Here now are these spacious halls like overhanging clouds and these lofty ridges whereon birds perch. If the jade thrones displayed therein are embellished with gold inlay, it is certain that dirt would no longer cloud the sunlike form, nor would tarnish blotch the moonlike countenance. If the glazed windows are close-set, then it would be impossible for the lightest breeze to enter. Finely woven "dragon-beard" matting would suffice to keep out swallows in their flight. At the same time it would ensure that the reasons for showing reverence would always be respected, and the desire to pay obeisance [to Buddha] would be strengthened. This is publicly decreed at once and is to be carried out forever. (*KHMC* 16; *YKC* 3001)

Occasionally, even in commonsense complaints like this, Hsiao Kang's rhetoric in passing casually hints at topics of major philosophical importance. For example, his references to "closed curtains" and "Tung Chung-shu's perverse teachings." Typically, these hints occur in lists of examples and similes, paired and balanced, illustrating some other concern under discussion. Hsiao Kang naturally assumed a high degree of shared experience and comprehension on the part of his colleagues, who formed his audience, and saw no necessity to explain his references. In any case, development and expansion of these remarks in such context would have been entirely out of place as, for example, an exegesis on Christian theology would be in a Shakespearean soliloquy.

The Han scholar, Tung Chung-shu (?179–?104 B.C.), was said

to have instructed his pupils from behind a closed curtain. His biography continues that for three years he never looked out into the garden, such was his diligence. His importance lay in his association with the establishment of state Confucianism under Emperor Wu (r. 140–87 B.C.) of Han, and with the founding of the eclectic, superstitious, and quasi-religious new text interpretation of the Confucian classics.

In criticizing Tung Chung-shu, Hsiao Kang seemed to favor the old text school skeptics—a rational stand characteristic of his commonsense attitudes. However, in Chapter Four we mentioned briefly a text concerning an exegesis of the *Mao Odes* in which he criticized in similarly casual reference the Han scholar Ma Yung (76–166) and his pupil Cheng Hsüan (127–200), both of whom were famous classical commentators and whose work mainly dealt with old text versions. In Hsiao Kang's context, though, Ma and Cheng were criticized for their orthodox moral-political utilitarian interpretation of the *Odes*—a concept shared by both new text and old text schools alike, and indeed by all orthodox Confucian scholar-bureaucrats—as opposed to Hsiao Kang's advocacy of all poetry, including the *Odes*, as the "free expression of personal emotion."[18]

Long before Liang, the old text school had more or less gained ascendancy and the controversy had ceased to be a burning issue (though it would be revived in later eras). Philosophical interests had moved on to Taoist metaphysics and the whole new universe of Buddhism. However, Hsiao Kang's incidental, allusive references to key figures in the dispute indicate that the subject was still a very familiar one, requiring no elucidation. In any case, Hsiao Kang had moved beyond partisanship in either new or old text schools, and, especially in regard to the *Odes*, questioned the validity of the very orthodoxy of Confucian utilitarianism. A rational man, with basically literary predilections, he appreciated the classics, histories, and philosophies, including the Buddhist canon, for the literary enjoyment to be derived therefrom and as a fount of reference and allusion to embellish his own literary production.

CHAPTER 7

The Fall of Chien-k'ang

FOR a century and a half the North had been under the rule of the Tartar Toba house of Wei. On November 8, 534, a Wei minister named Kao Huan formally declared the secession of territories in his control, established an emperor, and inaugurated the Eastern Wei dynasty. Kao Huan's principal aide in the coup was a Tartar soldier, Hou Ching.[1] Thirteen years later, in 547, Kao Huan died. His son, Kao Teng, was less well disposed toward his father's old ally, now in sole command of the area covering modern Honan and leading an army of a hundred thousand men, and planned to have Hou Ching recalled and stripped of his power. Hou Ching rejected the summons and offered to surrender his holdings to Yü-wen T'ai of the rival Western Wei regime. Yü-wen T'ai accepted Hou Ching's overtures, with the reservation that Hou Ching's loyalty was too much to expect. He made it clear that Hou Ching would be obliged to relinquish control of his forces and territory, and even bring the Eastern Wei capital at Ch'angan under the sway of the Western Wei court at Loyang. At this point, Kao Teng mobilized an army to attack Hou Ching. Caught between two foes, Hou Ching sent envoys to Emperor Wu in the south, offering submission if the Liang would assist him in this crisis.

Emperor Wu, forty-six years the sovereign of the South, saw in Hou Ching's entreaties the chance to fulfill his ambition of bringing all China under one power. But whatever opportunity there might have been to accomplish this grand design was undermined by Emperor Wu's choice of the man to lead the campaign. He originally intended to appoint Hsiao Fan, known for his martial vigor, and his grandson, Hsiao Hui-li, as co-commanders in chief. However, the emperor's close adviser, Chu I, eavesdropped on the deliberations, and at the mention of Hsiao Fan rushed in to object that Hsiao Fan was cruel and

rapacious and that the provincial populace from whom Hsiao
Fan's force would be recruited (in modern Kiangsu) was near
revolt. So Hsiao Fan was passed over; instead, Emperor Wu
appointed his nephew, Hsiao Yüan-ming, then garrison commander of Shou-yang (modern central Kiangsu), who had long
importuned the emperor for this command. Hsiao Yüan-ming and
Chu I then slandered the co-commander, Hsiao Hui-li (already
in disfavor with the emperor), for his proud and overbearing
manner toward his fellow officers. He was recalled, and Hsiao
Yüan-ming was left in sole command.

Such personal intrigue among the high command was to
enervate decision and disrupt strategy throughout the ensuing
hostilities. Furthermore, the Liang peasantry had long been
disaffected toward their rulers. Local revolts had occurred with
increasing frequency and on an increasingly large scale. And
so it was that Hsiao Yüan-ming's force was largely composed
of bankrupt peasantry. Morale was at its lowest ebb. The men
had to be driven into battle, and were they not chained and
fettered at the neck and wrists the whole army would have
melted away in desertion. Corruption was rife among the
officers. All vestige of discipline was neglected, and they plun-
dered and pillaged wherever the marches led their sorry hordes.
The decisive battle against the Eastern Wei came on December 10, 548. Hsiao Yüan-ming was in a drunken stupor and
could not be roused. His generals refused to obey any command
or to give battle. Individual heroics proved useless, and the
day ended when Hsiao Yüan-ming was captured and the Southern army virtually obliterated.

Following this rout of the Liang partner, Eastern Wei turned
upon Hou Ching. Shortly before, Hou Ching had rejected an
offer of truce from Eastern Wei, thus abandoning his mother,
wife, and children, held hostage by the Eastern Wei court, to
their fate. Now he fought his way out of the Northern encirclement, but stranded and faced with months of winter conditions
and shortages of supplies, his Northern soldiery began to desert
him. Finally, with only eight hundred followers, Hou Ching fled
south and tricked the commander of Shou-yang City, "a timorous
man, and none too bright" (NS 80.3b), into giving him sanctuary
in Liang territory.

News of this engagement reached the Southern capital as a rumor that Hou Ching and his entire general staff had been wiped out. The whole court was much upset, and Emperor Wu himself, now eighty-five years old, was so startled that he nearly fell out of bed! In the recording of this report is portrayed the basic Confucian historiography of the so-called "Hou Ching rebellion." Hou Ching went on to invest Chien-k'ang; Emperor Wu and Hsiao Kang died in captivity; and the Hsiao royalty were all but blotted out. Such a catastrophe posed a dilemma for the compilers of the exemplar histories. Hou Ching's campaign against the South was eventually unsuccessful; he did not control provincial Liang during his occupation of Chien-k'ang, and Liang sovereignty, even if largely only nominal, was restored after his death. The mandate clearly belonged to the Liang; Hou Ching was therefore a rebel. Yet he had been victorious over all the strategy and military might the throne could marshall against him.

The problem lay in apportioning the blame for the disaster. Emperor Wu died still emperor of the dynasty he had founded. He had administered one of the longest reigns in Chinese history, and until his last years he ruled vigorously. He was criticized by the historians for misrule and failure in his old age; but it was no less convenient to parade examples of villainy, ineptitude, and treachery on the part of members of the Hsiao clan and of ministers in the highest councils of the government to account for the debacle.

The role allotted to Hsiao Kang, however, was not so easy to contrive. While Emperor Wu lived, Hsiao Kang as the eldest son could bear the censure due his father; this would meet the demands of the Confucian code of filial piety. As heir apparent to an octogenarian monarch he could credibly have charge of state affairs and take the responsibility for the disaster. But after Emperor Wu's death, Hsiao Kang occupied the throne for two years as an accredited emperor, even though he was in fact merely a puppet under Hou Ching's domination. The historians begged the question; the biographies of Hsiao Kang the emperor merely state that "in the third year of T'ai-ch'ing [549] the imperial city fell."[2]

In other contexts, Hsiao Kang the crown prince epitomized the effete intellectualism into which the Hsiao ruling clique had degenerated. The collapse of the Chin regime in the early fourth century and the loss of the North to the tribes was considered largely the result of the Chin nobility's predilection for Taoist metaphysics at the expense of the devotion to administrative duty demanded by the orthodox Confucian doctrine. Hsiao Kang was known for his interest in Taoist philosophy, and so the orthodox historians could hold up the "mirror of history"[3] to show that the collapse of the Hsiao under barbarian attack stemmed from the same neglect of state affairs:

[In 548] news of Hou Ching's defeat [by Eastern Wei] reached the [Liang] court. Before the report was confirmed, a rumor spread that Hou Ching and his men had been wiped out. Everyone was dismayed. In a conversation with Ho Ching-jung, T'ai-tsung [Hsiao Kang] remarked, "Fresh news from north of the Huai has just come in. Hou Ching did actually escape. The rumor is unfounded." "If we can take Ching," said Ching-jung, "he must die at once." T'ai-tsung blanched, and asked what the man meant. Ching-jung replied, "Ching has no concept of loyalty; he ends by throwing the state into confusion." During this year [a time of crisis, especially in the North], T'ai-tsung had indulged in lecturing on the two [Taoist] texts, the *Lao-tzu* and the *Chuang-tzu*, in the Hsüan-fu. At this time, Wu Tzu was a scholar at the imperial library, and was a familiar figure at [Hsiao Kang's] lectures. Ching-jung said to Wu, "In the past the Chin dynasty came to ruin. To some extent this was a result of the royalty holding metaphysics in high esteem and permitting the Hu and Chieh barbarians to inundate the central plain [of North China]. Now the East Palace devotes itself to matters outside of human affairs. We can, no doubt, expect to fall to the Jung barbarians!" The troubles soon to be caused by Hou Ching bore out his words. In the first month of the third year of T'ai-ch'ing [549] [Ho Ching-jung] died in the siege. (*LS* 37.6b–7a; *NS* 30.17ab; *TCTC* 4972)

This conversation was recorded to illustrate that there were men of political acumen in the South who were willing to express their views even in the face of royal displeasure. Ho Ching-jung's name, too, lent credence to the incident: he had been a member of the council of three which endorsed Hsiao Kang's selection as crown prince, and so his frankness was quite credible.

With Hou Ching safe in Shou-yang under Emperor Wu's

protection, Eastern Wei resorted to diplomatic strategy to create a rift between the rebel and the emperor, hoping that one would eliminate the other and that no matter which side triumphed the resulting disorder would be to Eastern Wei's advantage. Hsiao Yüan-ming had been well treated in captivity and was now persuaded to write to Emperor Wu offering peace terms on behalf of Eastern Wei. The Liang court could not agree upon a strategy. Chu I and Chang Kuan, Hsiao Kang's brother-in-law, argued for accepting these overtures at face value, overriding more positive proposals. "Let's leave everyone in peace," they insisted, and it was advice from these favorites that the battle-shy Emperor Wu followed. But Hou Ching intercepted the Eastern Wei couriers. His own policy, outlined in a letter to Emperor Wu, was blocked by Chu I, who pocketed the three hundred taels of gold that accompanied the communication. After a series of correspondence with Emperor Wu, he finally forged a letter purporting to be from Eastern Wei offering to "ransom Yüan-ming for Hou Ching" to sound out the emperor's real intentions. One Liang minister spotted the trap, but again Chu I swayed the decision. "Ching is a beaten man on the run. He is quite powerless." Unsuspecting, the emperor agreed to the exchange: "Have Yüan-ming here in the morning, and by evening Hou Ching will be yours," he wrote. This note, too, was delivered into Hou Ching's hands. "I always knew that old rascal of Wu was a hard man," he remarked. "If we wait upon Emperor Wu's orders," his strategist Wang Wei counseled, "we shall die. And we'll die just the same if we raise rebellion against him." And so, early in 548, Hou Ching began his design against the Liang.

Events contrived to exacerbate the already strained relations between Hou Ching and the Southern court whose protection he had importuned. The central government had made no move to censure his unauthorized taxation of the local Shou-yang populace or the conscription of manpower into his armies. Now he requested a marriage alliance with the Wang and Hsieh families. Emperor Wu replied that these two families occupied peerless positions in the realm. "You'll have to try the Chu or Chang clans" (Chu I and Chang Kuan), he suggested. In a towering fury Hou Ching stormed, "I'll have those southern wenches for slaves!" He also requisitioned ten thousand bolts of brocade to uniform his army. Chu I sent blue dungaree. Hou Ching returned the inferior weaponry supplied him to be recast at the Eastern Foundry in the capital. Then, to make matters worse, news came to him that during the fifth month, Hsü Ling, star of Hsiao Kang's literary coterie, had been sent north to negotiate a renewed truce with Eastern Wei. At this, Hou Ching overtly intensified his preparations for battle.

His instrument for rebellion was Hsiao Cheng-te, the once-adopted son of Emperor Wu. Through the years Hsiao Cheng-te had nursed resentment at being set aside from his expectations of the heir-apparency and, in the meantime, had gathered about him a gang of desperados and had accumulated stocks of grain and military supplies. Delightedly, he fell in with Hou Ching's plans and entered an alliance with him whereby Hou Ching would support his claim on the throne. Hou Ching's own disaffection was no secret; the Liang court was fully apprised of the danger. But Emperor Wu had delegated border diplomacy to Chu I and his clique, and while many able ministers begged that Hou Ching be exterminated while yet relatively weak, intelligence reports of Hou Ching's preparations were ignored. Chu I merely mocked Hsiao Fan's urgent pleadings with "Must you deprive our court of even one guest?" and blocked Hsiao Fan's communications to the emperor. Chu I further condoned Hou Ching's suborning a provincial official to revolt. Hou Ching complained that the Liang government had been taken in by Eastern Wei's guile—which it had—and that he himself had become a laughingstock. Chu I's reply was meant to lead nowhere. The accompanying placation of silks and cloth was a feeble gesture, and on September 27, 548, hostilities began.

On the pretext that Chu I and his party had to be exterminated for the sake of the state, Hou Ching seized Shou-yang as the base of his operations. At this, Emperor Wu merely smiled. Quoting Chu I, he remarked that Hou Ching could never get away with it. It was obvious to Hou Ching, too, that he would be overwhelmed by the weight of numbers arrayed against him. He turned to Wang Wei for counsel, and this officer devised a daring plan whereby they would abandon Shou-yang and make a swift cavalry attack on Chien-k'ang itself. With fifth-column assistance from Hsiao Cheng-te inside the city, their coup stood a fair chance of success. On November 11 Hou Ching gave command of Shou-yang to his exogamic brother Wang Hsien-kuei and, pretending to go on a hunting trip, left Shou-yang without arousing suspicion. He won over the common people in the path of his advance by denouncing the local officials and distributing their wealth, and virtually unopposed he brought his small army to the banks of the Yangtze.

If the Liang side could be said to have a hero, it was the resourceful general Yang K'an (496–549). He pleaded with Emperor Wu to be allowed two thousand men to occupy a strategic position to check Hou Ching's advance, and advised that Hsiao Lun reoccupy Shou-yang. Hou Ching would then have been unable either to advance or retreat. But Chu I countered that Hou Ching had no intention of crossing the Yangtze, and Yang K'an's plan was shelved. "Now we are lost," he predicted. On December 6 Emperor Wu appointed Hsiao Cheng-te commander in chief of all the forces guarding the capital and stationed him in Tan-yang. Hou Ching's interests could hardly have been better served. Hsiao Cheng-te lost no time in sending several scores of large transport vessels, supposedly carrying reeds, to meet his clandestine ally on the north bank and ferry him across. Taken by surprise, outposts on the south side of the river fled before Hou Ching's advance, although at the time he had no more than several hundred horse and eight thousand men. Such an instance was the important guard mounted by Chiang Tzu-i, lying upstream from Hou Ching's crossing. He wanted to oppose Hou Ching with the several thousand men in his command, but when his aide, whose family lived north of the river, deserted, Chiang Tzu-i's own force had to retreat on foot to the capital. There Hsiao Kang took pity on him, recognizing his gallantry, and awarded him a palace appointment.

A conversation purported to have taken place between Hsiao Kang and Emperor Wu at this time unequivocally gave Hsiao Kang charge of the city's defenses:

The crown prince saw that the situation had become desperate. Donning battle dress, he presented himself to Emperor Wu and requested that the defense of the state be given into his charge so that the emperor need not disturb himself. The emperor replied, "This is your affair. Why do you ask! Military affairs at home and abroad are all delegated to you." The crown prince thereupon set up headquarters in the imperial secretariat and devoted himself to the situation, suddenly so desperate that no one could suggest a strategy. (NS 80.6b; TCTC 4984)

If Hsiao Kang received only random mention in running accounts of the battle, the historians intended that he, not Emperor Wu, be seen as the controlling voice in the Liang high command.

Hsiao Kang certainly appears consistent in the deployment of personnel. The frequency with which he was betrayed, however, shows him ill-equipped by training and temperament to be the leader of men expected of a Chinese gentleman-official. The most incredible appointment he made (as had Emperor Wu earlier) was the key post given to Hsiao Cheng-te. There is little doubt that Hsiao Cheng-te did betray his native land and join Hou Ching with the understanding that Hou Ching set him up as emperor. However, Emperor Wu's confidence and Hsiao Kang's trust in the man he had indirectly deprived of the succession does much to discredit the reports of Hsiao Cheng-te's earlier misdeeds. Whatever the truth, Hsiao Kang suspected nothing.

By December 9, 548, Hou Ching had reached the southern side of the Chu-chiao pontoon bridge. The crown prince transferred . . . Cheng-te to guard the Hsüan-yang gate, and appointed . . . Yü Hsin to guard the Chu-chiao gate. [Yü] had command of more than 3,000[4] civil and military personnel from the palace. They camped at the north of the pontoon. The crown prince ordered Hsin to sever the grand pontoon to check [Hou Ching's] spearhead. Cheng-te advised, "If the common people see the pontoon cut, there will be panic. For the time being leave things in peace." The crown prince followed his advice. Soon Ching was upon them. Hsin led his men forward to sever the pontoon, but scarcely had they cut away one of the floats than they caught sight of Hou Ching's army bristling with arms. They fled and hid in the gate. Hsin chewed on a stick of sugarcane [used as a sort of anodyne]. A flight of arrows followed them and stuck in the gate pillars. At the twang of the bowstrings, Hsin's lollipop fell to the ground. He abandoned his troops and

fled. . . . A member of . . . Cheng-te's faction closed the breach in
the pontoon and brought Ching across. The crown prince sent a
force of 3,000 crack troops under Wang Chih [to whom he had
given his own horse] to relieve Hsin, but coming upon the enemy
they broke and fled without even forming battle order. Cheng-te . . .
joined up with Ching, and their combined forces entered the Hsüan-
yang gate. (*LS* 56.13a; *NS* 80.7a; *TCTC* 4986)

Hsiao Cheng-te's treachery coincided with the defection of
other commanders appointed by Hsiao Kang. Even Hsiao Kang's
son, Hsiao Ta-ch'un, ran away, and Shih-t'ou with its stores of
grain and supplies was surrendered to Hou Ching. Yet another
emergency sortie that Hsiao Kang organized from the Ta-ssu-ma
gate collapsed when his entire attacking unit deserted to Hou
Ching.

Scattered reports show Hsiao Kang organizing the defense,
trying to raise morale, or taking part in the actual fighting.
These incidents, however, do little more than add color to the
narrative. For example, we are told that as Hou Ching closed
in he sent spies into the capital on the pretext of diplomatic
missions. These men were able to report that Chien-k'ang was
in panic. Looters jammed the carriage ways; slave labor at the
East and West Foundries and at the Mint were released and
amnesty was granted the inmates of the city prisons. Refugees
from the countryside were flocking to the safety of the city
walls; peasantry and nobility inextricably mobbed together with
no thought given to rank or precedence. Hsiao Kang established
a supply depot at the Te-yang Hall, accumulating stores there
from the temples and public treasuries. Everyone—men and
women, peasant and aristocrat—was mobilized to carry sacks
of rice, and forty thousand *tou* were stored away. Cash and
cloth amounted to five hundred thousand million. Curiously, we
are told, no thought was given to fuel, fodder, fish, or salt, and
when the fodder was exhausted the horses were fed on rice!
But little could be done to hold back the mob. Rank and file
militia raided the armories to equip themselves and the official
quartermasters were powerless to control them. Only when
General Yang K'an put several men to death was the free-for-all
stopped. And it was Yang K'an, we are told, and not Hsiao Kang

who managed to bring some semblance of organization to the influx of refugees.

Hou Ching threw a tight cordon around the city and attacked from all fronts. The clamor of his drums and trumpets shook the very ground. He set fire to the Ta-ssu-ma Gate and the Tung-hua and Hsi-hua gates, but Yang K'an managed to control the conflagration by making channels above the burning structures and releasing water down upon the blaze. Hsiao Kang himself, "grasping his silvered saddle," toured the defenses bestowing rewards on the fighting men. One source specified the gratuities as 5,000 taels of gold, 10,000 taels of silver, and 10,000 bolts of silk. This fortune was awarded to Yang K'an, now described as a personal friend upon whom Hsiao Kang much relied. The gift was of course recorded to illustrate the esteem in which Yang K'an was held by the royalty, and his refusal to accept it was cited to exemplify loyalty to the realm.

Then, on December 16, 548, although the outcome of the rebellion was by no means certain, Hou Ching felt confident enough to proclaim Hsiao Cheng-te emperor. The year-title was changed to Cheng-p'ing; Hsiao Cheng-te's eldest son, Hsiao Chien-li, was made crown prince; while Hou Ching was made prime minister and given one of Hsiao Cheng-te's daughters to wed. Just at this time, the rebel cause was aided by another defection from the Liang defense. Two thousand of Ching's troops had been deployed to attack the Tung-fu. The defenders held out for three days and the attackers were beaten off. Ching stepped in and directed the battle personally. Stone shot and arrows fell like rain. Then an officer in the service of Hsiao Kang's eldest son, Ta-ch'i, charged with holding the northeast tower, secretly led Ching to the top of the walls. On December 19 Ching broke in. He killed Hsiao T'ui, the commander of the garrison which had resisted so gallantly for so long, together with three thousand of the defenders. The corpses were exposed, and Ching spread the rumor that unless the garrison in the city surrendered forthwith, such would be its fate, too. He also spread a rumor that Emperor Wu was dead, and this was eventually believed inside the city. To scotch this demoralizing propaganda, on the next day, December 20, Hsiao Kang urged the old man to make a tour of the walls in person. But this was considered too dangerous; instead, the emperor visited the Ta-ssu-ma gate, and when the troops there heard the shouts of the officials clearing the emperor's path "they raised a great cheer and their tears flowed freely. The inspection did much to relieve the general anxiety." Other acts of individual heroism brightened the otherwise gloomy picture of cowardice and treachery. The three Chiang brothers, Tzu-i, Tzu-ssu, and Tzu-wu, re-employed by Hsiao Kang after their retreat from the Yangtze, died in sorties against the enemy, doomed from the start but useful as examples of faith in and loyalty to the throne. Hsiao Kang showed his appreciation in an order conferring posthumous honors upon them (*YKC* 2999).

It was such devotion to the state that upset Ching's calculations. Having penetrated to the imperial capital without serious resistance, Ching reasoned that Chien-k'ang could be taken in a day, and he maintained strict discipline in his forces. But now he found he could make no headway against the defenders and disaffection began to show among his men. He was also apprehensive lest relief forces should come to the emperor's aid from the outer provinces and wipe him out within the morning. Added to these concerns, the food supplies he had captured with the fall of Shih-t'ou were exhausted and his men were getting hungry. He solved this problem by allowing his armies to loot the food stores held by the common people. Of course the looting did not stop with food, and the townsfolk were robbed of their valuables and clothes, and even their sons and daughters were taken as slaves. The price of rice rose to seventy or eighty thousand cash per *sheng*. As so often reported by Chinese historians recounting desperate straits, there were occurrences of cannibalism. A good fifty or sixty percent of the people died of starvation. Gruesome details of the food shortage in the besieged garrison included the soldiers boiling the leather in their armor, smoking out rats, and catching sparrows to eat. They even ate dried moss. Horses were butchered and the meat adulterated with human flesh, but anyone who ate it surely fell ill. Exploiting Hsiao Kang's name and status as hyperbole in their description, the historians report that even his larder was down to its last strip of meat!

Hsiao Kang's name appears as similar hyperbole to illustrate the extremes to which the defenders were driven. Hou Ching

intensified his efforts to invest the palace complex, and on
December 23, 548 he began construction of earth mounds on
the east and west city walls. The labor force was conscripted
from civilian townsfolk, and no exceptions were permitted, even
those of noble birth. "The lash of the overseers fell unmercifully
and without discrimination. Those too exhausted or weak to continue their toil were killed and their bodies added to the
growing mounds. The sound of their cries moved the very earth.
No one dared hide himself away and evade conscription, and
within a week or two the labor force numbered several tens
of thousands" (NS 80.9a). The same device was adopted within
the city, where earth mounds were heaped up to meet the threat
from outside. But here the defenders were fighting for their
lives, and the reader of the histories is asked to visualize Hsiao
Kang and Hsiao Ta-ch'i—the two highest ranking personages in
the realm after the aged Emperor Wu—shouldering the hod and
wielding the shovel! (NS 80.8b). In any case, the defenders' luck
was out; a heavy rainfall washed away their mounds and the
rebels poured into the city. Then Yang K'an, resourceful as ever,
ordered firebrands hurled at the invaders and a wall of fire
built up to block them. At last the breach was repaired and
the enemy repelled.

Other citations of Hsiao Kang's activities in the defense of the
city range from ritual ceremony to the destruction of the East
Palace. Early in the siege, Hou Ching severed communications
between the city and the rescue missions standing off nearby.
The defenders constructed a paper kite to which was attached a
long cord. A legend in large lettering offered a reward of one
hundred taels of silver to anyone who retrieved the device and
dispatched a relief force. To the marvel of Hou Ching's rebels,
the kite was borne away on the northwest wind. Supposing
themselves endangered by the evil spells emanating from it—true
in a way—they shot it down with an arrow. The report adds that
Hsiao Kang released the kite in front of the T'ai-chi Hall—the
main hall of the imperial palace complex—which suggests that
the release was preceded by some sort of ceremony.

The barbarity of the campaign was perhaps best impressed
upon the historians' literati audience by the report that a man of
Hsiao Kang's sensibilities could be driven to incinerate the East

Palace library. When he first moved into the East Palace some twenty years previously, Hsiao Kang inherited Crown Prince Chao-ming's library of thirty thousand folios. On December 10, 548, Hou Ching invested the East Palace, which gave him a clear field of fire into the imperial palace. That night, while Hou Ching and his men were drinking and carousing with the palace women they had captured, Hsiao Kang sent a task force to burn down the palace. The T'ai-tien (Dais Hall) and the entire library of several hundred cases were destroyed. One source compares this calamity to the notorious "burning of the books" by the first emperor of Ch'in (Ch'in Shih Huang-ti, r. 221–210 B.C.):[5] "Previously, Chien-wen [Hsiao Kang] dreamed that someone painted a portrait of the first emperor of Ch'in, saying, 'This one will again burn books.' This came to pass" (*NS* 80.7b).

Investigation of Liang strategies reveals the most about Hsiao Kang's activities in the siege. It is here that he appears at his weakest. The leadership he might have been able to display seems to have been diminished by the endemic ill will between members of his entourage and Emperor Wu's favorite, Chu I. Chu I had become so secure in the emperor's favor that "although court officials looked askance at him, even the crown prince had no power over him."

Chu I was from a local family of Ch'ien-t'ang district in Wu, the metropolitan area, and hence was a member of the native southern gentry, one of the so-called "Wu surnames." This placed him fundamentally at odds with the émigré families from the north, and the feud with Hsiao Kang's men, incepted at least a quarter of a century earlier, characteristically arose over rivalry for the emperor's favor. Chu I felt the greatest threat to his position came from Hsü Ch'ih, incidentally from a relatively recently arrived émigré family and an upstart whom he doubtlessly considered could be attacked with a certain impunity. Hsü had impressed Emperor Wu during his interview about innovations in poetry, and he grew daily in the royal regard. Much displeased, Chu I remarked to his close associates that "Old man Hsü comes and goes between the two palaces [of Emperor Wu and Hsiao Kang]. By and by he will displace me. We had best do something about it at once!" (*LS* 30.9b). In 529 or 531[6] Chu I contrived to alienate Hsü Ch'ih from the emperor and have him rusticated. But before long, Hsü was back at the capital, and with added ranks into the bargain. The succeeding years of proximity between these rival factions, especially after control of state affairs passed to the East Palace—in effect, to Hsü Ch'ih—must have exacerbated jealousies beyond tolerance.

Another target of Chu I's displeasure was Wei Ts'an (496–549). He too is recorded as a personal friend of Hsiao Kang. He began his career in Hsiao Kang's service, followed him to Yung province, and thence into the East Palace. There he fell out with Chu I, who once insulted him for his rapid advance in rank. Sometime after 535, Emperor Wu fell ill and seemed on the point of death. Hsiao Kang and the whole court waited in attendance. It was popularly said that if the emperor died Wei Ts'an would assume *de jure* authority, such being his standing with the crown prince. Emperor Wu recovered. Hearing what had been said, he banished Wei Ts'an to a provincial governorship. In parting, Hsiao Kang "grasped his hand and said, 'We'll not be parted long'" (*LS* 43.2a; *NS* 58.7b).

Wei Ts'an was soon reprieved, and on his way back to the capital he learned of Hou Ching's rebellion. He joined forces with other loyal contingents, but through a series of mistakes he and his four sons were killed. Hsiao Kang wept when he heard of the disaster: "There was no more faithful a guardian of the altars of state than Master Wei," he told Hsiao K'ai. "How sad that he should die now in battle!" (*LS* 43.5a). He decreed that Wei Ts'an be awarded posthumous military honors; Wei Ts'an's eldest son, who also served in the East Palace, was given a military appointment.

In another engagement in the siege, Chu I and Chang Kuan were pitted against Hsiao Kang's trusty aide, Yang K'an. Hsiao Kang's rivals suggested sending a force outside the city to take the offensive. Yang K'an argued against the wisdom of this, but his counsel was overruled and a thousand men or so were sent to give battle. Just as Yang K'an had predicted, though, even before weapons were crossed the men turned and ran, fighting each other to cross the moat bridge to safety. Many fell into the water and were drowned and, in all, more than half the force was lost.

While the Liang defenders were thus being whittled away, Hou Ching's rebel army was increasing in numbers; his appeal to the disaffected peasantry and slave classes was irresistible. One man he captured was a slave formerly in the service of Chu I. This slave was advanced to a high official post and awarded his former master's family estate. He was richly dressed and mounted on a fine horse and paraded around the city walls to show off his new prosperity. Pouring recriminations upon Chu I, he called upon other slaves in the city to share in his good fortune, and within three days more than a thousand slaves had deserted to Hou Ching's side. Hou Ching sustained this barrage of propaganda, pointing out to the lesser officials and commoners among the defenders how their leaders had abused their authority, fleecing the taxpayers in order to satisfy their own rapacious cravings. He asked them to open their eyes to the private lakes and parklands of the privileged classes; their residences; their patronage of monasteries and nunneries and building of *stupas*; their inordinate harems and extensive residences; their thousands of servants, slaves, and retainers. After a statement sounding suspiciously like "they toil not, neither do they spin," he continued, "If not from robbing the people, then where does all their silken apparel, jade, and delicate food come from?" "These lords of the earth fear only for their skins now," he argued, "so why sacrifice your lives in such a worthless cause?" (*TCTC* 4992).

Hou Ching also exploited the notorious discord in the Liang high command. He shot an arrow into the city with a message promising to call off his attack and return north if Emperor Wu would execute Chu I and his faction, who, Hou Ching claimed, had usurped imperial authority. Emperor Wu asked Hsiao Kang for an opinion, and the crown prince agreed that Hou Ching was right. Emperor Wu was about to execute the ministers in question when Hsiao Kang interceded. "The rebels are only using Chu I and the others as an excuse," he said. "Killing them now will do nothing to help us out of this emergency, and we will only make ourselves a laughingstock. When we have dealt with the rebel Hou, it will not be too late to execute them" (*NS* 61.11b). The men were spared. Emperor Wu's gullibility is hard to believe. But if we accept the episode in its general outline—and it was a likely line of attack for Hou Ching to pursue—then Hsiao Kang showed objective judgment, putting state policy above personal differences and the opportunity to dispose of a powerful rival.

In another encounter with Chu I, Hsiao Kang appeared less magnanimous. Distrust of any overture by the attackers was now widespread in the city, and even in this respect Hou Ching had scored a victory in the extent to which Hsiao Kang's judgment was affected. An officer named Ch'en Hsin had been captured by Hou Ching but refused to serve him. Hou Ching then had one of his own men, Fan T'ao-pang, imprison Ch'en. But Ch'en talked Fan into a plot to assassinate two of Hou Ching's generals and defect to the Liang with his troops. As a preliminary step, Fan allowed Ch'en to escape to the city. When Hsiao Kang informed his father of the plot, the emperor was delighted. He had an engraved silver-mounted scroll prepared for presentation to Fan, with a message that on the day the operation was accomplished Fan would be enfeoffed as Prince of Honan and given command of Hou Ching's hosts, as well as being given gold, robes, and dancing-girls. But Hsiao Kang was suspicious and undecided. Emperor Wu addressed him angrily: "It is quite usual to accept a surrender. Why do you suddenly have suspicions?" Hsiao called a council to discuss what should be done. Chu I thought Fan's offer was genuine and that his desertion would throw Hou Ching into confusion. Hsiao Kang was obstinate toward any proposition made by Chu I: "We have staged an impenetrable defense while we await the relief forces. When they arrive there will be nothing left of the rebels worth exterminating! This strategy covers all contingencies. If we do open the gates to Fan, how can we know what Fan actually has in mind? If, as I suspect, he is bent on treachery, it will be too late for second thoughts. The altars of state are a serious matter. We ought to consider this more thoroughly" (NS 80.9ab). He remained adamant in the face of Chu I's arguments; pleading only increased his suspicions. Chu I shrugged: "If we fail in this, farewell to the altars of state!" In the delay, the plot was compromised. Fan was reported by a subordinate and summarily executed. Unaware of Fan's death, Ch'en emerged from the city at the scheduled time. Hou Ching seized him and tried to exploit the plot as a means to enter the city with his own men. Ch'en, realizing that his death was certain in any case, would not comply with Hou Ching's demands. He was killed there and then.

For all its historiographical problems, this episode illustrates Hsiao Kang's overriding power in policy and decision making. One can sympathize to some extent with his caution in this dilemma, but it is the caution of the pedant "going into things much more thoroughly," and he lacks the bold opportunism of an able general. His refusal to consider Chu I's proposals suggests a stubbornness growing out of factional jealousies. But why are these the only voices heard? And surely Chu I must have been a minority opinion, on any council convened by Hsiao Kang, even if Hsiao Kang could not exclude him altogether. Perhaps Hsiao Kang's distrust reflected the general consensus of the council.

Hsiao Kang's contempt for Chu I was categorically expressed in satirical verse ascribed to him:

> Regard the barren fields!
> Alas! That evil miasma!
> His erroneous counsel
> Usurps our imperial prerogative.[7]

("Poem Grieving over the Rebellion," *NS* 62.11b; *TFP* 1116)

High-hatted and shoes thick-soled;
Dining from tripods; astride a plump horse.
Ascending the cinnabar ground of the purple empyrean;
Opening the golden doors of the jade hall.
Enriching with the counsel of plans and policies;
Promulgating the blessing and awe of government and punishment.
Because of him the four-square suburbs are much fortified;
Because of him the myriad districts are not yet pacified.
Ask who is the wolf!
Enquire who is the serpent![8]
(Closing lines of "Besieged City *Fu*," *LS* 38.4b; *NS* 62.11b; *YKC* 2994)

The preservation of these items in Chu I's biographies is itself, however, tendentious. Chu I died at the height of the siege, on February 16, 549,[9] at the age of sixty-seven. With nothing else to go on, and wishing to finish him off with suitable retributive humiliation, the historians exploited these verses as the precise cause of his death. In so doing, they overlooked the fact that they also virtually indicted Hsiao Kang (who must have been aware of the likely effect of his castigations upon the proud old man) of a peculiarly cruel and premeditated murder! Soon after these verses were circulated, Emperor Wu himself was in the South Tower looking out over the rebel battalions. He turned to Chu I and remarked: "The four-square suburbs are much fortified. I wonder whose fault this is?" (*NS* 62.11b). Chu choked on his furious humiliation and broke into a sweat. Unable to think of some retort to turn the tables, he fell ill and died.

Hsiao Kang did no better in his next assessment of strategy. Things had not gone smoothly for the attackers. They had failed to crack the determination of the defenders; they were hungry and battle weary; and they were in increasing danger of being overrun by the converging rescue missions. Clearly it was time for diplomacy. Hou Ching now pretended to seek an armistice and permission to return to his garrison in Shou-yang. He calculated that while his proposal was being considered he could rest his men and horses, re-equip, and lay in provisions. Hsiao Kang saw only the exhaustion in the capital and proposed to Emperor Wu that they accept Hou Ching's terms. The old man flew into a rage. "Better death than a truce!" he exclaimed. "Hou Ching has besieged us for a long time," Hsiao Kang persisted. "The relief forces are quarreling among themselves and will not fight. We could do better to agree to an armistice and work out a plan later." After a silence, the emperor capitulated. "You think it over for yourself," he replied, "but do not become the laughingstock of a thousand generations."[10]

Hou Ching then requested the command of the four territories of Nan-yü, Hsi-yü, Ho and Kuang provinces, lying north of the Yangtze. He also asked that Hsiao Ta-ch'i accompany him on the way. Hsiao Kang's only show of resistance to these demands was to send Hsiao Ta-k'uan in place of Hsiao Ta-ch'i. An edict halted the advancing relief forces; high ranks were conferred upon Hou Ching, and he was restored to his former eminence as Prince of Honan.

On March 27 an altar was set up outside the Hsi-hua gate and officers from both camps attended a ceremony of ratification.

A blood sacrifice was performed; the lips of the principals were smeared to seal the covenant. Hou Ching, however, made no move to raise the siege. "We cannot evacuate our men," he dissembled. "I am afraid too that we may be set upon by the relief forces camped on the banks of the Ch'in-huai" (*LS* 56.17b). Nor would he accept the substitution of Hsiao Ta-k'uan for Hsiao Ta-ch'i; Hsiao Ta-k'uan was sent back to the city with a renewed demand that his eldest brother be delivered to Hou Ching.

Hsiao Kang now realized that Hou Ching had no intention of keeping his word, but there was nothing he could do to break the deadlock. More Liang forces were arriving, among them Hsiao Hui-li and his thirty thousand men. To counter Hou Ching's protest that they would prevent him crossing the Yangtze, Hsiao Kang ordered Hsiao Hui-li to reroute his army. He also raised no objections when Hou Ching proposed that in return for recapturing areas of Shou-yang and Chung-li from Northern control he be given command of Kuang-ling and Chiao province. Hou Ching was also allowed his own choice of location for crossing the Yangtze.

Whether or not we accept the conversations and other detail as authentic, in acquiescing to Hou Ching's seemingly preposterous demands Hsiao Kang relinquished control of both rebel and government troop movements outside the capital. One may admire Hou Ching's assessment of the Liang commanders or condemn his duplicity, but it is difficult to sympathize with the equally insincere but less resolute Liang counsel of "wait and see."

Hsiao Kang's trump strategy was of course to hold out until the relief forces arrived; and had any determined effort been made by the many columns converging on the capital, Hou Ching would have been brushed away. But just as the war councils at the capital were wrecked by factional jealousies and disaffection, so the Hsiao governors in the provinces were reluctant to come to the aid of the senile emperor and his favorite, Hsiao Kang, nominated out of turn to the heir-apparency. Rather, at most they proceeded tardily, hesitated to commit their forces (quite apart from bungling opportunities), and generally held back in the hope of some personal profit from the outcome of events between besieged and besiegers.

News of the battle reached the Prince of Hsiang-tung upstream at Chiang-ling. None too early, on December 24 he proclaimed martial law and summoned to arms his nephews Hsiao Yü and Hsiao Ch'a (sons of Crown Prince Chao-ming), and Hsiao Kang's son Ta-hsin, serving in the provinces. On December 27 a rescue force set out from Chiang-ling; however, this army never arrived in time and, with the cessation of hostilities in Chien-k'ang, the various contingents split up under their respective leaders and turned to fighting among themselves.

No more effective was the hundred-thousand-man army that had rallied to Emperor Wu's call and that, by the Chinese New Year, February 13, 549, was encamped on the Grand Pontoon. The contingent under Hsiao Kang's friend, Wei Ts'an, was defeated in the muddle of a night fog—the engagement in which Wei Ts'an was killed. However, Hsiao Lun, who had been routed during his pursuit of Hou Ching from Shou-yang, joined up with Hsiao Kang's sons, Hsiao Ta-lien and Hsiao Ta-ch'eng, in Wei Ts'an's camp south of the Grand Pontoon. Other reinforcements were arriving daily, including advance units from the massive army mobilized by the Prince of Hsiang-tung under his son Hsiao Fang-teng and the renowned General Wang Seng-pien. It was these forces that Hsiao Kang immobilized by his agreement to a truce with Hou Ching. And now, the dissension, rivalry, and jealousies among the Liang generals placed the initiative back into Hou Ching's hands. Hsiao Lun and Hsiao Ta-lien developed a hatred for the one-armed Liu Chung-li, unfortunately an arrogant man. Hsiao Ta-lien was also at odds with other commanders and there was a damaging lack of rapport between the troops and their leaders, which seriously affected the soldiers' willingness to go into battle. No discipline was exerted on the common troops, who wandered about pilfering and looting. The formerly welcoming populace lost heart, and the demoralized Liang officers began to turn to the rebels.

With his own troops rested and fed during the truce and his siege machines in good repair, and with the opposing Liang armies inside and outside the city torn between rival factions, Hou Ching now took the advice of his aides and the urgings of his appointed monarch, Hsiao Cheng-te, to launch a surprise attack on the capital. Concerned with justifying the "legality" of his rebellion, he issued a statement cataloguing the ten faults of which the emperor was guilty, and included criticisms of the royal scions. Concerning Hsiao Kang he said: "The crown prince's delights are pearls and jade; his pleasures are wine and women. He speaks of nothing but the frivolous and shallow. His literary compositions do not rise above such libertine ideas as are expressed in the poem 'Sang-chung'."[11] Using a phrase that Hsiao Kang had once quoted, he summed up other prominent members of the Hsiao clan as "monkeys bathed and capped." The infuriated emperor set up an altar in the T'ai-chi Hall and, on April 13, 549, announced to heaven and earth that Hou Ching had foresworn his sacred oath. The emperor's call to arms was greeted with cheers and acclamation (*LS* 56.23a).

At the beginning of the siege, there were some hundred thousand and more inhabitants within the city walls and twenty or thirty thousand men under arms. The prolonged encirclement reduced this number by eighty or ninety per cent. The survivors were totally exhausted, and no more than four thousand men could be mustered with strength enough to defend the city. Corpses littered the streets, and corruption flowed in the ditches. Yet, continued the historians, the hardy defense was determined to resist while awaiting the deliverance by rescue missions.

Hou Ching released the waters of Hsüan-wu Lake to flood the imperial city, and coordinated an attack from all directions. Day and night the fighting continued. Hsiao Lun's eldest son. Hsiao Chien, commanded the garrison at the T'ai-yang Gate, one of the six gates to the city. However, he did nothing but gamble at dice and indulge in drinking bouts, caring nothing for his men and officers. Two of his aides resented the inept corruption of their leader. Shortly before dawn on April 24, 549, the two men led a column of Hou Ching's troops onto the wall by the northwest tower. A loyal officer tried to hold off the incursion in a hand-to-hand sword fight, but, outnumbered, he retreated to the emperor's residence. "The city has fallen," he gasped. Unperturbed, the emperor sighed: "In this way I gained the empire; in this way I lose it. There is no cause for regret" (*NS* 80.14b).

Hou Ching came face to face with his royal foe. Beaten in battle, the Liang highest royalty now appeared as the epitome of the Chinese gentleman in adversity: unafraid of Hou Ching's

bodyguard of tribesmen, articulate in contrast to Hou Ching's
bluster. The description of his meeting with Hsiao Kang in the
Yung-fu sheng, whence Hsiao Kang had moved on January 25, is
recorded in the biographies of Hsü Ch'ih and Yin Pu-hai to display their loyalty to the throne. Thus even in this ordeal Hsiao
Kang was relegated to the background. His courtiers and bodyguard had already fled in terror, but Hsiao Kang showed no
fear when, still in his armor, Hou Ching confronted him. Only
his old tutor, Hsü Ch'ih, and Yin Pu-hai remained at his side.
Hsü Ch'ih, unperturbed, called Hou Ching to task for his lack
of respect in the presence of the crown prince. "Your Excellency
Hou should observe the rules of etiquette during an audience.
How dare you behave like this!" Hou Ching prostrated himself,
outfaced by Hsü Ch'ih's fierce demeanor, and he never after-
wards lost his uneasiness in front of Hsü. He had been at a loss
to answer the emperor's leading questions about the wife and
children he had abandoned to their fate as hostages in Eastern
Wei. He fared no better with Hsiao Kang's inquiries.[12]

Hsiao Cheng-te was not even conceded Hou Ching's martial
qualities. He had agreed with Hou Ching that on the day the
capital fell, "two palaces should not co-exist"—that Emperor Wu
would be eliminated and Hsiao Cheng-te established as the sole
emperor. When the rebels finally broke in, Hsiao Cheng-te
headed a band of soldiers and, sword in hand, tried to force his
way into the imperial palace. Hou Ching forestalled him by
setting a guard at the palace gates and preventing him from
entering. He then demoted Cheng-te from his imperial eminence
to an honorary rank. Only then was he permitted to see the
emperor. In tears, he made his obeisance. Emperor Wu sneered,
and quoted the *Odes* at him: "Ever flow her tears, but of what
avail is her lament?"[13]

In the histories, Emperor Wu is represented as being properly
intransigent towards his captors. Hsiao Kang, naturally, was given
the part of the filial son concerned for his father's welfare. However, to achieve this impression, Hsiao Kang's image is made to
suffer. Reports state that, in tears, he tried to persuade his father
to be more amenable. Emperor Wu exclaimed, "Who sent you?
If our altars of state still possess divine power then our empire
will recover. If not then what need of tears?" (*NS* 80.16a).

Emperor Wu's requirements were restricted and he soon fell sick. Hsiao Kang inquired after him every day, tears streaming down his face. Even the rebels could not restrain their weeping. Realizing that matters were approaching a climax, Hsiao Kang gave his youngest son, Hsiao Ta-huan, nail and hair clippings (tokens of eternal parting) and sent him to stay, no doubt secretly, with the Prince of Hsiang-tung in Chiang-ling.

Hsiao Kang's opposition was characteristically literary. Still extant are a complete verse, and a fragment of another, which are glossed as referring to this situation:

> The wings of the cavernous gates are yet unbarred;
> Drips from the golden clepsydra have run out.
> Evening mists are born of a winding creek,
> Shaded hues rise from a thicket's edge.
> Blossoms of snow, quite rootless;
> Mirrors of ice, no stable plinth.
> Now are the willows on the steps inverted,
> And the cassia by the banks newly halved.
> Spreading roots are burdened with fallen orchid,
> Delicate foliage exhales fragrant plum.
> Migrating geese in line above the reeds;
> Monkeys sporting among the branches.
> ("Winter's Eve in the Park of Mysteries," *NS* 80.15a;
> *TFP* 1133)

The fragment reads: "The flying wheel in the end made no tracks; / A bright mirror, no stable plinth."[14]

Within two months of the fall of the capital, Emperor Wu had starved to death. Under the circumstances, official descriptions of his death could not but be tendentious. The most heinous crime against the Confucian code was to conceal the death of an emperor, and this the rebels were said to have done. Sources vary in detail, and it is uncertain whether Hsiao Kang was aware of his father's death and privy to its concealment. Emperor Wu's biography says that Hsiao Kang continued to make a daily call on his father, but was not allowed to see him and could only express his grief outside the chamber. Another account says that the emperor's bier was moved into Hou Ching's quarters in the Chao-yang Hall. Hsiao Kang was intercepted in the Yung-fu-sheng and forced to attend court as usual. He was kept under close surveillance by Hou Ching's chief aides, and though he maintained his weeping and wailing, he dared not disclose his bereavement. None of the civil and military officers inside or out of the palace was told anything.

On June 12, 549, Emperor Wu was laid on his sickbed in the Cheng-chü Hall. His mouth tasted so bitter that even the finest honey could not relieve him. He murmured *"uh, uh"* over and over, and died. (*NS* 7.17b) He was eighty-six. Sources agree on the date of his demise and also on the date, July 7, twenty-six days later, when his death was revealed. It is not said, however, which date the rebels gave for his death, nor is there any apparent reason for the timing of the release. Whatever the case may be, it was on the latter date that Hsiao Kang was proclaimed emperor.[15]

CHAPTER 8

The Emperor

H SIAO Kang occupied the Liang throne for nearly two and a half years. Under the domination of Hou Ching, however, his reign was only nominal and his recorded activities were confined mainly to ceremonial occasions. Doubtlessly he endured his equivocal position in the hope of some turn of events that would restore his sovereignty. But, as in his defense of the capital, he failed to exploit his chances for a coup, and his supporters were eliminated. Some of his literary pieces, whether or not intended to do so, were construed as criticism of the rebels. But, like the proclamation on his accession to the throne, the diction was too subtle and too negative for the spirited call to arms the situation demanded:

My destiny was ill-omened; I mourn this harsh bereavement. The emperor has abandoned the ten thousand states [of the empire]. I honor him and grieve over his demise. Whither shall I turn! I have but few virtues, and yet I am placed above the people. "Dispirited I am, and full of distress"; I know not where I may find support. Now I depend upon the provincial officials so that the altars of state will be at peace. Out of regard for the mandate, and having inherited this favor, it is fitting that I pass on auspicious blessings. I hereby proclaim a general amnesty throughout the empire.[1] ("Proclamation Declaring a General Amnesty," LS 4.2b; YKC 2999)

Similar sentiments were expressed in Hsiao Kang's edict declaring an amnesty and inaugurating the year-title Ta-pao (Great Treasure). Under normal circumstances, the year-title would have been changed on his accession to the throne; but it was promulgated, very belatedly, on New Year's Day (February 2, 550). At this time, too, the seven-month period of national mourning for Emperor Wu was still in effect, and so the court was not convened.[2] It had been Hsiao Kang's intention to adopt the year-title Wen-ming, glossed in the histories as a means by which Hsiao Kang hoped to control the nobility in the provinces. But he was afraid the rebels might understand the implications of the phrase, and instead adopted the year-title Ta-pao. In any case, the edict failed in its purpose. The Prince of Hsiang-tung, the most important of the provincial administrators, refused to accept the change. He argued that Hsiao Kang had been coerced by the rebels, who had no authority to assume an imperial prerogative. He continued to calculate by the former year-title and recognized the new year as the fourth year of T'ai-ch'ing.[3]

The rebels exploited Hsiao Kang's imperial authority to issue an edict releasing slaves of northern origin held in the South:

Only by magnanimity is matter fostered; only by grace are the people led.[4] The Way glorifies and inspires the sovereign. They were not bondsmen by origin. Some were pioneers opening up new territory, but were captured and made slaves. Others dwelled on state borders and were taken prisoner and conscripted into labor. In wars between two nations, wherein lies the fault of the common people? I, the emperor, in my humble blindness create and succeed to the great undertakings of a sovereign. Being ruler of the empire, I exert my transforming influence over the universe. Indeed, I may not contrive to be partial in awarding appointments, while exclusively making vagabonds of the common people. Those prisoners and slaves of northern origin within our realm, together with their womenfolk and children, may all be freed. ("Proclamation Releasing Slaves of Northern Origin," LS 4.3a; YKC 2999)

Presumably Hou Ching had already freed the slaves in the areas under his control. Through Hsiao Kang's edict, he confirmed his actions with the sanction of legitimate Liang authority, and placed the provincial nobility in the position of either submitting to rebel policies or disobeying an imperial decree.

Matters of court protocol at Chien-k'ang continued to function. New honors were distributed among Hsiao Kang's family, commensurate with his own increased station. His mother, Lady Ting, was raised posthumously to the rank of empress, with the canonical appellation "Mu." His wife, Ling-pin, had died in April or May, a few weeks before Emperor Wu, just at the fall of the capital. She was forty-five years old and had been Hsiao Kang's consort for thirty-seven years. She died in the Yung-fu-sheng, to which Hsiao Kang had moved earlier in the siege. On July 9, 549, the day following Hsiao Kang's accession to the throne, she too was posthumously raised to the rank of empress and was given the appellation "Chien." A year later, in September or October 550, she was interred at Chuang-ling. Hsiao Kang's edict on that occasion reflected the harshness of the times upon which the capital had fallen.

Empress Chien's interment is now due [after one year]. In the past, the Pa-ling tombs of the western capital [Loyang], the hills themselves formed the mausoleum. The Shou-ling tombs of Eastern Han were no more than running streams.[5] I, the Emperor, appreciate that times now are hard. Poor harvests have brought famine, and the common people are in extreme distress. It is my wish to illustrate my personal example for my subjects, and forever manifest my esteem of simplicity. Currently in this interment at Chuang-ling we make a point of preserving frugality. ("Proclamation on the Interment at Chuang-ling," *LS* 7.5a; *YKC* 2999)

Hsiao Kang also commissioned one of Hsiao Tzu-hsien's brothers, Hsiao Tzu-fan, and Chang Tsan to prepare the funeral oration. Congratulating them on their literary skill, he remarked: "Though the present burial ceremony be frugal, this text lacks nothing in comparison with those of antiquity" (*LS* 35.6a).

Hsiao Kang's eldest son, Hsiao Ta-ch'i, became crown prince on July 13, 549, and the promotions of the other imperial sons were announced a few days later. Hsiao Tzu-fan was to be given additional honors, but this was blocked by Hou Ching, no doubt to forestall the formation of a loyalist clique at court.[6]

Hsiao Cheng-te, Hou Ching's puppet emperor during the siege, fared less well. Betrayed by the man for whom he had betrayed his native land, he communicated secretly with Hsiao Kang's cousin, Hsiao Fan (499-550), one of Hsiao Hui's sons. Rightly or wrongly, Hsiao Fan was known for his designs upon the throne, and Hsiao Cheng-te hoped to enlist his aid in an attack on Hou Ching. The communication was intercepted, and on August 8 Hou Ching had Hsiao Cheng-te strangled.[7]

The collapse of resistance at Chien-k'ang and Hsiao Kang's enthronement signaled the outbreak of overt hostilities among the emperor's brothers and nephews in the provinces. Chief contestants in the struggles were the Prince of Hsiang-tung, long ensconced at Chiang-ling; Hsiao Chi, nearly two decades in the far west at Ssuchuan; Hsiao Lun; and Crown Prince Chaoming's sons, Hsiao Yü, governor of Hsiang-tung, and Hsiao Ch'a in Hsiang-yang. Other Hsiao nobility, including Hsiao Fan and Hsiao Kang's sons, Hsiao Ta-hsin and Hsiao Ta-lien, were instrumental in affecting the plans of their more powerful rivals. In the uncertainties of the time, they too must have awaited their chance of gaining supreme power.

The histories record vivid details of the attritive campaigns fought among the princes, during which Hsiao Yu was killed and Hsiao Ch'a was driven to seek asylum in the Northern court. Hsiao Lun was pursued from town to town, until he too was captured and executed (on February 21, 551)[8] by Northern forces. His body was cast on a river bank and for days no decomposition took place. Neither carrion birds nor animals dared approach. It was left to the dead man's nephew, Hsiao Ch'a, to retrieve the corpse and have it decently buried. Hsiao Fan met his death at the hands of Hsiao Kang's son, Hsiao Ta-hsin. Hsiao Ta-lien was taken prisoner by Hou Ching's men in the provinces and sent to Chien-k'ang. It was said that he was so drunk at the time that he had no recollection of these events. Emperor Wu had once remarked: "Ta-lin and Ta-lien are most likeable boys. They will be a comfort to me in my old age" (LS 44.4b). Hearing of his son's predicament, Hsiao Kang covered his face and wept behind his sleeve.

While his relatives eliminated each other in the provinces, Hsiao Kang, for whatever reasons, cooperated with his rebel captors. Following his enthronement, he accompanied Hou Ching into the Ch'ung-yun Hall in the Hua-lin Garden. Together they made obeisance to Buddha, swearing a formal oath that "from this day sovereign and subject will be of one mind. The subject will never abandon his liege lord; the liege lord likewise may never abandon his subject" (TCTC 5057). Tension at court was indeed lessened, and early in the new year, on March 9, an end to martial law was decreed:

Recently the eastern territories of the state were in confusion; and areas north of the [Yangtze] River degenerated into idle indulgence. High officers plotted and planned while brave warriors were inspired with impetuous valor. The Wu and Kuai districts are now pacified; Chi and Yen provinces are at peace. In the capital and the home countries there is no cause for the donning of arms. Senior officials of the court and staff of the inner palaces may be relieved from martial law. (*LS* 4.5a; *YKC* 2999)

On April 6, 550,[9] Hsiao Kang attended a banquet given by Hou Ching in the Lo-yu Park to celebrate his nuptials with Hsiao Kang's daughter, the Li-yang princess. She was a graceful young maiden and Hou Ching was infatuated with her. The festivities and drinking continued for three days, while Hou Ching's men caroused with the palace women The imperial princes and the lesser ranks competed in mounted archery, and winners received prizes of gold coin. Toward dawn, Hsiao Kang returned to the palace; he refused to remain, even though Hou Ching begged him on bended knee. Hou Ching and his bride sat on the imperial couch, facing south as only a sovereign might do, while the civil and military officers of the court, seated according to precedence, attended their pleasure.

On May 28, 550,[10] Hou Ching had Hsiao Kang make an imperial inspection of Hsi-chou, the district outside the imperial palace in Chien-k'ang where the imperial princes resided. The emperor, dressed in undyed inferior cloth, rode in an unadorned coach and was attended by few more than four hundred guards; Hou Ching, decked in purple brocades over which he had added a golden sash, was flanked by a retinue of several thousand guards "bathed in iron." Obeisance to the nominal emperor on his arrival at Hsi-chou was a mockery. Hou Ching sat with Ch'en Ch'ing and So Ch'ao-shih and others of his entourage facing west, while the Li-yang princess and her mother, the Virtuous Consort Fan, faced east.[11] Hsiao Kang heard the sound of music and tears rolled down his face. "Why is Your Majesty not happy?" apologized Hou Ching. Hsiao Kang sighed and, showing his contempt for Hou Ching's barbarian entourage by punning on their names, he said: "Tell me, Prime Minister, when So Ch'ao-shih [supramortal] hears this, what kind of noise does he think it is?" Hou Ching replied: "How should I know? Am I the only

'supramortal'?" (NS 80.17a). Hsiao Kang then commanded Hou
Ching to commence the dancing. Hou Ching descended from his
seat and sang to the music of the strings. Hsiao Kang turned
and issued an order to the Virtuous Consort Fan, but desisted
when she vehemently declined. Hou Ching offered courtesies
and had Hsiao Kang begin the dance. Wine flowed, and the
revelers reeled in their seats. Hsiao Kang embraced Hou Ching
on his couch and said: "I have great affection for you, Prime
Minister." "If Your Majesty did not have great affection for me,"
replied Hou Ching, "how could I have come to this?" Then Hsiao
Kang called for a bamboo chowry and said: "I will lecture to
you, sir." He commanded Hou Ching to leave his seat and sing a
sutra. Hou Ching asked So Ch'ao-shih what was the shortest
sutra, to which So Ch'ao-shih replied that the "Kuan-shih-yin
Sutra" was short. Hou Ching thereupon sang, "At that time, the
Inexhaustible-Mind Boddhisattva," to Hsiao Kang's great distress.
Only when night fell did the gathering end[12] (NS 80.17a).

In these encounters, Hou Ching was patently made to emerge
as the better man. Such repartee, known as "pure-talk," was a
particular feature of Chinese aristocratic society during the
Six Dynasties and a man of Hsiao Kang's standing would be expected to excel at it. The historians could hardly have expressed
greater contempt than by showing him worsted by a barbarian.

Hou Ching had Hsiao Kang make another imperial inspection
of Hsi-chou during the winter, on November 13, 550. Just before
this, on October 24, Hou Ching had promoted himself to the rank
of chancellor (hsiang-kuo). He appropriated a huge appanage of
twenty prefectures and gave himself the title Prince of Han. He
conferred exceptional dignities upon himself, such as entering the
court without obligatory haste, tabooing his given name, and
wearing a sword in the palace. On the day Hsiao Kang was sent
off on his tour, Hou Ching openly flouted imperial prerogatives
and usurped the offices of Universal Generalissimo, Commander-
in-Chief of the Universe Over All Military Affairs, while retain-
ing his former titles. These were precedented steps toward
usurping the throne itself. He notified Hsiao Kang in an edict.
"How can the general now take the appellation 'universal'?"
(NS 80.18a), Hsiao Kang asked in great alarm. At this point, the
younger princes received their first enfeoffments.

While there is no doubt that Hsiao Kang was denied even nominal authority, a question of the restrictions on his personal freedom is raised by a literary item attributed to him:

I take advantage of my leisure time to team up my coach and ramble there [in the Hsiu-lin mountain, some twenty *li* northwest of Hua-t'ing]. I regard the splendid view and am deeply touched by what I see.... Contributing to the atmosphere, quite at ease; relaxed in pleasure, rejoicing at heart. (Composed on the fifteenth day of the third month, in the spring of the *keng-wu* year, the first year of Ta-pao [April 16, 550].) ("Inscription on Luxuriant Forest Mountain,"[13] *WYYH* [?]; *YKC* 3025)

According to historical accounts, Hsiao Kang's circumstances were more harsh. Hou Ching kept him in close confinement; no one from outside the palace was permitted to see him; correspondence was forbidden. Only Hsiao Tzu (Hsiao Fan's younger brother), Wang K'e and, at Hsiao Kang's request, Yin Pu-hai were allowed to enter his private apartments. The expert administrator, Yin Pu-hai, had formerly been appointed to relieve his more literary-minded colleagues of administrative responsibilities. Now in isolation with his patron, their differing interests are again significant. Since Yin Pu-hai's literary attainments were weak, Hsiao Kang could only deliver one-sided lectures: from morning to night he discoursed on the Six Arts. Then a plot was disclosed involving Hsiao Hui-li, who was put to death. Wang K'e and Yin Pu-hai were terrified that their association with Hsiao Kang would put them in jeopardy, and from that time on they kept their distance. Only Hsiao Tzu persisted in his loyalty to Hsiao Kang, and this earned him Hou Ching's enmity. Hou Ching suspected that Hsiao Tzu had kept Hsiao Kang informed of Hsiao Hui-li's debacle and that he encouraged the emperor to hope for restoration of his sovereignty. Therefore Hou Ching contrived to have an enemy of Hsiao Tzu stab him to death. When Hsiao Kang learned of the murder, he pointed to his residence and said to Yin Pu-hai, "P'ang Chüan ought to die here"[14] (*TCTC* 5057).

Hsiao Hui-li had departed to the provinces after the fall of Chien-k'ang, taking with him the better part of his army. Later he surrendered to a detachment of Hou Ching's army and was sent back to the capital. Here, like other members of the royalty, he steadily gained official promotion. Early in the spring of 550, after a series of meteorological portents,[15] a provincial magistrate, Tsu Hao, rallied to the Liang cause. Hsiao Hui-li agreed to support the uprising by a coup in the capital. But Hou Ching besieged Tsu Hao and within three days, by March 6, had eliminated the resistance. He wreaked barbaric vengeance on the survivors. Tsu Hao was bound and riddled with arrows, after which his body was torn to fragments by chariots driven in different directions. Citizens, young and old alike, were partially buried in the ground to serve as targets for Hou Ching's mounted archers. Hou Ching then returned to Chien-k'ang to enjoy his nuptials with the Li-yang princess.

So swiftly had the uprising been suppressed that Hsiao Hui-li had not had time to show his hand. But that winter his luck changed. Hou Ching's general, Jen Yüeh, had conducted a sweeping campaign in the west, forcing Hsiao Ta-hsin to surrender his command in Chiang province, and Hsiao Ta-lien, after his own capture earlier, was entrusted with the governorship of these territories. Jen Yüeh continued to make incursions into other areas held by the Liang princes until on December 15, 550, in a river battle with the Prince of Hsiang-tung's forces, he met a serious defeat. Hou Ching sent troops to reinforce Jen Yüeh, and he himself set out from Chien-k'ang and did not return to the capital for another month.

Hsiao Hui-li calculated that the depleted garrison at Chen-k'ang numbered no more than a thousand men. With several other loyal officers he planned to raise troops, execute Hou Ching's second in command at the capital, Wang Wei, and thus leave Hou Ching stranded in the provinces. But the strategy failed through lack of secrecy; two other Hsiao scions, Hsiao Pi (Hsiao Cheng-te's nephew) and Hsiao Tzu-yung (Hsiao Tan's grandson), forewarned Wang Wei. On December 31, 550, Wang Wei had the conspirators, including Hsiao Hui-li, put to death.[16]

Soon after Hou Ching returned to the capital, early in the new year of 551, he received another urgent call from Jen Yüeh requesting help. Jen Yüeh's position seemed desperate enough to warrant Hou Ching's personal participation in the expedition;

and in the intercalary month of 551, between April and May, he set out for the west once more. As a precaution against a recurrence of intrigue in the capital, he took with him as hostage the heir apparent, Hsiao Ta-ch'i, and left Wang Wei in charge of the city garrison.

Things went badly for Hou Ching. Outwitted at Paling, he was decisively beaten by the Prince of Hsiang-tung's forces. In the rout, Hsiao Ta-ch'i had a chance to escape. He preferred, however, to place duty to the throne above considerations of personal safety: "Since our state was overthrown," he said, "I have given no thought to my own life. The throne is usurped, the rightful sovereign fallen as into the dust; how could he bear to be parted from those around him! If I were now to escape, I would be disloyal to my father. It would be of no account that I save myself from the rebels" (*TCTC* 5068). Thus he remained Hou Ching's captive; and on September 1, 551, they arrived in Chien-k'ang.[17]

Despite Hou Ching's reverses in the west, his hold on the capital was not yet threatened and the status quo might have continued without further alarms to upset Hsiao Kang's tenuous position. The turning point in his fortunes, leading to his deposition and assassination, arose from an unexpected direction. Like so many of the great events in the histories, Hsiao Kang's fall was attributed to the most trivial and mundane causes.

Hou Ching's adored princess bride was said to have distracted her husband from his administrative duties. Wang Wei remonstrated with Hou Ching; Hou Ching relayed the complaints to his bride. The girl made an insulting retort, and Hsiao Kang's fate was sealed. Wang Wei saw a danger that the girl's slander would lead to his own estrangement from Hou Ching and his certain execution. To forestall the possibility, he advised Hou Ching to dispose of the emperor. Afterward, he reasoned, he could separate the princess from Hou Ching.

Hou Ching made no secret of his ambition for the throne. After his defeat and retreat from Paling and the loss of his two best generals, he must have appreciated the insecurity of his hold on the South. Wang Wei played on these apprehensions. He advised Hou Ching to dethrone Hsiao Kang not only to demonstrate the rebels' power but also to remove any lingering hopes the populace might entertain of a resurgence of Liang rule. Hsiao Hui-li's near success would have been fresh in Hou Ching's mind to add cogency to Wang Wei's counsel.

Intrigue was rife at the capital, and no doubt Hou Ching was influenced by many other factors that were passed over by the chroniclers or were unknown to them. But in broad outline, speculations about the motives that governed events were reasonable. Hou Ching had an edict drafted in which it was claimed that the princes were contesting the throne and that the firmament was in disorder because of the wrongful selection of Hsiao Kang to the succession. As a result, calamities and disasters were brought upon the empire. To set matters aright, Hsiao Kang would be deposed in favor of Hsiao Tung, son of the deceased Hsiao Huan and grandson of the original Liang crown prince, Hsiao T'ung. Hsiao Kang was compelled to write out the edict in his own hand. He copied it as far as this passage: "The former emperor bore in mind the importance of the sacred vessels and recalled the antiquity of the altars of state. I was promoted out of turn and followed the sovereign in the east [the East Palace of the crown prince]" (NS 8.3a). So moved was he, the tale continues, that he burst into uncontrollable sobbing. The rebels turned their backs to hide their own tears!

The historians intended the reader to be moved by Hsiao Kang's tears. Objectively, however, the altars of state stood a better chance of restoration under Hsiao Tung than under his predecessor. Hsiao Kang's removal and the enthronement of Hsiao Tung would at last rectify the succession. Theoretically at least, the provincial lords would cease their rivalry for the throne and would unite under the banner of the legitimate incumbent. Although Hou Ching would undoubtedly manipulate Hsiao Tung, as he had Hsiao Kang, the "hopes of the people" would be confirmed rather than cut off.

On October 2, 551, Hou Ching sent a detachment of soldiers under P'eng Chün and Wang Seng-kuei to demote Hsiao Kang to his former rank of Prince of Chin-an and sequester him in the Yung-fu-sheng. Armed guards were posted inside and out; cavalry maintained strict surveillance; even the walls of the building were fortified with an abatis of thorns. His old tutor Hsü Ch'ih, who had served him for nearly half a century, was denied access.

In chagrin the old man, now seventy-eight, sickened and died. Within a week, Hsiao Tung was crowned. On October 6 the new monarch declared an amnesty, and the year-title was changed from the second year of Ta-pao to the first year of T'ien-cheng (Rectifying the Heavens).[18] The historical sources relate that during the ceremony a whirlwind sprang up from the Yung-fu-sheng where Hsiao Kang was imprisoned. "Ceremonial vessels were blown over and smashed and the onlookers were filled with terror" (*NS* 80.19a). Former honors lists now became death lists. The first victims were the princes Ta-chün, a lad of twelve; Ta-wei, also twelve; Ta-ch'iu, ten; Ta-hsin, ten; Ta-chih, nine; and the eldest son, Crown Prince Ta-ch'i, twenty-eight. These princes, together with Ta-hsin and his sons, were murdered at Hou Ching's orders. Hsiao Ta-ch'i's death was described in a tale of stoicism and dignity befitting a crown prince. On the eve of his execution, he rose to a defiant last word. "If the rebels conduct their affairs correctly," he said in private to some of his men, "it is not entirely certain I shall be killed. Although I pay them no deference and hold them in derision, in the end I dare not express my feelings in words. If the day comes when I am to be executed, even though I were to make a hundred obeisances in a day, that would still count for nothing in my favor." "Your Highness' situation is very precarious," his attendants persisted, "and yet you appear perfectly happy and content and never make any complaint. Why is this?" Hsiao Ta-ch'i replied, "I reason that I am to die before the rebels. If you, my uncles, can wipe out the rebels, the rebels will first kill me before they themselves die. If you cannot, then the rebels will certainly kill me to gain riches and position. Why should I, fated to die, waste myself on fruitless lamentation?"

The day of execution did indeed arrive, but Hsiao Ta-ch'i betrayed no emotion. Gravely, he remarked, "I have long expected this; I am surprised only that it comes so late." The executioners prepared to strangle him with his sash, but he exclaimed, "You will not be able to kill me with that!" (*TCTC* 5071). He ordered curtain cord to be brought, and with this he was strangled. Later, after the Prince of Hsiang-tung gained the throne, Hsiao Ta-ch'i was posthumously honored as the Ill-fated Crown Prince (Ai T'ai-tzu). Hsiao Ta-k'uan, Hsiao Ta-ch'eng,

and Hsiao Ta-feng had fled to the Prince of Hsiang-tung's court
in Chiang-ling in July 550, and so escaped the massacre.

The first phase of Wang Wei's machinations was accomplished.
But another of Hou Ching's officers, Kuo Yüan-chien, who had
earlier led the force against Hsiao Hui-li's ally Tsu Hao, learned
about the dethronement and hurried back to the capital from
his post in the provinces. "The emperor was the rightful heir of
the former sovereign," he argued. "What reason was there for
deposing him?" "It was Wang Wei's idea," Hou Ching supposedly replied. "He told me to put an end to the people's hopes
of a restoration as soon as possible. I followed his advice to bring
peace to the empire." "I sympathized with the emperor," replied
Kuo Yüan-chien. "The feudal lords still fear that matters cannot be set right. You have deposed the emperor for nothing, and
in so doing you have further endangered your own position. How
can you talk of bringing peace?" Hou Ching was apparently
ready to reinstate Hsiao Kang as emperor. Hsiao Tung was
to be allowed the rank of T'ai-sun (grandson of the crown), but
Wang Wei put a stop to this. "Deposing an emperor is no slight
matter. How can you keep changing about like this?" So Hou
Ching left things as they were (*TCTC* 5072).

On October 9 Hou Ching sent men to kill the princes serving
outside the capital. Hsiao Ta-lin, twenty-four, was killed in
Wu-chün, Ta-lien, also twenty-four, met his end in Ku-shu;
Ta-ch'un, twenty-one, died in Kuai-chi; and the seventeen-year-
old Ta-chuang was murdered at Ching-k'ou. The next day Crown
Prince Chao-ming was posthumously canonized as Emperor
Chao-ming, and his line received commensurate promotions.

Wang Wei, still pursuing his objectives, suggested that Hsiao
Kang be killed in order to remove him as a focus of antirebel
loyalty. Hou Ching agreed. Hsiao Kang also knew that after
Hsiao Hui-li's execution it was only a matter of time until Hou
Ching disposed of him as well. Portents confirming his fears
are recorded: "Last night," he remarked to Yin Pu-hai, "I
dreamed of swallowing earth. How do you interpret this?" Yin
Pu-hai replied: "In the past Chung Erh was given a clod of earth
to eat. In the end he returned to Chin State. Does not what Your
Majesty dreamed tally with this?" The emperor said: "If in hell

there is proof of this, then I expect these words will not be in vain."[19]

On November 15, 551, Wang Wei, P'eng Chün, and Wang Hsiu-tsuan presented some wine to Hsiao Kang. "The Prime Minister has kept Your Majesty imprisoned a long time. He herewith sends us with this wine to wish you long life." Hsiao Kang smiled. "I have already been deposed. Why do you address me as 'Your Majesty'? And as for this toast to my longevity," he punned, "I doubt that I can finish it!" P'eng Chün and the others served the wine and savouries, and to the accompaniment of a crook-necked lute they drank heavily. Hsiao Kang had no illusions but that this was his death sentence, and he drank himself into a stupor. "I did not think that music could attain to this," he remarked.[20] Intoxicated, he retired to bed. The assassins Wang Wei and P'eng Chün brought in a large sandbag which was thrown onto Hsiao Kang's chest.[21] Wang Hsiu-tsuan sat on top, and thus they smothered the sleeping monarch. The dream of "swallowing earth" was realized. Hsiao Kang was forty-nine years old by Chinese count; in the Western calendar he was seventeen days short of his forty-eighth birthday. Wang Wei and his henchmen wrapped the corpse in a monk's robe and, using the panel of a door as a bier, secretly buried it in a wine cellar north of the city wall.

Throughout his imprisonment, Hsiao Kang had been denied personal attendants and even such amenities as writing paper. To give vent to his urge for literary expression he wrote on the red-lacquered wall-posts of his prison, composing several hundred items of prose and poetry, the phraseology of which, we are told, was pitifully sad. One item reads: "There is a true gentleman of Liang, Hsiao Shih-tsan of Lan-ling. He established himself in the Way. Beginning and end are as one. 'Through the wind and rain all looks dark, and the cock crows without ceasing.' He did not deceive in the darkened room; how much less would he do so in the Three Brilliances [of sun, moon, and stars]. Destined to come to this, how strange is Fate!"[22] (*LS* 4.8a; *KHMC* 30; *YKC* 3018).

Having mentioned Hsiao Kang's literary occupation in the face of his material deprivations, the historians enlarged upon the disappearance of most of these items and at the same time

provided a convincing reason for the survival of a few verses
(which still appear in his collected works). Even after his death,
said the historians, Wang Wei's hostility remained implacable.
When he noticed these writings he was furious at the aptness of
the sentiments, and he had them scraped off. Before the writing
was obliterated, however, one of his entourage memorized three
lien-chu ("strung pearls"), four *shih,* and five *chüeh-chü* verses.

> Hazily the evening mists disperse;
> Soughing winds in the shadowing pines.
> In mountains remote, white willows age;
> On desolate roads yellow dust lies deep.
> In the end, no thousand-moon fate;
> What use is the gold of the Nine Elixirs?
> Ch'üeh-li lies o'ergrown with lengthy weeds;[23]
> In vain the blue sky reflects my heart.
> ("A Poem Expressing My Thoughts in My Imprisonment,"
> *KHMC* 30; *TFP* 1158)

Hou Ching had Hsiao Kang canonized as Emperor Ming, with
the temple name Kao-tsung. In the provinces, Wang Seng-pien
heard of Hsiao Kang's death, and on November 29, 551, he petitioned the Prince of Hsiang-tung to accord proper honors for
the murdered sovereign. Probably because the situation was
not resolved, the prince refused permission.[24] However, within
months of the regicide, Chien-k'ang came under the Prince of
Hsiang-tung's control. On April 30, 552, Wang Seng-pien, now
the Prince of Hsiang-tung's garrison commander at the capital,
escorted Hsiao Kang's cortege into the Hall of Court and led
the assembled officials in weeping and obeisance according to
prescribed etiquette.[25]

On June 5, 552, Hsiao Kang's body was interred beside that of
his empress in the mausoleum at Chuang-ling. With the rebels
dislodged from the capital, the Prince of Hsiang-tung legitimized
Hsiao Kang's reign by permitting the unauthorized appellations
to be revoked and changed to Chien-wen huang-ti, with the
temple-name T'ai-tsung.[26]

The assessment of the T'ang historians was not far from the
truth:

As a youth T'ai-tsung was intelligent and perceptive and had an excellent reputation. He was talented and had broad aptitude, crowning past and present times. His literary composition, however, at times became involved in frivolity and ornate embellishment. No gentleman would choose it. As for fostering virtue in the East Court, his name spread through the I and Hsia tribes, and continues in unbroken tradition. Indeed, he had the manner of a ruler of men. He could have hoped to compare with the Emperors Wen and Ching [of the Han, father and son] in their peaceful and virtuous rule, but he was fated to meet an era of decline. He was controlled by rebels and could not realize his true capacity. In the end he suffered the cruel fate of [the Chin emperors] Min and Huai[27] (*LS* 4.9b).

Chien-wen had a highly cultivated disposition and was endowed with inherent ability. Though not in line for the succession, he occupied the Double Brightness position. No one has ever heard of such state policy. Palace-style composition was propagated, transforming court and countryside. He was a ruler in name only; how could he rescue [the state] from oblivion? (*NS* 8.20a)

CHAPTER 9

Epilogue

THE six years between Hsiao Kang's death and the formal end of the dynasty his father had established saw the acceleration of the internecine struggle for power in the South. All considerations of rightful claim, kinship, and even common humanity were ignored. The dignity of the imperial seat was degraded in the very numbers of "emperors" who seized this supreme prize, only to be overthrown in a few months. Not infrequently there were two or more emperors competing with each other from their respective strongholds in the South. Whenever expedient, the surviving Hsiao claimants did not hesitate to make alliances with their common enemy in the North. Yet in every case, after some temporary gain for the southern partner in the intrigue, it was the North that benefited in the acquisition of southern territory.

Hsiao Kang's successor and puppet emperor for Hou Ching, Hsiao Tung, occupied his throne for less than three months. On January 1, 552, Hou Ching forced his abdication and proclaimed himself Emperor of Han. But three months later, Hou Ching was in turn forced to flee from Chien-k'ang by troops led by Wang Seng-pien. Treachery secured his end and he was dispatched with appropriate savagery. (His wife, Hsiao Kang's daughter, is seen leading the populace in devouring every last shred of the corpse. Another source says that she too was boiled alive.)

Wang Wei, too, fell into the Prince of Hsiang-tung's hands, and might have earned reprieve, but a literary insult—a slur on the prince's partial blindness—enraged his captor, and he was done to death in the marketplace. One of Hsiao Kang's assassins, P'eng Chün, ended his own life; and the luckless Hsiao Tung, together with his two brothers, was released from confinement

174

only to be thrown into a river by Wang Seng-pien's men and drowned.

Three principal contenders for the vacant throne remained: the seventh brother, the Prince of Hsiang-tung, in Chiang-ling; the eighth brother, Hsiao Chi, in Ssuchuan; and Hsiao T'ung's son, Hsiao Ch'a, in Yung province. Hsiao Chi moved first. On May 16, 552, he assumed the imperial title; in September he began his advance eastwards.

Alarmed by the news, on December 13, 552, the Prince of Hsiang-tung proclaimed himself emperor. Hoping to forestall his younger brother, he hired a magician to draw a portrait of Hsiao Chi on a board and with his own hand drove a nail into it and cast spells upon it. As a more practical measure, he wrote to the enemy Wei regime, quoting the classics and requesting that Hsiao Chi be killed. In August 553, the deed was accomplished, and Ssuchuan and the West fell to Wei. The capital was transferred to Chiang-ling. A year later, at the end of 554, this city, too, fell siege to Wei. Survivors of former campaigns reappear; even Yin Pu-hai turns up, searching for his dead mother among the frozen corpses in the streets and ditches. (He later joined Hsiao Ch'a's court, and died in 589, at the age of eighty-five.) The surrender of the city witnessed another bibliotecal catastrophe, with the destruction of the books, scrolls, paintings, calligraphy, antiques, and artifacts accumulated at the prince's court over the years or salvaged from the ruins of Chien-k'ang.

Hsiao Ch'a, under the protection of Northern Wei, had his uncle, the Prince of Hsiang-tung (Emperor Yüan), sandbagged to death and buried in a common grave outside the city gates. He was rewarded with three hundred *li* of territory and the title Lord of Liang; a Wei garrison was detailed to "assist" him. On New Year's Day (February 7, 555) he was proclaimed emperor.

Meanwhile in Chien-k'ang, Weng Seng-pien and Ch'en Pa-hsien, formerly commanders of the Prince of Hsiang-tung's forces, brought Hsiao Yüang-ming back from Northern Ch'i where he had been held in semicaptivity. On July 1, 555, he too was established as emperor. The Prince of Hsiang-tung's son, Hsiao Fang-chih, was promoted to crown prince. Then Ch'en Pa-hsien killed Wang Seng-pien, deposed Hsiao Yüan-ming, and, on November 1, instated Hsiao Fang-chih as emperor in his place. This fifteen-year-old boy maintained his position for two years, but in the end he, too, was forced to abdicate. On November 16, 557, Ch'en Pa-hsien was proclaimed emperor of the Ch'en dynasty, the event that signified the formal conclusion of the Liang.

LIST OF ABBREVIATIONS

BMFEA	*Bulletin of the Museum of Far Eastern Antiquities*
CHC	*Ch'u-hsüeh chi*
HHS	*Hou Han shu*
HJAS	*Harvard Journal of Asiatic Studies*
HS	*Han shu*
IWLC	*I-wen lei chü*
JAOS	*Journal of the American Oriental Society*
JAS	*Journal of Asian Studies*
KHMC	*Kuang Hung-ming chi*
LS	*Liang shu*
NS	*Nan shih*
SC	*Shih chi*
SPTK	*Ssu-pu ts'ung-k'an*
TCTC	*Tzu-chih t'ung-chien*
TFP	Ting Fu-pao, *Ch'üan Han San-kuo Chin Nan-Pei-ch'ao shih*
TPYL	*T'ai-p'ing yü-lan*
WYYH	*Wen-yüan ying-hua*
YKC	Yen K'o-chün, *Ch'üan Shang-ku San-tai Ch'in Han San-kuo Liu-ch'ao wen*
YSCH	*Yen-shih chia-hsün*
YT	*Yü-t'ai hsin-yung*

Notes and References

Chapter One

1. See Teng Ssu-yü, trans., *The Family Instructions for the Yen Clan, Yen-shih chia-hsün by Yen Chih-t'ui* (Leiden, 1968), pp. 12–15, for contemporaneous descriptions of the difficulties engendered by remarriage.

2. *LS* 4.1a; *NS* 8.1a (both in *Erh-shih-ssu shih*, Po-na ed.). The name Kang means "controlling rope of a net," "principle." He also bore the style-name Shih-tsan (Laud of the Generation); and the minor-style Liu-T'ung (Six Perspicacities). The form of these names—the "silk" signific; the *shih* and the "speech" signific; and the numerical unit—was continued in the names of his seven brothers. See Appendix I.

3. In 504 Ting Ling-kuang bore her third son, Emperor Wu's fifth, Hsiao Hsü.

4. In 282 Emperor Wu of the Chin dynasty divided Chien-an prefecture and established Chin-an there.

5. Hsiao Kang's "8,000" (*pa ch'ien*) might be a graphic error for "2,000" (*erh ch'ien*), in which case his appanage would equal those of his brothers.

6. Chu Hsieh, *Chin-ling ku-chi t'u k'ao* (Illustrated Study of the Archaeology of Chin-ling) (Shanghai, 1936), includes a portrait of Hsiao Kang. The source is unidentified, but it may be the work of Ma Lin (thirteenth century). The original seems to have been lost in the disturbances of 1947–49. See also Alexander C. Soper, *Textual Evidence for the Secular Arts of China in the Period from Liu Sung through Sui* (Ascona, Switzerland: Artibus Asiae, 1968), p. 21.

7. *Ibid.*

8. "Memorial on Behalf of the Prince of Chin-an in Thanks for [the governorship] of South Yen Province" (*CHC* 10; *YKC* 3017).

9. Liu Ch'ien, "Memorial on Behalf of the Prince of Chin-an on Declining the Prefectship of Tan-yang" (*IWLC* 50; *YKC* 3314).

10. Po-na ed. has *chia* "additional" for Palace ed. *ju* "be like."

11. Chang K'an brought order and peace to his border district administration, and the populace sang of his achievements. *HHS* 31 (in *Erh-shih-ssu shih*).

12. So successfully did Lien Fan conduct his administration that the people were enriched and sang, "In my life I have never had a shirt, but now I have five pairs of trousers."

13. A folk song referring to Chang K'an states that so prosperous had the people become that "each cornstalk had double ears of grain."

14. The willow is a symbol of parting. See *Shih-shuo hsin-yü* (Popular Sayings and New Tales), "Yen-yü" (On Speech), "Huan Wen shih" (Affairs of Huan Wen). Shao Po was an honest official of the Chou dynasty. He once rested in the shade of an apple tree, and after his death the people were unwilling to cut down the tree. Another tradition says that Shao Po conducted his law practice under the tree. See James Legge, *The Chinese Classics* (London, 1871), IV, 26.

15. This term refers to the merciful attitude of the sovereign even when hunting wild game. See Richard Wilhelm, *I Ching or Book of Changes* (London, 1951), "Pi kua" (Holding Together), I, 40.

16. *Sui shu* 25.2a; 5a (in *Erh-shih-wu shih*, Palace ed.) records that after 502 and 512 punishments could be redeemed by payment of fines. See also Ch'eng Shu-te, *Chiu-ch'ao lü k'ao* (Study of the Legal Systems of the Nine Dynasties) (Taipei: Taiwan Commercial Press, 1965), II, 374.

17. "Dictum on Painting the Portraits of the Able Governors of Yung Province" (*IWLC* 52; *YKC* 3000). See Eli Lancman, *Chinese Portraiture* (Rutland, Vt., 1966), pp. 36–37.

18. See, for example, Han Kuo-p'an, *Nan-ch'ao ching-chi shih-t'an* (A Study of the Economics of the Southern Dynasties) (Shanghai: Jen-min ch'u-pan she, 1963).

19. *LS* 4.8b; *TCTC* 4690. *LS* 30.9a says, "at the beginning of A.D. 527." But at this time Hsiao Kang was in mourning for his mother and could not have undertaken the campaign as stated in this source.

20. *LS* 4.9a says, "The governor of South Ching province, Li Chih, garrison commander of An-ch'ang city." Li Chih's biography is in *Wei shu* 62 (in *Erh-shih-ssu shih*).

21. See Arthur Waley, *Analects of Confucius* (London, 1938), 12.12.

22. Wilhelm, *Changes*, "Feng kua" (Abundance), I, 227.

23. *HS* 51.28b (in *Erh-shih-ssu shih*). Lu Wen-shu's biography here includes a powerful treatise on prison reform.

24. This item and Emperor Wu's correspondence are translated into Japanese in Uchida Tomoo, "Yakuchu Zuisho keihōshi" (Annotated Translation of the Treatise on the Criminal Code in the Dynastic History of the Sui). *Dōshisha hōgaku,* 87 (1964), 225–226. Original

sources of the text are variously abridged. Uchida notes that these were all minor offices. There was a commissariat (*ts'ai-kuan*) general, second of the eighteen official grades during Liang; the *ch'e-fu* were transport officials or keepers of the coaches, and by Liang times they were attached to the *shang-shu chia-pu;* the caterers (*t'ai-kuan*) belonged to the first (i.e., the lowest) rank in the Liang official hierarchy, along with the officials of the East and West Foundries and the transport officials; the *hsia-sheng* were probably part of the chancellery.

25. Elements of this term appear in *Shih-ching* (Book of Odes), "Yü wu cheng" and "Hsiao min." One context has to do with injustice; the other tells of the "recklessness and incapacity of the king's plans." Legge, *Classics,* IV, 325, 330.

26. Uchida (see n. 24) notes that during Han times such insignia of office were attached to ranks having an income of between six hundred and one thousand bushels of grain. Prison officials held ranks which qualified for a salary of between six hundred and one thousand bushels. The cords were one foot two inches long and three inches broad. Prison officials endorsed their judgments in red ink.

27. *YKC* and *Sui shu* have *li* "establish"; *IWLC* has *wu* "five."

28. "Imperial Report to the Crown Prince' ((*YKC* 2970).

29. *Han Wei Liu-ch'ao chu-chia wen-chi* (Collected Works of the Han, Wei, and Six Dynasties), comp. Wang Shih-hsien, Wang shih k'an pen ed.; and *YKC* 3016.

30. "Memorial from the Provinces Requesting Compassionate Leave" (*IWLC* 75; *YKC* 3002).

31. *LS* 7.8b. Ting Ling-kuang died at age forty-one. She was given the posthumous name Mu (*LS* 7.10a). Upon Hsiao Kang's enthronement in 549, she was posthumously elevated to the rank of empress dowager (*t'ai-hou*).

32. *LS* 34.19a (Po-na ed.) says, "T'ai-tsung's tenth daughter"; the Palace ed. says "eleventh."

33. In "Grieving for My Son Ta-t'ung" (*IWLC* 34; *WYYH* 999; *YKC* 3026), Hsiao Kang refers to Ta-t'ung as his nineteenth son. In the histories the nineteenth is Hsiao Ta-chih.

34. The word *jang* "decline" appears in a number of titles referring to the award of an appointment, although the recipient clearly accepts the honor. See Masuda Kiyohide, "Nan-boku-chō ni okeru kosui-kashi no jitsujō" (What the Presentation of a Military Band in the Northern and Southern Dynasties Really Meant), *Ōsaka gakugei daigaku kiyō,* XV (1967), 10–21.

35. Wu Ching, *Yüeh-fu ku-t'i yao-chieh* (Explanation of the Ancient Titles of Yüeh-fu Poetry), in *Hsüeh-chin t'ao-yüan ts'ung-shu,*

n.d. explains the title "Morning Birds" by reference to the septuagenarian bachelor, Tu Mu-tzu, during the time of King Hsüan of Ch'i, who, observing a pheasant leading its hen, sighed that although the sage kings had so graced the birds and beasts, they had neglected him. He thereupon composed this song to express his sadness. Wu Ching's text continues that in mentioning "flying birds" in his poem, Hsiao Kang remained faithful to the original intent.

36. LS 3.12a. The fifth brother, Hsiao Hsü, took over the governorship of Yung province at this time. Perhaps the "south" in LS 4.2a, "military governor of the two provinces of South Yang and Hsü," is misplaced and should read "the two provinces of Yang and South Hsü."

37. "Memorial Declining [the appointment to] Daring Cavalry [general] and Governor of Yang Province" (IWLC 18; TPYL 238; YKC 3001).

38. These emblems were the privilege of the governor of Yang province. The baton was made of bronze and mounted with gold at each end. Crops held by lesser ranks were made of wood. See Ku-chin-chu, Comp. Ts'ui Pao, Sec. 1, "Yü-fu" (Vehicles and Attire).

Chapter Two

1. Yen Chih-t'ui, "Kuan wo sheng fu" (Rhymeprose on "My Life"), in "Biography of Yen Chih-tui," trans. Albert E. Dien (unpublished), presents an epic chronicle of the fall of Liang. Yen sees the collapse of the dynasty as a result of Hsiao Kang's selection for the heir-apparency.

2. See Yang Lien-sheng, Money and Credit in China, Harvard-Yenching Institute Monograph Series No. 12 (1952), p. 27 and passim.

3. NS 53.6a says yen-jen; TCTC 4808 says huan-che. Both terms mean "eunuch" and this variety of vocabulary indicates that "eunuch" was indeed intended.

4. That is, five months short of his thirtieth birthday. The histories say thirty-one.

5. Hsiao Huan died on February 11, 541. The date is given as Ta-tung VI.12 jen-tzu, which is actually Ta-t'ung VII.1.1. NS 7.10a.

6. LS 29.1a–2a; NS 53.12a; TCTC 4763. IWLC 20; YKC 3004. IWLC 22; YKC 3047.

7. LS 36.3a. See LS 36.5a and YKC 2999 for the complimentary obituary Hsiao Kang composed on K'ung Hsiu-yüan's death in 532. Since the only source for this piece is K'ung's official biography, and

since it is cited to demonstrate K'ung's favor in royal circles, the authenticity of Hsiao Kang's authorship could be questioned.

8. *LS* 4.2a; *NS* 8.6b. Crown Prince Chao-ming was buried on June 21, 531; on this day Hsiao Huan was returned to his provincial duties.

9. T'ai-tsung is the most easterly of the five sacred mountains in Shantung. Hsiao Kang's quotation comes from the *Odes*. See Legge, *Classics*, IV, 416.

10. *Ibid.*, 451–452.

11. For "innate knowledge," see Waley, *Analects*, 7.19. For "abundant blessings," see Wilhelm, *Changes*, II, 26. The next two sentences occur in *CHC*.

12. Waley, *Analects*, 13.12.

13. *Mencius* 6B.5 refers to the way people follow a sure example; see Legge, *Classics*, II, 434.

14. *Ch'en shu* 24.2a (in *Erh-shih-ssu shih*); *YKC* 3426.

15. See Herbert A. Giles, *Chuangtzu*, 2nd rev. ed. (1929; rpt. London, 1961), pp. 27, 30.

16. *Kuo-yü* (Sayings of the States), "Ch'u-yü" (Sayings of the State of Ch'u), B, 18.8a. Reference to Chao Chien-tzu, who "tinkled his jade insignia in an audience at the Chin court."

17. The terms for crown prince come from the *Changes*. See Wilhelm, *Changes*, I, 127, 210; II, 179, 296. In December 522 Hsiao Kang's uncle, Hsiao Tan, died. The crown prince customarily conducted the rites on the death of an uncle, but Crown Prince Chao-ming, uncertain of the protocol, solicited opinions from his courtiers. *LS* 8.2a.

18. For this term, see n. 17, above.

19. Said in respect of Chün-ch'en. See Legge, *Classics*, III, 535.

20. Waley, *Analects*, 2.4.

21. See Giles, *Chuangtzu*, pp. 272–273. This refers to a prince of Yüeh who, because of the fate of his predecessors, was unwilling to accept the throne.

22. As crown prince, King Wen of Chou inquired about his father's health at dawn each day. He showed joy at a favorable response and grief at an unfavorable one. He also inspected the emperor's food to see if it were too hot or too cold. The crown prince's attention to official documents seems to anticipate the function of the board of censors in the government organization of later dynasties.

23. As crown prince, Emperor Ming of the Han dynasty received a summons from the emperor. He left his palace via the Dragon Tower Gate (so named because of the brazen dragon set upon the

upper story like a flying white crane) but dared not cross the Imperial Highway, which was reserved for the emperor. In answer to the emperor's complaints of his tardy arrival, he mentioned his roundabout route. The emperor was pleased and granted him access to the highway. The emperor paid reverence at the chapel of Confucius. He personally ascended the lecture dais and commanded the crown prince and other princes to expound the classics. *HS* 10.1b.

24. *IWLC* 50; *YKC* 3002. Hsiao Kang wrote two pieces to or about Hsiao Chi. See *TFP* 1149; *YT* 10.19b; *TFP* 1151.

25. The poem is in *TFP* 1183.

26. *NS* 52.9b–10a; *TCTC* 4939–4940. See also Kikuchi Hideo, "Riku-chō gunshi no shingun ni tsuite no ikkōsatsu" (A Study of the Bodyguards of the Warlords of the Six Dynasties), *Tōyōshi kenkyū*, XVIII, no. 1, 17–38.

27. *TFP* 1082 wrongly dates Hsiao Kang's appointment to the governorship of South Hsü province.

28. E.g., Yen Yen-chih (384–456), "Preface to the [poems on the] Serpentine on the Third Day of the Third Month" (*YKC* 2640).

29. The "three excellences" were the proper relations between sovereign and subject, father and son, elder and younger. See *Li-chi* (Book of Ritual), "Wen wang shih-tzu" (King Wen's Heir Apparent) (in *Shih-san ching chu-su*). The eight districts are otherwise interpreted as the name of the eight inner palaces.

30. *IWLC* 16, 55; *CHC* 10; *YKC* 3002.

31. *LS* 8.1b says that on T'ien-chien V.5 *keng-hsü*, Hsiao T'ung took up residence in the East Palace (at the age of nearly five years). *NS* 53.1b agrees with this date, but there is no *keng-hsü* day in the fifth month of this year. *TCTC* 4562 is probably correct in giving the date as the *keng-hsü* day of the sixth month (July 22, 506).

32. *LS* 50.22a. "Rhymeprose on Returning to Death" (*IWLC* 27; *YKC* 2995).

Chapter Three

1. See "Letter to the Prince of Hsiang-tung," pp. 80–82.

2. Legge, *Classics*, V, 684a.

3. Wilhelm, *Changes*, I, 7.

4. Legge, *Classics*, V, 209a.

5. Waley, Analects, 11.23. In ancient times, records were inscribed on wooden tablets. Graphic errors were erased by scraping the tablet with a knife.

6. David Hawkes, *Ch'u-tz'u: The Songs of the South* (Oxford, 1957), p. 89.

7. This is repeated almost word for word in respect of Crown Prince Chao-ming. *LS* 8.4b.

8. *Han Wei Liu-ch'ao pai-san chia chi* (A Hundred and Three Authors of the Han, Wei, and Six Dynasties), comp. Chang P'u, "Liang Chien-wen ti chi hsü" (Preface to the Collected Works of Emperor Chien-wen of Liang).

9. Okamura Shigeru, "Ken-an bundan e no shikaku" (A View of the Literary Forum of the Chien-an Era), *Chūgoku chūsei bungaku kenkyū*, V (June 1966), 1–16.

10. Morino Shigeo, "Ryō-shō no bungaku shūdan" (Literary Salons in Early Liang), *Chūgoku bungaku-hō*, XXI (October 1966), 83–108.

11. Hsiao Kang's works include the "Epitaph for the Prince of An-ch'eng" (*IWLC* 45; *YKC* 3027). Hsiao Hsiu held the title An-ch'eng k'ang wang. He died in 518 (*LS* 22.4b–10a; *NS* 52.1a–3b). His son, Hsiao Chi (d. 528), was An-ch'eng yang wang; his grandson, Hsiao Ts'ao, was An-ch'eng wang. No An-ch'eng fan wang appears among the Liang nobility. The content of the item seems to refer to Hsiao Hsiu.

12. See Morino, "Literary Salons," p. 94.

13. *KHMC* 20; *YKC* 3051. The Prince of Hsiang-tung's (Hsiao I) preface dates from 534 or 535.

14. "Hazelnuts and spiced meats" and "crosspins and jewels" are classical references—e.g., see Legge, *Classics*, IV, 76. In V, 187b, Huai Ying and four other ladies were presented to the prince, Chung-erh, who made her hold a goblet and pour water from it for him to wash his hands. But since the Chin and Ch'in states were equals, he should not have demanded this of her.

15. *YSCH*, "Yin-tz'u" 18.7b–8a. See Legge, *Classics*, V, 753, for the invasion of Ying; *HHS* 59 for Pao Yung as *ssu-li chiao-wei*; and Teng, *Family Instructions*, p. 196. In n. 4 Teng mistakenly gives Liang Yüan-ti (Prince of Hsiang-tung) as Hsiao Kang's son.

16. See Teng, *Family Instructions*, p. 98. Yin Yün (*LS* 41.19ab; *NS* 60.22a) was a member of Hsiao Kang's entourage in the East Palace. See also Richard B. Mather, "A Note on the Dialect of Loyang and Nanking During the Six Dynasties," in *Wen-lin*, ed. Chow Tse-tsung (Madison, 1968), pp. 247–256.

17. Prince Chao-ming's collection of some thirty thousand folios in the East Palace (*LS* 8.4b; *NS* 53.4a) was stored in several hundred bookcases (*NS* 80.7b). These were burned by Hsiao Kang during the siege of the capital. Another private collection exceeded ten thousand folios, many of which were rare (*NS* 59.16a). This collection compared favorably with those of Shen Yüeh and Jen Fang. See also Alexander Wylie, *Notes on Chinese Literature* (Shanghai,

1867), "Introduction," p. xvii, for a list of bibliographic collections in Liang and the catastrophe that befell them.

18. *Shu-pin* (Classification of Calligraphy); *Kuang Han Wei ts'ung-shu*, 86.

19. E.g., Hsiao Tzu-yün (487–549).

20. *Ch'i-p'in* (Classification on Chess), 5 fols.; *T'an-ch'i p'u* (On Playing Chess), 1 fol. *NS* 8.4a; *IWLC* 74; *YKC* 3017.

21. Joseph Needham, *Science and Civilization in China* (Cambridge: Cambridge University Press, 1965), IV, Part 1, 314–330.

22. The most common epithet was *neng chu wen* "capable of literary composition." This was applied to the five-year-old Hsiao Kang. The term was varied as *kung chu wen* "skilled at literary composition" and *shan chu wen* "excels at literary composition."

23. "Letter to Liu Hsiao-i Mourning Liu Tsun [d. 535]" (*LS* 41.15b; *NS* 39.8b–9a; *YKC* 2999).

24. This echoes Ts'ao P'ei, "Letter to Wu Chih" (*YKC* 1089), which mourned the deaths of several of Ts'ao P'ei's friends. For reference to poetry, see Legge, *Classics*, III, 48. *Ch'ing-i* and *ch'ing-t'an* (discussions of character and ability) were still in vogue as a salon pastime.

25. E.g., Hsiao Kang's poem, "Presented to Chang Tsan" (*TFP* 1118), and "Letter to Hsiao Lin-ch'uan" (*IWLC* 30; *YKC* 3010). *Liu-ch'ao wen-hsieh chien-chu* (Notes on Literary Works of the Six Dynasties), comp. Hsü Lien, offers evidence that the letter was addressed to Hsiao Tzu-yün.

26. Elaborate literary composition was compared with "dragon patterns," hence such writing was called "dragon carving." See Liu Hsiang, "Pieh-lu" (Bibliography in Seven Categories).

27. Legge, *Classics*, IV, 364.

28. *Hsiung-hsin* "heroic heart," varied as *pien-hsin* "frontier heart" and *hsiang-ssu* "homesickness," were key concepts in the literature of the period. See Lin Wen-yüeh, "Nan-ch'ao kung-t'i-shih yen-chiu" (A Study of the Palace-Style Poetry of the Southern Courts), *Wen shih che hsüeh-pao*, XV (1966), 407–458.

29. *LS* 35.12b. Hsiao T'e died at age twenty-four, and Hsiao Kang composed the "Epitaph for the t'ai-tzu she-jen Hsiao T'e" (*IWLC* 49; *YKC* 3028).

Chapter Four

1. Yen Chih-t'ui points to an inaccurate reference in one of Hsiao Kang's poems. See Teng, *Family Instructions*, p. 104.

2. Legge, *Classics*, IV, "Prologomena," p. 36.

3. *Han Wei Liu-ch'ao pai-san chia chi,* "Liang Chien-wen ti chi hsü."

4. Teng, *Family Instructions,* p. 107.

5. See Obi Koichi, *Chūgoku bungaku ni arawareta shizen to shizenkan* (Nature and Its View Revealed in [medieval] Chinese Literature) (Tokyo, 1962), pp. 530–571, for a discussion of aristocratic pleasures during the Six Dynasties as expressed in nature poetry. On p. 552 Obi notes the word "enjoyment" (*shang-hsin*) in the last line of Hsiao Kang's "Rhymes on the 'Ninth Day'" (*TFP* 1141). See also Hsiao Kang, "The Stroll," in which the word "happiness" (*huan-lo*) appears (*YT* 10.20a; *TFP* 1151).

6. See below, n. 78.

7. The *chih-tien* (administrative code), *li-tien* (code of rites), *chiao-tien* (education code), *cheng-tien* (code of regulations), *hsing-tien* (criminal code), and *shih-tien* (service code).

8. The *Chou-li, I-li, and Li-chi.*

9. Prosodically only four characters are allowed. Hsiao Kang characteristically omits "military action" from the set five-character phrase.

10. See below, n. 78.

11. *Li-chi,* chap. 12.

12. Legge, *Classics,* III, 48.

13. *Ibid.,* Book X, part 5.

14. *Ibid.,* IV, 228.

15. One of the three ancient books of *Changes.*

16. Hawkes, *Songs of the South,* p. 109.

17. A section of the *Changes.*

18. See below, n. 78.

19. See below, n. 79.

20. Waley, *Analects,* 5.26.

21. This nickname was apparently uncommon enough in early Liang for Chung Hung to gloss it in his already brief criticism of Hsieh Ling-yün's literary style. See *Shih-p'in* (Classification of Poets), Part A.

22. See pp. 91, 190.

23. See below, n. 65.

24. Achilles Fang, trans., "Rhymeprose on Literature: The *Wen-fu* of Lu Chi (A.D. 261–303)," *HJAS,* XIV (1951), 536.

25. *Ibid.,* p. 544.

26. *Ming* (name) and its antithesis *shih* (reality), like *wen* (embellishment) and *chih* (substance), are common antitheses in Chinese literary theory.

27. The *lin* was said to be a virtuous beast that neither treads on

live insects nor crushes living herbs. No other creature shared its prey like the *lin,* hence the meaning of extreme philanthropy. See Legge, *Classics,* V, 834–835.

28. *Chuang-tzu,* "Ch'iu-shui p'ien" (Autumn Waters), contains the story of the boy of Shou-ling who went to Han-tan to learn the Han-tan walk. Before he mastered what the people there had to teach him, he forgot his native walk and had to crawl back home.

29. "Companionship with a good man is like entering a fragrant room. After a time, one becomes used to the fragrance and no longer notices it. Companionship with an evil man is like entering a fish market. But after a while, one becomes used to the stench and, in the same way, no longer notices it." *K'ung-tzu chia-yü* (Family Sayings of Confucius).

30. Legge, *Classics,* V, 229. In this series of references Hsiao Kang asserts that the original models, P'ei and Hsieh, are faulty to begin with. Imitators merely repeat the mistakes of their models.

31. Confucius had three thousand disciples. Hsiao Kang is saying that Hsieh Ling-yün is inimitable.

32. T'ang Lin and T'ang Tsun are recorded in *HS* 88 and 99B–C as the "Two T'ang." The reference is so obscure that it cannot be assumed to have been Hsiao Kang's intention, even though during Liang the *Han shu* attracted attention for its rarity. The references to the "Rules for Women" and the "Injunctions against Drunkenness" in Liang poetry are probably specific attacks. Some of Hsiao Kang's targets can be identified, but the target in his reference to the Two T'ang is unknown. P'ei Tzu-yeh was a historian.

33. Fang, "Rhymepose on Literature," p. 543.

34. "A musician was traveling in Ying [capital of Ch'u]. First he performed the 'Hsia-li Pa-jen,' and there were several thousand people in the state who could accompany him. Then he performed the 'Yang-ch'un Pai-hsüeh,' and in the whole state there were not more than a score of men who could accompany him." Sung Yü, "Tui Ch'u Wang wen" (Questioning the King of Ch'u). See also Fang, "Rhymeprose on Literature," p. 540. In Hsiao Kang's letter, the word order is changed to "Pa-jen Hsia-li."

35. Fang, "Rhymeprose on Literature," p. 538.

36. *Ibid.,* p. 543.

37. See Hawkes, *Songs of the South,* p. 71. The continuation of the reference, which Hsiao Kang intended his readers to notice, is Ch'ü Yüan's complaint about the ignorant rustics at the Ch'u court who could not appreciate ability and refinement in the true master.

38. Cheng and Man were barbarian territories. Cheng was known for its licentious musical entertainments; Man was associated with

the crude "Hsia-li Pa-jen" ditties. A man of Ch'ü Yüan's sophistication, says Hsiao Kang, cannot elevate such savage tastes and can only sigh and retire.

39. See *LS* 33.9b and *LS* 25.2a.

40. The text is scrambled. *LS* (Palace ed.) 49.7a and *NS* (Palace ed.) 50.13b say "ssu yen Tzu-chien" (I think of speaking of Tzu-chien). *LS* (Po-na ed.) 49.9a says "wu Tzu-chien" (My Tzu-chien). *NS* (Po-na ed.) 50.12b–13a says "ssu wu Tzu-chien" (I think of my Tzu-chien). *YKC* follows *NS* (Po-na ed.). The similarity between the graphs *yen* and *wu* is conducive to error.

41. See below, n. 71.

42. Reference is to Hsü Shao and his brother, Hsü Ching, who, on the first day of every month, discussed their neighbors' conduct. Thus in Ju-nan, where they lived, the term "first of the month" came to mean "criticize." *HHS* 98.7b–9a.

43. Waley, *Analects*, 17.18. The primary color red was considered orthodox; the secondary color purple was considered to represent deviant tendencies.

44. See Ch'ü Wan-li and Ch'ang Pei-te, *T'u-shu pan-pen hsüeh yao-lüeh* (A Survey of the Study of Editions) (Peking: Chung-hua Wen-hua ch'u-pan shih-yeh wei-yüan hui, 1955), pp. 12–13, for a discussion of the use of a yellow dye to preserve paper from insect damage, the methods of correcting graphic errors with another yellow substance, and the association of the process with criticism.

45. The people of Cheng said that before polishing, jade is *p'o* (uncut gem). The people of Chou said that before drying, rat (meat) is *p'o*. A Chou man, clasping his *p'o* to his chest, said to a Cheng merchant, "I have some *p'o* for sale. Do you want it?" The merchant said he did. The Chou man produced his *p'o*—a rat—for inspection. The merchant refused it. *Yin-wen-tzu*, "Ta-tao" (The Great Way), part 2. The rat-sellers in Hsiao Kang's context are his literary opponents who, like Ch'ü Yüan's persecutors, do not appreciate refinement.

46. This refers to the Hermit of the Southern Wall who played the flute in King Hsüan's orchestra. King Hsüan died, and King Min succeeded to the throne. King Min preferred to hear solo performances by his musicians, and the hermit found himself out of work again. This refers to an imposter. *Han Fei-tzu*, "Nei-ch'u-shuo" (Inner Congeries of Sayings).

47. Hsü Shao (Tzu-chiang) was admired for his just administration. A local nobleman named Yüan Shao was returning home with a retinue of personnel and carriages. Just as Yüan reached his home district, he dismissed his followers with the apology, "How can

I let Hsü Tzu-chiang see all my coaches and fine apparel!" *HHS* 98.7b–9a.

48. Wang Lieh had a reputation for probity. A villager who was arrested for stealing an ox was willing to submit to any punishment, provided that Wang was not informed. Wang did hear, and out of consideration for the man's embarrassment sent him a gift of cloth. *HHS* 111.26ab.

49. *Shih-p'in*, Part A, "Preface."

50. "Preface to the Collected Works of the Princess of Lin-an" (*IWLC* 55; *YKC* 3017). The Princess of Lin-an was one of Emperor Wu's three daughters, known for their literary accomplishments. *NS* 51.18b. In Hsiao Kang's context here, *yün* means "style."

51. The term is *ch'an-huan*. Morino Shigeo, "Kanbun tei no bunshōkan" (Emperor Chien-wen's View of Literary Composition), *Chūgoku chūsei bungaku kenkyū*, V (June 1966), 47, finds no mention of tonality in the letter.

52. *Shih-p'in*, Part B. Discussion of Jen Fang's poetry. *NS* 59.9a.

53. *Ibid.* Discussion of Shen Yüeh's poetry. Lu Ch'ui was still alive when the *Shih-p'in* was completed, and he was not mentioned there.

54. Vincent Yu-chung Shih, trans., *The Literary Mind and the Carving of Dragons* (New York, 1959), "Introduction," p. xxxv.

55. *HS* 30.36b; Shih, *Literary Mind*, p. 48.

56. Fang, "Rhymeprose on Literature," p. 536.

57. Legge, *Classics*, III, 48.

58. This probably refers to the poem "Huang-chu shih" (Yellow Bamboo) attributed to King Mu of Chou. See *Mu T'ien-tzu chuan.*

59. Reference to the theme of Mei Sheng's "Ch'i fa" (Seven Stimuli).

60. Unlike K'ung Yung (153–208), who could not sustain an argument. See Ts'ao P'ei, "Tien-lun lun-wen" (Discourse on Literature).

61. These terms are discussed in Shih, *Literary Mind*, pp. 176ff., 195–202.

62. *LS* 30.5a says: "In the first year of Ta-t'ung [527], [P'ei] Tzu-yeh was appointed Grand Nuncio Gentleman [*hung-lu-ch'ing*]. . . . In the second year of Chung-ta-t'ung [530], he died in office at the age of sixty-two." The preface to his essay, "On Insect Carving," reads: "The Grand Nuncio Gentleman of Liang, P'ei Tzu-yeh, wrote. . . ." Thus, the essay was written between 527 and 530, antedating Hsiao Kang's letter, which was written after 531. Chu Tung-jun, *Chung-kuo wen-hsüeh p'i-p'ing shih ta-kang* (Brief History of Chinese Literary Criticism) (Hong Kong: Chien-wen shu-chü, 1959), suggests that P'ei completed his essay about the same time as his *Sung-lüeh*, during the Ch'i. But the mention of his official position in

the preface seems to preclude this possibility. Lo Ken-tse, *Chung-kuo wen-hsüeh p'i-p'ing shih* (History of Chinese Literary Criticism) (Peking: Ku-tien wen-hsüeh ch'u-pan she, 1958), p. 135, in a footnote states that "P'ei assumed the office of *hung-lu* in Yüan-t'ung yüan-nien [first year of Yüan-t'ung, one year before his death]. One year after his death, Hsiao T'ung also died. Thus, this essay was perhaps composed after the compilation of the *Wen-hsüan*." This note is in error. Even allowing that Yüan-t'ung is a misprint for Ta-t'ung, the first year of Ta-t'ung (527) is still three years before P'ei's death and four years before the death of Hsiao T'ung. "Insect carving" was a term coined by Yang Hsiung of the Han dynasty, parodying the nobility of "dragon carving" (the composition of great and beautiful literature) to criticize the intricate triviality of his own *fu* compositions. The term came into common use during the Six Dynasties period. See Yang Hsiung, *Fa-yen* (Model Sayings), "Wu-tzu p'ien" (My Son) (in *Han Wei ts'ung-shu*).

63. The term *tien* was generally taken to describe the unadorned severity of the style of the *Documents*. Shih, *Literary Mind*, p. 159, says that this style "models itself after the classical form and adopts the Confucian principles." *Ibid.*, pp. 154–158, deals with the speed or tardiness with which individual writers are able to compose their works.

64. *LS* 30.4b–5a. The activities of the ancient school are described in *LS* 40.7a–10b (Biography of Liu Chih-lin). *LS* 40.5a (Biography of Liu Hsien) also describes the fraternity of this group in the Forbidden Palace, and adds: "There was no one at the time who did not admire them."

65. In *Shih-p'in*, Part A, "Preface," Chung Hung says: "Only Pan Ku [32–92] versified history. [His style] was unadorned and wooden, and devoid of embellishment." (Ch'en Yen-chieh notes that Pan Ku wrote a poem entitled "On History." See *TFP* 83.) Chung Hung's criticism of the Han historian, Pan Ku, is echoed in Hsiao Kang's attack on the Liang historian, P'ei Tzu-yeh.

66. For example, Hsiao Kang's "Letter to Chang Tsan, Thanking Him for Showing His Collected Works" (*IWLC* 58; *CHC* 21; *YKC* 3010); "Letter in Reply to the Marquis of Hsin-yü on Matching Poems" (*IWLC* 58; *YKC* 3010).

67. These antonyms are pejorative in early Confucian texts. *Chih* means "substance"; too much "substance" becomes "unadorned." In literary terms it is more commonly the antonym of *wen* "embellishment." Waley, *Analects*, 6.18, asserts that when "substance" predominates over "embellishment," then "uncouthness" (*yeh*) results. The text continues: "When 'embellishment' predominates over 'sub-

stance,' then 'pedantry' [*shih*—also the word for "history"] results."
The text concludes with the watchword of the orthodox school: "a
balance of embellishment and substance." In criticizing P'ei's work
for its "splendid pedantry," its "unadorned" style, and its lack of
"beauty" (*mei*), Hsiao Kang may have intended these references as
puns on P'ei Tzu-yeh's personal name *yeh* "uncouthness," and his
profession *shih* "history." In Waley, *Analects*, 1.3, "artful" (*ch'iao*)
has the idea of "specious" or "tricky." In describing Hsieh Ling-yun's
work with this word, and going on to say that metropolitan writers
do not balance embellishment and substance, "differing from the
artistic mind [*chiao-hsin*]," Hsiao Kang probably had Lu Chi's "Wen
fu" in mind. See Fang, "Rhymeprose on Literature," p. 543.

68. K'ang-lo was one of Hsieh Ling-yün's names, as Confucius
had the names Ch'iu-ming and Chung-ni, and Lao-tzu bore the name
Lao-tan.

69. *TFP* 1427; Teng, *Family Instructions*, p. 105.

70. *Shih-p'in*, Part B. Discussion of Hsieh Ling-yün's poetry.

71. *Hsieh K'o wen ching-wei* (The Limpid and the Muddy in the
Works of Hsieh Ling-yün). This work has not survived nor is it
mentioned in the *Sui shu*, "Ching-chi chih" (Treatise on Literature).
The *ching-wei* in the title refers to the rivers Ching and Wei. At
their confluence the clear water of the Ching flows with the muddy
water of the Wei for three hundred *li* without commingling. See
Legge, *Classics*, III, 123–124;IV, 56. Chang P'u places Hsiao Kang
"after Hsieh [Ling-yün] and before P'ei Tzu-yeh." *Tzu-jan* "spontaneity" was the watchword of Yang Hsiung's theory of literary
creation. Yang Hsiung, *T'ai hsüan* 7.17. Yang Hsiung appears in
Hsiao Kang's list of worthy models. In another context, he criticized
Yang Hsiung for requiring a writer to model his composition on
the Confucian classics.

72. Shih, *Literary Mind*, pp. 31–38.

73. *Mao Shih shih-wu Kuo-feng i* (Exegesis on the 'Fifteen Airs
of the States' of the *Mao Odes*), in Ma Kuo-han, *Yü-han-shan-fang
chi i shu*, "Ching pien, shih-lei." Hsiao Kang's piece is given as
glossing the line "ko i hsün chih" ("And I sing [this song] to admonish him"), from Ode 141 ("Mu-men" [Gate to the Tombs]), in
"Ch'en Feng" (Airs of Ch'en). The text of Legge, *Classics*, IV, 210,
is misprinted.

74. *Ibid.*, IV. 34.

75. "Memorial Requesting that the Assistant Director of the Left
to the President of the Board, Ho Ch'en, Present an Exegesis of the
Odes" (*IWLC* 55; *YKC* 3003). Ho Ch'en (481–549) came from a
poor family but gained a reputation for classical erudition. He came

to Emperor Wu's notice in the 520s and twice held the post mentioned in the title of Hsiao Kang's memorial. Thus we can only be certain that this memorial was written after 520.

76. "Letter to Chang Tsan." See above, n. 66.

77. *HS* 87A-B. Yang Hsiung, *Fa-yen* 2.4. Hsiao Kang specifically quotes *Fa-yen* 5.3, which required a writer to model his composition on the Confucian classics.

78. This passage contains many important terms in the literary theory of the time. "Homesickness" (*ssu-hsiang* or *hsiang-ssu*) and "heroism" (*hsiung-hsin* or *pien-hsin*) referred to poetry about soldiers on active duty, or the lonely life of the traveler. "Short verse" (*tuan-han* or *tuan-yung*) and "commonplace sounds" (*yung-yin*) appear in Lu Chi's "Wen Fu," (Fang, "Rhymeprose on Literature," p. 543); and in Chung Hung's "Shih-p'in, Part C, where Hsü Yao-chih of the Ch'i dynasty, two of whose poems appear in *YT* 10, was said to be "good at short stanzas and still-life description." "Commonplace sounds and mixed forms" were faults Chung Hung saw in Liang literary practice (*Shih-p'in*, Part A, "Preface"). Liu Hsieh, *Wen-hsin tiao-lung*, mentions "factual reality" (*yin-shih*) (Shih, *Literary Mind*, p. 202); Hsiao Kang's views on this appear in Yen Chih-t'ui, *Yen-shih chia-hsün* (Teng, *Family Instructions*, p. 98). Jen Fang's poetry is criticized in *Shih-p'in*, Part B, discussion of his poetry. Hsiao Kang's deferential self-criticism in his letter to Hsiao I, "I am a clumsy writer," is reminiscent of Lu Chi (Fang, p. 542); and his hesitation to make "specific and individual criticisms" recalls Ts'ao Chih's "Letter to Yang Te-tsu," quoted verbatim in *Shih-p'in*, Part B.

79. Cf. the opening lines of Lu Chi's "Wen fu," (Fang, "Rhymeprose on Literature" pp. 530 and 543).

80. A collection of works by Crown Prince Chao-ming in five folios dating from Ming times is extant, but it bears little resemblance to the original compilation which, according to his biography, consisted of twenty folios. Hsiao Kang's memorial accompanying the presentation of his unofficial biography of the crown prince mentions that a collected works (*wen-chi*) was also included in his presentation. It is uncertain whether Hsiao Kang's preface was to this particular collection. The Ming version of the crown prince's collection roughly follows the arrangement of (modern versions of) his *Wen-hsüan*. Hsiao Kang names eight genres: poetry (*shih*), lament (*sao*), inscription (*ming*), appreciation (*tsan*), sevens (*ch'i*), memorial (*piao*), epitaph (*pei*), and discussion (*i*). Examples of only three—poetry, appreciation, and discussion—appear in the surviving collection and are complemented by only a single sevens in the comprehensive compilations of *YKC* and Chang P'u. For discussion

of the status of poetry and rhymeprose, see Ami Yuji, *Chūgoku chūsei bungaku kenkyū* (A Study of Medieval Chinese Literature) (Tokyo, 1960).

81. See Ts'ao P'ei, "Tien-lun lun-wen."

82. Hsiao Ta-hsin was enfeoffed as Duke of Tang-yang in 532. *LS* 44.1b.

83. Waley, *Analects,* 15.30, p. 199.

84. *Ibid.,* 17.10, p. 212. Po Yü was Confucius' son. Hsiao Kang's reference is then apt, being addressed to his own son. He must have found the quotation even more fortuitous in that the "Chou Nan" and the "Shao Nan" are the first two books of the *Odes,* a curriculum that would have met his fullest approval. In *Analects* 16.13, Confucius again recommends the *Odes* to his son as a subject for study.

85. *SC* 7.17a. This remark, criticizing the cruel nature of the Ch'u people, was especially directed against the Ch'u general, Hsiang Yü.

86. *NS* 54.2b. See Chapter 2, p. 53.

87. See Teng, *Family Instructions,* pp. 53–54; *NS* 51.19b.

88. Shih, *Literary Mind,* p. 224.

89. The term *fang-tang* had long been in common use, both in the literary sense that Hsiao Kang adopts and in the concept of a code of behavior. Tung-fang Shuo's work was criticized for being "uninhibited [*fang-tang*]" and for its "unbecoming levity." *HS* 65. A sketch of Ts'ao Ts'ao in his youth relates the term *fang-tang* to unrestrained behavior. The variant *yu-tang* appears here with the same meaning. *San-kuo chih* (History of the Three Kingdoms) (in *Erh-shih-ssu shih*) 1.1a. *Fang-tang* appears in the *Shih-shuo hsin-yü* in a description of a famous drunkard, Liu Ling, a prominent member of the Seven Sages of the Bamboo Grove, whose unpredictable eccentricities shocked and amused their more staid contemporaries of the third century. Liu was "reckless and uninhibited."

90. Chou Tso-jen, "Wen-chang ti fang-tang" (Literary Dissoluteness), quoted by Hayashida Shinnosuke, "Nan-chō hō-tō bungakuron no bi-ishiki" (Sense of Beauty in the Southern Dynasties Stressed in the Discussion of Dissoluteness in Literature), *Tōhōgaku,* XXVII (February 1964), 3.

91. Wang Yao, *Chung-ku wen-hsüeh feng-mao* (The Spirit of Medieval Literature), quoted by Hayashida, "Sense of Beauty," p. 3, who considers them "crude theories."

Chapter Five

1. Tu Ch'üeh (T'ang), "Ts'en Chia-chou chi hsü" (Preface to the Collected Works of Ts'en Chia-chou).

2. Morino Shigeo, "Ryō no bungaku no yūgisei" (Literary Games of the Liang), *Chūgoku chūsei bungaku kenkyū*, VI (June, 1967), 27–40.

3. *Ibid.* See also Tabei Fumio, "Riku-chō kyūtai no shi ni tsuite" (On the Palace-Style Poetry of the Six Dynasties Period), *Kanbun gakkai-hō*, XVIII (1959), 9.

4. *YT* (new ed.); *Yüeh-fu-shih chi* (Collected Yüeh-fu Poetry) (Taipei, 1961); and *WYYH* attribute these verses to Crown Prince Chao-ming. *IWLC* attributes them to Hsiao Kang. *TFP* 1128 explains that *YT* (old ed.) referred to Hsiao Kang as *t'ai-tzu* (crown prince), and that later editors assumed this to mean Crown Prince Chao-ming.

5. See *TFP* 1064–1068. *TFP* notes the *Ku-chin yüeh-lu* (Record of Songs Old and New), which says that in the winter of 512 Emperor Wu revised some western melodies (*hsi-ch'ü*) and composed fourteen songs to the music of "The Clouds over Chiang-nan" ("Chiang-nan shang yün") and seven "Songs of Chiang-nan."

6. Attributed to Wu Chün (469–520) in *WYYH*. *YT* and *Yüeh-fu-shih chi* say Emperor Wu.

7. Tabei, "Palace-Style Poetry." See also Shiba Rokurō, " 'Fu-toku' no imi ni tsuite" (On the Meaning of "Fu-te"), *Chūgoku bungaku-hō*, III (October 1955), 33–49.

8. Tabei, "Palace-Style Poetry."

9. *TFP* follows *Yüeh-fu-shih chi* in attributing the item to Hsiao Kang.

10. See Lin, "Palace-Style Poetry."

11. "The Lady of Ch'u Sighs" (*YT* 7.9a; TFP 1105). This is one of a group of three *tai yüeh-fu* and the title is one of the Han *yüeh-fu* titles. See also Hsiao Kang's "Plucking Lotus Song" (*YT* 7.27b; *WYYH* 1291; *TFP* 1102). This poem does not seem to be connected with the one that forms part of Emperor Wu's cycle of seven songs titled "Song of Chiang-nan." *TFP* notes that *YT* continues this song with six lines of the "Plucking Lotus Song" appended to Hsiao Kang's "Rhymeprose on Plucking Lotus" in *IWLC* 82 and *YKC* 2998.

12. *YT* 9.26a titles this piece "Tsa-chü ch'un-ch'ing i-shou" (A Poem, in Irregular Lines, on Spring Feelings). *TFP* 1157 follows *Yüeh-fu-shih chi* as "Ch'un-ch'ing ch'ü" (A Song about Spring Feelings), but omits "ch'u" (song).

13. J. R. Hightower, "Some Characteristics of Parallel Prose," *Studia Serica Bernhard Karlgren Dedicata* (Copenhagen), (1959), pp. 60–91.

14. Suzuki Torao, *Fushi taiyō* (Outline History of Rhymeprose) (Tokyo, 1963). See also Li T'iao-yüan, *Fu-hua* (An Exegesis of

Rhymeprose) (Taipei, 1961); and Ch'iu Ch'iung-sun, *Shih fu tz'u ch'ü kai-lun* (Outline of Poetry, Rhymeprose, Lyrics, and Songs) (Shanghai, 1934), esp. pp. 160–170.

15. E.g., *Shui-ching chu* (Classic of the Rivers), comp. Li Tao-yüan; and Hsiao Kang, "History of Thatch Hall" (*YKC* 3026).

16. *Han Wei Liu-ch'ao pai-san chia chi.*

17. The *k'ung-hou* was originally a harp, but during the Six Dynasties period it was also the name for a small lute. See John D. Frodsham and Ch'eng Hsi, *Anthology of Chinese Verse* (London, 1967), p. 40n; and *YT* 1.24a. See also John Marney, "A Criticism of the Kung-t'i Poetry of Liang Chien-wen Ti," International Conference of Orientalists in Japan, *Transactions*, no. 14 (1969), pp. 108–115; see John Marney, "Life and Literature of Emperor Chien-wen of Liang" (Dissertation, University of Wisconsin, 1972), for a study of Hsiao Kang's rhyme technique.

18. *IWLC* notes that Tsai Yung of Han had an interest in lute technique. The *Ch'in li ch'in ch'ü* records five songs by him. The fifth line is reminiscent of the one from *Songs of the South*. See Hawkes, p. 92. During the T'ien-chien era (502–519) a decree ordered palace women to wear white powder and blue-black mascara.

19. Lin, "Palace-Style Poetry," p. 430.

20. See Obi, "Nature in Chinese Literature," Also see J. Frodsham, *The Murmuring Stream* (Kuala Lumpur: Oxford University Press 1967), which concerns the life and work of Hsieh Ling-yün.

21. "Mountain ranges form precipitous gorges, with outcrops resembling flying buttresses, hence the name 'Chien-ko' [Towers of Chien]." *Shui-ching chu* 20.13b. In modern Ssuchuan province. Ch'en-yang was a district on the north side of the Ch'en River (modern Hunan province). The Hsüan-fu (Park of Mysteries) adjoined the East Palace. The name was derived during the preceding Ch'i dynasty from comparison of the imperial palace complex with the triple stages in altitude of the Kun-lun mountains. The lowest stage was called Fan-t'ung (enclosed T'ung tree); the second, Hsüan-fu; and the third and highest, Ts'eng-ch'eng (tiered city), where the emperor dwelt. The East Palace adjoined the emperor's residence and thus corresponded to the intermediate stage. Hence the garden of the East Palace was the Hsüan-fu. *TCTC* 4972 (Hu San-sheng's note). *Shui-ching chu* 1.1a notes variant names.

22. Lin, "Palace-Style Poetry."

23. These terms appear in Hsiao Kang's "Reply to Chang Tsan" (*YKC* 3010) and "Letter to Liu Hsiao-cho" (*YKC* 3010). Examples of this theme are in *TFP* 1094–1096.

24. Wu Ching, *Yüeh-fu ku-t'i yao chieh*, cites Hsiao Kang eight times for his adherence to the subject matter of the original title.
25. *YT* 7.26b; *WYYH* 1255; *TFP* 1097.
26. Tabei, "Palace-Style Poetry."
27. Lin, "Palace-Style Poetry," p. 428.
28. *Ibid.*, pp. 427, 428.
29. *TFP* notes that there is also a poem "Your Sad One Grieves Alone at Night" and that *Yüeh-fu-shih chi* 76 attributes it to Wang Yen of the T'ang dynasty. Wu Chao-i in *YT* notes that it has been attributed to Shen Yüeh.
30. Hsiao Kang's texts are in *YKC* 3020 and 3004. After the Buddha died, the First Patriarch came to the twin trees and wept. The Buddha revealed his feet from within his golden bier, "Silver'd grasses" and "gilded clouds" appear in Hsiao Kang's eulogy. In *YKC* *ken* "roots" occurs as a variant for *yün* "clouds." "Clouds" are confirmed in Crown Prince Chao-ming's reply.
31. *TCTC* 5007. Legge, *Classics*, IV, 78.
32. Lin, "Palace-Style Poetry."
33. Hsiao Kang's complete poetry is translated in John Marney, *Beyond the Mulberries* (forthcoming).
34. *Ta-T'ang hsin-yü* (New Tales of the Great T'ang).
35. Lo Ken-tse, *History of Chinese Literary Criticism*, p. 137.
36. Hsiao Kang contributed one hundred and nine items, arranged in fols. 7, 9, and 10. Emperor Wu has fifty-three items, Shen Yüeh forty-one, and Wu Chün thirty; Jen Fang is not represented. Works by Crown Prince Chao-ming and P'ei Tzu-yeh are included. Yü Chien-wu has seventeen items; his son, Yü Hsin, thirteen.
37. Hightower, "Parallel Prose," p. 85.
38. Tabei, "Palace-Style Poetry."
39. Wang Po, Yang Chiung, Lu Chao-lin, and Lo Pin-wang.
40. Prince Ch'a of Wu was enfeoffed at Yen-ling. For his evaluation of music, see Legge, *Classics*, V, 549–550.
41. Lu Shih-yung, *Shih-ching tsung-lun*, noted in Lin, "Palace-Style Poetry," p. 438.
42. *Han Wei Liu-ch'ao pai-san chia chi*, "Liang Chien-wen ti chi hsü."
43. See Wen I-to, "Kung-t'i-shih ti tzu-shu" (Palace-Style Poetry Puts Itself Up for Sale), in his *T'ang-shih tsa-lun, Wen I-to ch'üan-chi*, III.
44. Chang P'u doubts whether a single word of criticism by students of the Six Dynasties could be leveled at Hsiao Kang's work.
45. *CHC, IWLC, TPYL, WYYH*. For discussion of the influence

of *lei-shu* (encyclopedias) upon poetry, see Wen I-to, *Wen I-to ch'üan-chi,* III, 3–10.

Chapter Six

1. Teng, *Family Instructions,* p. 70. Hsiao Kang has a poem matching a verse by Emperor Wu, "Matching Poem on the Three Teachings" (*TFP* 1148).

2. See Mou Jun-sun, *Lun Wei Chin i-lai chih sung-shang t'an-pien chi ch'i ying-hsiang* (The Esteem Given to Discourse during Wei, Chin, and Thereafter and Its Influence) (Hong Kong, H. K. Univ. Press 1966). See also Hsiao Kang, "Preface to the Collected Works of Crown Prince Chao-ming," section 11.

3. See Kenneth Ch'en, *Buddhism in China* (Princeton, 1964), pp. 121–209. See also Arthur F. Wright, *Buddhism in Chinese History* (Stanford Univ. Press, 1959), chap. iii; and T'ang Yung-t'ung, *Han Wei Liang-Chin Nan-Pei-ch'ao fo-chiao shih* (History of Buddhism in the Han Wei, Two-Chin, and Northern and Southern Dynasties), 2 vols. (1938; rpt. Taipei, 1965).

4. The phraseology of the reference to enjoyment is from *Chuang-tzu* 17, "Autumn Floods." See Giles, *Chuangtzu,* p. 171. The Prince of Hsiang-tung's bibliography, *LS* 5.31a, lists *Chu Han shu* (Annotated History of the Han Dynasty) in 115 fols. *Sui shu* 33.1a notes that by the Sui dynasty the compilation was lost. The P'ing-teng temple was a metropolitan establishment, but its location is uncertain. See Liu Shih-heng, *Nan-ch'ao ssu k'ao* (A Study of the Temples of the Southern Dynasties) (in *Sheng-ching ts'ung-shu*). The reference to Tzu-lu is in *Analects* 5:13.

5. *Hsü Kao-seng chuan* (More Lives of Eminent Monks), comp. Tao Hsüan (of T'ang), folio 1, "Biography of Pao Ch'ang."

6. See Ch'en, *Buddhism in China,* p. 127. LS, NS, and *Sui shu* list *Fa-pao lien-pi* (Linked Jade of the Buddha Jewel) in 300 fols.; *Yü-chien* (The Jade Tablets) in 50 fols.; *Kuang-ming fu* (The Brilliant Tally) in 20 fols.; and *Mu-yü ching* (Sutra on the Bathing [on the eighth day of the fourth lunar month]) in 3 fols. All four works are lost. Of Hsiao Kang's 197 items in *YKC,* some 60 are on Buddhist topics.

7. See Alexander C. Soper, *Literary Evidence for Early Buddhist Art in China* (Ascona: Artibus Asiae, 1959), pp. 9–10, 12. Original text is in *Kao-seng chuan* (Lives of Eminent Monks), comp. Hui Chao, folio 12, "Biography of Hui-ta."

8. The fishery terms are from the *Odes.* See Legge, *Classics,* IV, 241.

9. See Waley, *Analects*, 17.18; and Giles, *Chuangtzu*, p. 44.

10. Yang Hsiung uses the phrase "three-inch tongue" in his poem "Understanding Ridicule" (*WH* 45). Buddhist references are from the *Vimalakīrtisūtra*.

11. "Gentry Buddhism" in the Southern dynasties is studied in E. Zurcher, *The Buddhist Conquest of China* (Leiden, 1959). Controversies provoked by Buddhist doctrine are discussed in *ibid.*, pp. 106–108, 156–157, 231–239; Leon Hurvitz, " 'Render unto Caesar' in Early Chinese Buddhism," Sino-Indian Studies, *Liebenthal Festschrift* (1957); and W. Liebenthal, "Chinese Buddhism during the Fourth and Fifth Centuries," *Monumenta Nipponica*, VI (1955), 44–83.

12. *KHMC* 16; *YKC* 3007–3008, 3034. See Soper, *Literary Evidence*, pp. 77–78.

13. Examples of the interminable numerical categories that characterized Buddhist texts of the time. The first two of the "eight divisions" are heaven and the serpents. The "six paths" begin with heaven above and the mortal world. The "four forms of birth" are creatures born of an egg, of a womb, of moisture (i.e., insects, which were believed to come into existence spontaneously in damp places), and by transformation (again, insects, or Buddhist birth without parentage).

14. *KHMC* 17; *YKC* 3024. See Soper, *Literary Evidence*, p. 77.

15. *Ibid.*, pp. 78–79, has a translation of this item. The references to the sages and the spirits are in *Analects* 3.12 and in Legge, *Classics*, II, 502.

16. The text has *hsiang* "elephant" for *hsiang* "image." The king of Yüeh was defeated by the king of Wu in 494 B. C. He "ate gall and slept on reeds" until, in 473 B.C., he returned to annex the state of Wu. *Chin shu* 36.12b–13a (Palace ed.) (in *Erh-shih-wu shih*) relates how a pair of magic swords, inscribed with the names Lung-ch'üan and T'ai-a, were discovered in a luminescent stone coffer buried deep beneath a prison vault. The phrase "escaped from their cages" is from Waley, *Analects*, Book xvi, 1.7, p. 202. See Soper, *Literary Evidence*, pp. 78–79.

17. "Closed curtains" are explained below in text. Pin-ch'ing was the style-name of the great commentator on *Mencius*, Chao Ch'i (d. 201). Once, escaping from a court intrigue, he fled to the countryside, changed his name, and subsisted as a cake-seller. He was rescued from this predicament by Sun Sung, who hid him "between two walls" for several years. *HHS* 94 (Palace ed.); *HHS* (Chunghua shu-chü ed.) (Peking, 1965), ch. 64, p. 2122.

18. *HS* 56.1a. See Feng Yu-lan, *History of Chinese Philosophy* (Princeton, 1953), II, 7–87.

Chapter Seven

1. Hou Ching's nationality is discussed in Takeda Ryōji, "Kō Kei no ran ni tsuite no ikkōsatsu" (A Study of Hou Ching's Rebellion), *Shigaku*, XXIX, no. 3 (1956), 34–59. See *LS* 56; *NS* 80; *TCTC* 4855–5017. *TCTC* is the abbreviation for *Tzu-chih t'ung-chien* (Comprehensive Mirror as an Aid to Government), compiled by Ssu-ma Kuang.

2. *NS* 8.1a. *LS* 4 does not even mention it.

3. A Confucian concept, hence the title of Ssu-ma Kuang's compilation (see n. 1, above). *TCTC* 5117 mentions that Emperor Yüan of Liang (Prince of Hsiang-tung Hsiao I) lectured on the *Lao-tzu* just before his dynasty was overthrown by the North.

4. *TCTC* 4986 gives this figure. *LS* 56.13a and *NS* 80.7a say one thousand and more. Perhaps *TCTC* confused the number in Yü Hsin's force with that of Wang Chih's mentioned a few lines later. W. T. Graham suggested to me that the reference to Yü Hsin is perhaps libelous, since Hsiao Shao, compiler of the *Tai-ch'ing chi* (in *TCTC*), whence this record derives, was at odds with Yü Hsin. *NS* 51.10a–11b.

5. *LS* 8.4b; *NS* 53.4a describe Crown Prince Chao-ming's library. Also see Hsiao Kang's "Preface to the Collected Works of Crown Prince Chao-ming," sec. 13 (*YKC* 3017), for a description of the preservation of books, "each in its blue silk binding." *LS* 56.13b; *NS* 80.7b. In the fall of Chiang-ling in 554, the Prince of Hsiang-tung was held responsible for similar destruction (*TCTC* 5121).

6. Po-na ed. *LS* 30.9b and *NS* 62.14b say Chung Ta-t'ung III (531). Palace ed. *LS* 30.7b says Ta-t'ung III (529). Po-na ed. seems to be correct; by 531 Hsü Ch'ih was serving in the East Palace.

7. The first line is from the *Odes*. See Legge, *Classics*, IV, 317, and 314n. *TFP* follows the *Odes* in using *chan* for *NS min*. "Evil miasma" is a metaphor for a national traitor. Legge (p. 330) says, "Counsels which are good he will not follow, and those which are not good he employs." The last line evokes thoughts of the sage emperor Shao. See Legge, *Classics* V, 641.

8. Line 2 is from the *Analects*; see Waley, *Analects*, 6.3. *HS* 67.7b says the floor of the imperial palace was plastered with reddened wattle. "Purple empyrean" was another name for the palace. "Plans and policies" come from the *Documents*. See Legge, *Classics*, III, 252. The "four-square suburbs" were environs of the

imperial city (see *Li-chi* 1A). Line 8 is from the *Odes* (see Legge, IV, 607). Hsiao Kang's negation of the original, together with his other quotations from the *Odes* in these pieces, demonstrates his expertise in exploiting the *Odes* for their traditional function: to satirize. During the time of Emperor An of Han, Chang Kang was still a youth and occupied the lowest official post. Upon being promoted, he buried the wheels of his carriage in Loyang, saying, "There's a wolf blocking the road. Why not ask a fox?" (*HHS* 46). For the last line, see Legge, *Classics*, IV, 317.

9. *TCTC* 5001 gives this date; *LS* 3.35a gives February 22.

10. *TCTC* 5003. *NS* 80.13a text is scrambled. Emperor Wu says "Better death than truce" twice; after the second time, Hsiao Kang says, "This covenant beneath the city walls is a profound disgrace. I do not care about the naked blades before us and the flow of arrows." This is the opposite of what he has been advocating. *TCTC* omits this altogether.

11. "Sang-chung" is the ode in which "a gentleman sings of his intimacy and intrigues with various noble ladies." See Legge, *Classics*, IV, 78.

12. *Ch'en shu* 32.2b says Chung-shu sheng. Yung-fu sheng is more likely, since Hsiao Kang had moved there on January 25, 549 (*NS* 80.12a; *TCTC* 5001).

13. Legge, *Classics*, IV, 117.

14. This fragment is not in Hsiao Kang's collected works. *Wu-ti* "rootless" is a pun on *wu-ti* "emperorless." *Pu-an-t'ai* "no stable plinth" is a pun on *T'ai-ch'eng pu-an* "the Dais City was unsettled." *Lun-wu-ch'e* "the wheel made no tracks" is a pun on the name Hsiao Lun: he failed to relieve the siege though he was on hand to do so, and thus left no evidence of having been there.

15. *LS* 56.25b and *NS* 80.16a say "more than twenty days."

Chapter Eight

1. See Legge, *Classics*, V, 318b, 846a.

2. Emperor Wu's interment at Hsiu-ling took place on December 8, 549, six months after his death. *T'ai-ch'ing chi*, in *TCTC* 5030, gives the fourteenth day, i.e., ten days later, on December 18.

3. The phrase *wen-ming* occurs in the "T'ung-jen kua" (Fellowship with Man) hexagon in the *Changes*: "Clarity within and yielding without," interpreted as "the character of a peaceful union, which, in order to hold together, needs one yielding nature among many firm and independent spirited persons" (Wilhelm, *Changes*, I, 58). The phrase also occurs in the "Ke kua" (Revolution) hexagon,

which aptly represents Hsiao Kang's intentions. See Wilhelm, *Changes*, I, 202. Hsiao Kang's intentions concerning the year-titles are glossed in *NS* 8.4b. *LS* 5.1a mentions the secret commission the Prince of Hsiang-tung received from Emperor Wu just after the fall of the capital.

4. Wilhelm, *Changes*, I, 108. *Chou li*, "T'ien-kuan ta tsai." (in *Shih-san ching chu-su*). H. Wist, "Sklaverei in China," *Artibus Asiae*, VIII (1945), 255–256, translates this item into German.

5. When Emperor Wen of Han (r. 179–156 B.C.) had the Pa-ling mausoleum constructed, he forbade the use of precious metals and permitted only pottery burial furnishings. The hills themselves (east of Ch'ang-an district of Shensi province) formed the tumuli (*HS* 4.19b). The word *ling* in Pa-ling, Hsui-ling, etc., means "tomb."

6. *LS* 4.3a. *T'ai-ch'ing chi* says "seventh month," i.e., August-September 549, for the promotion of Hsiao Ta-ch'i. For the other princes, *LS* 4.3ab says July 18. *T'ai-ch'ing chi* and *Tien-lüeh* (in *TCTC* 5019) say that these promotions were awarded on the day that Hsiao Ta-ch'i became crown prince. Individual biographies in *LS* 44 and *NS* 54 usually give Ta-pao I (550).

7. *NS* 52.10a; *TCTC* 5021. *Tien-lüeh* says "fifth month" (June-July 549); *NS* 80.16a says "sixth month . . . in the Yung-fu sheng."

8. *LS* 29 gives Hsiao Lun's age as 33; this is incompatible with his being enfeoffed in 514.

9. No *chia-shen* day appears in the third month. Ta-pao I.3.6 *chia-yin* gives April 6, 550.

10. *NS* 80.16b gives May 13, 550. *LS* 4.5a; *NS* 8.2a; *TCTC* 5039 all give May 28, 550. *LS* and *NS* say "forced" (*pi*); *NS* 80.16b has "summon" (*chao*); *TCTC* says "invited" (*ch'ing*).

11. Lady Fan also bore Hsiao Kang's fifteenth son, Hsiao Ta-wei. Po-na ed. of *NS* 54.1a mistakenly gives *sheng* for *wei*.

12. *So* is a barbarian name. Hsiao Kang punned on the word, attempting to scorn the man's ignorance of Chinese culture.

13. This mountain is in modern Kiangsu province, to the west of Sung-chiang district. *YKC* gives the source of the item as *WYYH*, but gives no folio reference. It does not appear in the Hua-wen shu-chü collated ed. (Taipei, 1965) of *WYYH*.

14. P'ang Chüan of the Warring States kingdom of Wei was a military rival of Sun Pin. Before their battle at Ma-ling Tao, Sun carved on a tree, "P'ang Chüan will die beneath this tree." Sun ambushed P'ang, and the latter committed suicide (*SC* 46.12a).

15. See Hans Bielenstein, "An Interpretation of the Portents in the Ts'ien-Han-Shu," *BMFEA* (Stockholm), XX (1950), 127–143.

16. TCTC 5057. Hu San-sheng notes that *T'ai-ch'ing chi* gives this date. *LS.* 4.6a says November 20, 550.

17. *Tien-lüeh* (in *TCTC* 5070) gives the date of Hou Ching's return as August 7, 551; *T'ai-ch'ing chi* says Septmber 5, 551.

18. *TCTC* 5072, Hu San-sheng notes an error in the date given in *Tien-lüeh.*

19. *Ch'en shu* 32.2b glosses the reference: "In the past Duke Wen of Chin fled into the wilderness where he was given a clod of earth to eat. In the end he returned to Chin. Does Your Highness' dream tally with this?" See Legge, *Classics,* V, 186b.

20. Hsiao Kang's remark is a pun. Legge, *Classics,* I, 199, translates: "I did not think," [the Master] said, "that music could have been made so excellent as this." The original text reads, "pu t'u wei yüeh chih chih yü ssu yeh," featuring a common pun on *yüeh/lo* "music/pleasure" in the "pleasure" of the Shao "music." Hsiao Kang's utterance varies as "yüeh i chih." To present Hsiao Kang as an articulate Confucian gentleman, the historians reduced the "pleasure" of the wine party by introducing a "crook-necked lute," which provided the "music" necessary for conformity with the analect. This interpretation adds significance to an otherwise merely descriptive detail in the chronicle. Later commentators either took this for granted or overlooked it and, like Hu San-sheng—who glossed *yüeh* definitively as *lo*—described the lute itself in detail (*TCTC* 5073).

21. *LS* 4.8a text is scrambled here. See also Chang Yüan-chi, *Chiao-shih sui-pi* (Shanghai, 1938; rpt. 1957), pp. 39b–40a.

22. References are to the *Hsiao-ching* (Book of Filial Piety), "Kuang-yang ming" (Amplification of "Raising the Reputation"): "Establish oneself in the Way and spread one's reputation through later generations"; *Hsün-tzu,* "Li lun" (Discussion of Rites): "Rites are strictest in their ordering of birth and death. Birth is the beginning of man, death his end. When both beginning and end are good, man's way is complete," trans. Burton Watson, *Hsün Tzu Basic Writings* (New York: Columbia Univ. Press, 1963), pp. 96–97. Legge, *Classics,* IV, 143, notes the old tradition which interprets the ode allusively: the speaker is "longing for superior men to arise and settle the disturbed state of Ch'ing, men who should do their duty as the cocks in the darkest and stormiest night." *Shih-shuo hsin-yü,* "Te-hsing" (Noble Actions), tells the story of Juan Chang-chih, who made a mistake in protocol. It was night and he might have been undetected, but he could not bear any form of deception.

23. The poem by Kuo P'u, "The Roving Immortal," has the couplet, "In this world no thousand moons / A fate like an autumn leaf" (*TFP* 563). The essence of the nine heavens and the vitality

of the positive *yang* and negative *yin* elements combine as the nine elixirs and form the human body—the "gold" of Hsiao Kang's line. Ch'üeh-li was Confucius' native village (modern Shantung province, Ch'ü-fu district city).

24. *TCTC* 5074, *Tien-lüeh,* says November 28, 551.

25. *TCTC* 5082 gives April 29, 552. *LS* 4.8a says "on the *k'uei-ch'ou* day of the third month of the following year." No such day appears in the calendar. *NS* 8.3b gives the *ssu-ch'ou* day, i.e., April 30, 552.

26. *TCTC* 5087. Chu Hsieh, *Chien-k'ang Lan-ling Liu-ch'ao Ling-mu t'u k'ao* (Illustrated Study of the Tombs of the Six Dynasties at Lan-ling, Chien-k'ang), (Shanghai, 1936), pp. 26–27, notes that historical sources give no precise details of the location of Chuang-ling. He says: "Near modern Nanking there are two stone unicorns [*ch'i-lin*] twenty-seven *li* southeast of Tan-yang, to the east of Ling-k'ou-chen, at the confluence of the Hsiao-Liang River and the Yün-ho [canal]. They are situated one each on the east and west sides of the river; both have long since collapsed. The one on the east is eroded by the weather, although its form is still distinguishable; the one on the west is half buried in the ground and is relatively well preserved. They have generally been considered to mark Hsiao Kang's grave. Problems arise from there being two monuments—i.e., if they are headstones, which one indicates the actual burial site? Further-more, they are set some thirteen *li* from the other imperial sepul-chres, including that of Emperor Wu. A contemporaneous Liang source [Ku Yeh-wang, *Yü-ti chih*] says that the imperial barge would have passed along this river during Emperor Wu's visit to the Hsiao clan's native district of Lan-ling. These stone unicorns may then merely have been a lavish spectacle to delight the royal eye. The theory accepting this area as the ancient Chuang-ling mausoleum derives from a history of the Tan-yang district [*Tan-yang hsien-chih*] which describes how the local topography curves into a bay, called Hsiao-t'ang Cove, in front of which are stone unicorns about ten feet high. These are positively identified as marking the graves of Empress Chien and Emperor Chien-wen of Liang."

Neither rebel nor authorized formuli were original. "Kao-tsung Ming huang-ti," the title conferred by Hou Ching, had been applied to the fifth emperor of the Ch'i dynasty, Hsiao Lun (r. 494–499) (*Ch'i shu* 6 in *Erh-shih-ssu shih*; *NS* 5.8a–13a). The Prince of Hsiang-tung's amendment came from an earlier source: "T'ai-tsung Chien-wen huang-ti" was the posthumous appellation of Ssu-ma Yü (r. 371–373) (*Chin shu* 9), the ninth emperor of the Eastern Chin dynasty. The significance of this title is explained by Hsieh An (*Chin shu* 79.2b–5b), and while his reference is to the Chin emperor, the same interpretation is applicable to Hsiao Kang:

> Unremiss in pure virtue is called *chien*; widely versed in the Way and in Virtue is called *wen*. [Legge, *Classics*, III, 213.] By means of the easy and simple [*chien*] we grasp the laws of the whole world. [Wilhelm, *Changes*, I, 308.] Through contemplation of the forms [*wen*] existing in human society it becomes possible to shape the world. [Wilhelm, *Changes*, I, 97.] The ceremonies of the "great road" [Legge, *Classics*, IV, 393] still have some resemblance. The posthumous title "T'ai-tsung" and appellation "Chien-wen" may be conferred. ("On the Posthumous Appellation 'Chien-wen ti,'" *YKC* 1938)

This text appears in the *Shih-shuo hsin-yü*, "Wen-hsüeh" (On Literature) 4.1b–34a, in the commentary quoting Liu Ch'ien, *Chin chi*. "Huan Wen showed the piece to his honored guests and remarked, 'These are An-shih's gold filings [literary gems]'." The *t'ai-tsung* was an office during the Chou dynasty. Centuries later, in the Han, the title acquired its imperial functions. *Hsin-shu*, "Shu-ning," (in *Han Wei ts'ung-shu*), says: "The founder [*tsu*] has accomplishments; the descendant [*tsung*] has moral virtue. The former's accomplishment lies in his first gaining the empire; the latter's moral virtue lies in his first governing the empire. On account of the [descendant's] forming the court, he called the Great Descendant [*t'ai-tsung*] of the empire and receives the empire from the Great Founder [*t'ai-tsu*]." Such was the relationship between Emperor Wu and Hsiao Kang. Another interpretation is in Hu San-sheng's commentary in *TCTC* 5034: "Tranquil and at ease and without malice is called '*chien*.' Diligent in study and fond of enquiry is called '*wen*'."

27. Emperors Min and Huai (r. 307–313; 313) were the last rulers of the Western Chin dynasty. In their reigns the North was lost to barbarian control.

Selected Bibliography

I. Works by Emperor Chien-wen that are no longer extant:

Chao-ming T'ai-tzu chuan (Biography of Crown Prince Chao-ming). 5 fols. Title in *LS* 4.9a; *NS* 8.4a.

Chu wang chuan (Biographies of the Princes). 30 fols. Title in *LS* 4.9a; *NS* 8.4a.

Li ta i (General Exegesis of the Book of Ritual). 20 fols. Title in *LS* 4.9a; *NS* 8.4a.

Lao-tzu i (Exegesis on the Lao-tzu). 20 fols. Title in *LS* 4.9a. Yao Chen-tsung, *Sui shu ching-chi chih k'ao-cheng*, notes that this and the following titles were included in Hsiao Kang's *Ch'ang-ch'un tien i chi* and hence were not listed in *NS*.

Chuang-tzu i (Exegesis on the Chuang-tzu). 20 fols. Title in *LS* 4.9a.

Ch'ang-ch'un i chi (Tales of the [Palace of] Eternal Spring). 100 fols. Title in *LS* 4.9a; *NS* 8.4a; *Sui shu* 32.16b.

Fa-pao lien-pi (Linked Jade of the Buddha-Jewel). 300 fols. Title in *LS* 4.9a; *NS* 8.4a.

Hsieh K'o wen ching-wei (The Limpid and Muddy in the Works of Hsieh Ling-yün). 3 fols. Title in *NS* 8.4a.

Yü chien (The Jade Tablets). 50 fols. Title in *NS* 8.4a.

Kuang-ming fu (The Brilliant Tally). 12 fols. Title in *NS* 8.4a; *Sui shu* 34.13b (listed with an additional folio, table of contents).

I lin (The Forest of Changes), 17 fols. Title in *NS* 8.4a.

Tsao ching (Classic of the Kitchen God). 2 fols. Title in *NS* 8.4a; *Sui shu* 34.15b (listed as 14 fols.).

Mu-yü ching (Classic, or Sutra, on the Bathing [of Buddha on the Eighth Day of the Fourth Lunar Month]). 3 fols. Title in *NS* 8.4a.

Ma-shuo p'u (Treatise on Chess). 1 fol. Title in *NS* 8.4a.

Ch'i-p'in (Classification on Chess). 5 fols. Title in *NS* 8.4a.

T'an-ch'i p'u (On Playing Chess). 1 fol. Title in *NS* 8.4a.

Hsin Seng pai ts'e t'u (Chart for the Purification of a Newly Ordained Monk). 5 fols. Title in *NS* 8.4a.

Ju-i fang (On the Handling of a *Ju-i* Baton). 10 fols. Title in *NS* 8.4a.

Wen chi (Collected Works). 100 fols. Title in *NS* 8.4a.

Mao Shih shih-wu Kuo-feng i (Exegesis on the Fifteen "Airs of the States" of the *Mao Odes*). 20 fols. Title in *Sui shu* 32.8a.

Ch'un-ch'iu fa-t'i (Themes from the *Spring and Autumn Annals*). 1 fol. Title in *Sui shu* 32.13a.

Hsiao-ching i-shu (Commentary on the *Classic of Filial Piety*). 5 fols. Title in *Sui shu* 32.15a.

Lao-tzu ssu chi (Personal Records of Lao-tzu). 10 fols. Title in *Sui shu* 34.2a.

Chuang-tzu chiang-shu (Lectures on the *Chuang-tzu*). 10 fols. Title in *Sui shu* 34.2b (listed as a fragment of the 20 fols. of the *Chuang-tzu i*). Listed as 13 fols. in *T'ang shu,* "Ching-chi chih."

Liang Chien-wen ti chi (Collected Works of Emperor Chien-wen of Liang). 85 fols. Title in *Sui shu* 35.9b (listed as compiled by Lu Chao).

Ch'un-ch'iu Tso-shih-chuan li-yüan (Collected Extracts from the *Tso Commentary* to the *Spring and Autumn Annals*). 18 fols. Title in *T'ang shu,* "Ching-chi chih."

Liang Chien-wen ti chi (Collected Works of Emperor Chien-wen of Liang). 80 fols. Title in *T'ang shu,* "Ching-chi chih."

Liang Chien-wen ti chi. 14 fols. Title in *Chiang-su sheng ti-i tz'u shu-mu* and *Chiang-su ts'ai-chi i-shu mu-lu chien-mu.*

Liang Chien-wen ti chi. 2 fols. Title in *Liang Chiang ti-i tz'u shu-mu.*

II. Editions of Emperor Chien-wen's Extant Works:

Mao Shih shih-wu Kuo-feng i. 1 fol. In Ma Kuo-han, *Yü-han-shan-fang chi i-shu,* "Ching pien, shih lei." Editions: Lang-huan kuan pen; Ch'ung yin pen; Ch'u-nan shu-chü pen.

Liang Chien-wen ti chi. 2 fols. *Liu-ch'ao shih chi; Wen-hsüan i-chi.*

Liang Chien-wen ti yü-chih chi. 2 fols. *Han Wei Liu-ch'ao pai-san ming-chia chi.* Editions: Chang shih pen; Shou-k'ao-t'ang pen; Hsin-shu-t'ang pen; Ching chi t'ang pen; Han-mo shan fang pen; Sao-yeh-shan-fang shih yin pen; Ssu-ch'uan kuan yin chü pen.

Liang Chien-wen ti chi. Tseng-ting Han Wei Liu-ch'ao pieh chieh, "Chi pu."

Liang Chien-wen ti chi. 8 fols. *Han Wei Liu-ch'ao ming-chia chi ch'u-k'e.*

Liang Chien-wen ti chi hsüan. 1 fol. Wu Ju-lun, *Han Wei Liu-ch'ao pai-san chia chi hsüan.*

Liang Chien-wen ti wen chi. 6 fols. Yen K'o-chün, *Ch'üan Shang-ku San-tai Ch'in Han San-kuo Liu-ch'ao wen.* 741 fols. Kuang-ya shu-chü k'an pen edition, 1886–1893. Reprinted Chung-hua shu-chü. 4 vols. Peking: Chung-hua shu-chü, 1958. Vol. III: "Ch'üan Liang wen," fols. 8–14.

Liang Chien-wen ti shih chi. Ting Fu-pao, *Ch'üan Han San-kuo Chin Nan-Pei-ch'ao shih.* 54 fols. Wu-hsi Ting shih p'ai yin pen edition, 1916. Reprinted Yee-wen yin-shu-kuan. 6 vols. Taipei: Yee-wen yin-shu-kuan, n.d. Vol. IV: "Ch'üan Liang shih."

III. Primary Sources:

Chang P'u. See *Han Wei Liu-ch'ao pai-san chia chi.*

Chien-chu Yü-t'ai hsin-yung (New Songs of the Jade Terrace, with Annotations). Compiled by Hsü Ling (507–583). Annotated by Wu Chao-i (fl. 1672). 2 vols. Taipei: Kuang-wen shu-chü, 1967.

Ch'üan Han San-kuo Chin Nan-Pei-ch'ao shih (Complete Poetry of the Han, Three Kingdoms, Chin, Northern and Southern Dynasties). Ting Fu-pao. 6 vols. Taipei: Yee-wen yin-shu-kuan, n. d.

Ch'üan Shang-ku San-tai Ch'in Han San-kuo Liu-ch'ao wen (Complete Prose of High Antiquity, the Three Eras, Ch'in, Han, Three Kingdoms, and Six Dynasties). Yen K'o-chün (1762–1843). 4 vols. Peking: Chung-hua shu-chü, 1958.

Erh-shih-ssu shih (Twenty-Four Dynastic Histories). Po-na edition. Taiwan: Commercial Press.

Erh-shih-wu shih (Twenty-Five Dynastic Histories). Palace edition. Ch'ing Ch'ien-lung Wu-ying Palace edition photo reprint, Taiwan: Yee-wen yin-shu-kuan.

Han Wei Liu-ch'ao pai-san chia chi (Collected Works of One Hundred and Three Authors of the Han, Wei, and Six Dynasties). Compiled by Chang P'u (1602–1641). 14 vols. Taipei: Hsin-hsing shu-chü, n.d.

Han Wei Liu-ch'ao chu-chia wen-chi (Collected Works of the Authors of the Han, Wei, and Six Dynasties). Compiled by Wang Shih-hsien (Ming). Wang shih k'an pen edition.

Hung-ming chi. Compiled by Shih Seng-yu (Liang). In *Taisho* 2102.

I-wen lei-chü. Compiled by Ou-yang Hsün (557–641). 2 vols. Peking: Chung-hua shu-chü, 1965.

Kao-seng chuan (Lives of Eminent Monks). Compiled by Hui Chiao (497–554).

Ku-chin-chu. Compiled by Ts'ui Pao. SPTK edition.

Kuang Hung-ming chi. Compiled by Tao Hsüan (T'ang). In *Taisho* 2103.

Liu-ch'ao wen-hsieh chien-chu. Compiled by Hsü Lien (Ch'ing). Peking: Chung-hua shu-chü, 1962.

Lo-yang chia-lan chi chiao-shih. Yang Hsien-chih (Northern Wei). Annotated by Chou Tsu-mo. Peking: Chung-hua shu-chü, 1963.

Shih-p'in chu. Chung Hung (d. 518). Annotated by Ch'en Yen-chieh. Shanghai: Kai-ming shu-tien, 1927. Reprinted Hong Kong: Commercial Press, 1959.

Shih-san ching chu-su fu chiao-k'an chi (The Thirteen Classics with Collated Commentaries). Edited by Juan Yüan (1764–1849). Woodblock edition, 1826.

Shih-shuo hsin-yü (Popular Sayings and New Tales). Compiled by Liu I-ch'ing (403–444). SPTK edition.

Shui-ching chu (Classic of the Rivers). Compiled by Li Tao-yüan (d. 527). SPTK edition.

Tzu-chih t'ung-chien (Comprehensive Mirror as an Aid to Government). Compiled by Ssu-ma Kuang (1019–1086). 2nd printing. Peking: Chung-hua shu-chü, 1963.

Wen-hsin tiao-lung. Liu Hsieh (ca. 465–522). SPTK edition.

Wen-hsüan. Compiled by Liang Chao-ming T'ai-tzu (Hsiao T'ung) (501–531). Taipei: Yee-wen yin-shu-kuan, 1967.

Wen-yüan ying-hua. Compiled by P'eng Shu-hsia (fl. 1204). 12 vols. Taipei: Hua-wen shu-chü, 1965. Vol. XIII: Index. 1967.

Yen Chih-t'ui. See *Yen-shih chia-hsün.*

Yen-shih chia-hsün. Yen Chih-t'ui (531–591). SPTK edition.

Yü-p'ien. Ku Yeh-wang (519–581). SPTK edition.

Yü-t'ai hsin-yung. See *Chien-chu Yü-t'ai hsin-yung.*

Yüeh-fu-shih chi (Collected Yüeh-fu Poetry). Kuo Mao-ch'ien. 3 vols. Taipei: Shih-chieh shu-chü, 1961.

IV. Secondary Sources in Western Languages:

ACKER, WILLIAM. *Some T'ang and Pre-T'ang Texts in Chinese Painting.* Leiden: Brill, 1955.

CH'EN, KENNETH. *Buddhism in China.* Princeton: Princeton University Press, 1964.

CH'EN SHIH-HSIANG, trans. "Essay on Literature." By Lu Chi. *Anthology of Chinese Literature.* Edited by C. Birch and D. Keene. New York: Grove Press, 1965.

DIEN, ALBERT E. "Biography of Yen Chih-t'ui." Unpublished.

FANG, ACHILLES, trans., "Rhymeprose on Literature: The *Wen-fu* of Lu Chi (A.D. 261–303)." *HJAS,* XIV (1951), 527–566.

FRODSHAM, JOHN D., and CH'ENG HSI. *Anthology of Chinese Verse.* London: Oxford University Press, 1967.

GILES, HERBERT A., trans. *Chuangtzu.* 2nd rev. ed. London: Allen & Unwin, 1961.

HAWKES, DAVID. *Ch'u Tz'u: The Songs of the South.* London: Oxford University Press, 1957.

HIGHTOWER, JAMES ROBERT. "Some Characteristics of Parallel Prose." *Studia Serica Bernhard Karlgren Dedicata* (Copenhagen) (1959).

————. "The Wen-hsüan and Genre Theory." *HJAS,* XX (1957), 512–533.

HUGHES, E. R. *The Art of Letters: Lu Chi's "Wen Fu,"* A. D. 302. Bollingen Series No. 29. New York: Pantheon Press, 1951.

LANCMAN, ELI. *Chinese Portraiture.* Rutland, Vt.: Tuttle, 1966.

LEGGE, JAMES, trans. *The Chinese Classics.* 7 vols. London: Trübner, 1861–1872.

MATHER, RICHARD. "The Landscape Buddhism of the Fifth Century Poet, Hsieh Ling-yün." *JAS* 18.1 (1958), 67–79.

MIYAKAWA HISAYUKI. "The Confucianization of South China." *The Confucian Persuasion.* Edited by A. F. Wright. Stanford: Stanford University Press, 1960.

SHIH YU-CHUNG,VINCENT, trans. *The Literary Mind and the Carving of Dragons.* New York: Columbia University Press, 1959.

SOPER, ALEXANDER C. *Literary Evidence for Early Buddhist Art in China.* Ascona: Artibus Asiae, 1959.

————. "South Chinese Influence on the Buddhist Art of the Six Dynasties Period." *BMFEA,* XXXII (1960).

————. *Textual Evidence for the Secular Arts of China in the Period from Liu Sung through Sui.* Ascona: Artibus Asiae, 1968.

TENG SSU-YÜ, trans. *The Family Instructions for the Yen Clan, Yen-shih chia-hsün, by Yen Chih-t'ui.* Leiden: Brill, 1968.

WALEY, ARTHUR. *The Analects of Confucius.* London: Allen & Unwin, 1938.

WILHELM, HELMUT. "A Note on Chung Hung and His Shih-p'in." In *Wen-lin.* Edited by Chow Tse-tsung. Madison: University of Wisconsin Press, 1958.

WILHELM, RICHARD. *The I Ching or Book of Changes.* Translated by Cary F. Baynes. 2 vols. London: Routledge & Kegan Paul, 1951.

WIST, H. "Sklaverei in China." *Artibus Asiae,* VIII (1945), 238–257.

ZURCHER, EMIL. *The Buddhist Conquest of China: The Spread and Adaptation of Buddhism in Early Medieval China.* 2 vols. Leiden: Brill, 1959.

V. Secondary Sources in Chinese and Japanese:

AMI YUJI. *Chūgoku chūsei bungaku kenkyū* (A Study of Medieval Chinese Literature). Tokyo: Shinjusha, 1960.

CHANG HSIANG-KUANG. "Kuan-yü Tung-Chin Nan-ch'ao men-fa shih-tsu ti shuai-wang wen-t'i" (The Problem of the Decline of the Nobility of the Eastern Chin and Southern Dynasties). *Li-shih chiao-hsüeh* (December 1964), pp. 106–108.

CHANG HUANG. *Liang-tai ling-mu k'ao* (On the Tombs of the Liang Era). Shanghai, 1930.

CH'EN I (Ming). *Chin-ling ku-chin t'u k'ao* (Illustrated Description of Nanking). Nanking, 1928. Reprint of Cheng-te woodblock edition, 1516.

CH'IU CH'IUNG-SUN. *Shih fu tz'u ch'ü kai-lun* (Outline of Poetry, Rhymeprose, Lyrics, and Songs). Shanghai, 1934. Reprinted Taipei: Chung-hua shu-chü, 1966.

CHOU TSO-JEN. "Wen-chang ti fang-tang" (Literary Dissoluteness). In *K'u-chu tsa-chi*. N.p., n.d.

CHOU YIN-CH'U. "Kuan-yü kung-t'i-shih ti jo-kan wen-t'i" (Some Problems Concerning Palace-Style Poetry). *Hsin-chien she,* III (1965), 54–61.

CHU HSIEH. *Chien-k'ang Lan-ling Liu-ch'ao ling-mu t'u k'ao* (Illustrated Study of the Tombs of the Six Dynasties at Lan-ling, Chien-k'ang). Shanghai, 1936.

————. *Chin-ling ku-chi t'u k'ao* (Illustrated Study of the Archeology of Chin-ling). Shanghai, 1936.

FUNATSU TOMIHIKO. "Ryō-dai bungakuron ni arawareta keijisetsu ni tsuite" (Concerning Theories Apparent in the Literary Discussions of the Liang Era). *Tōyō bungaku kenkyū,* XV (1967), 80–97.

HAYASHIDA SHINNOSUKE. "Nan-chō hō-tō bungakuron no bi-ishiki" (Sense of Beauty in the Southern Dynasties Stressed in the Discussions of Dissoluteness in Literature). *Tōhōgaku,* XXVII (February 1964), 1–14.

————. "Shō Kō no 'Sō tō ō shō ataeru' o megutte Morino-shi ronbun 'Kanbuntei no bunshōkan' hihan" (Criticism of Mr. Morino's Article "Emperor Chien-wen's View of Literary Composition" which Centered upon Hsiao Kang's "Letter to the Prince of Hsiang-tung"). *Chūgoku chūsei bungaku kenkyū,* VII (1968), 16–25.

HU NIEN-I. "Lun kung-t'i-shih ti wen-t'i" (Discussion of the Problems of Palace-Style Poetry). *Hsin-chien she,* III (March 1964), 167–173.

KAWAKATSU YOSHIO. "Kō Kei no ran to Nan-chō no kahei keizai" (Hou Ching's Rebellion and the Money Economy of the Southern Dynasties). *Tōhō gaku-hō* (Tokyo), XXXII (March 1962), 69–118.

——————. "Nan-chō kizoku-sei no botsuraku ni kansuru ikkōsatsu" (Decline of the Nobility in the Southern Dynasties). *Tōyōshi kenkyū*, XX (April 1962), 120–144.

KIKUCHI HIDEO. "Riku-chō gunshi no shingun ni tsuite no ikkōsatsu" (A Study of the Bodyguards of the Warlords of the Six Dynasties). *Tōyōshi kenkyū*, XVIII, no. 1 (January 1959), 17–38.

KUNG TUN. "Pu-yao tsai tsao-p'o chung chao ching-hua" (Do Not Seek the Finest Essence Among Dregs). *Kuang-ming jih-pao* October 10, 1965.

LI CH'UN-SHENG. "Liang ku-chiao-heng-ch'ui ch'ü" (The Drum, Horn, and Fife Songs of Liang). *Ta-lu tsa-chih*, XXVIII:12 (June 1964), 14–17.

LI T'IAO-YÜAN. *Fu-hua* (An Exegesis of Rhymeprose). Taipei, 1961.

LIN WEN-YÜEH. "Nan-ch'ao kung-t'i-shih yen-chiu" (A Study of the Palace-Style Poetry of the Southern Courts). *Wen shih che hsüeh-pao*, XV (1966), 407–458.

LU SSU-MIEN. *Liang-Chin Nan-Pei-ch'ao shih* (History of the Two Chin and Northern and Southern Dynasties). 2 vols. Shanghai, 1948. Reprinted Hong Kong: T'ai-p'ing shu-chü, 1962.

MAO HAN-KUANG. *Liang-Chin Nan-Pei-ch'ao shih-tsu cheng-chih chih yen-chiu* (A Study of the Government by the Nobility During the Two Chin and the Northern and Southern Dynasties). 2 vols. Taipei: Taiwan Commercial Press, 1966.

MASUDA KIYOHIDE. "Nan-boku-chō ni okeru kosui-kashi no jitsujō" (What the Presentation of a Military Band in the Northern and Southern Dynasties Really Meant). *Ōsaka gakugei daigaku kiyō*, XV (1967), 10–21.

MIYAKAWA HISAYUKI. "Ryō no Gen tei" (Emperor Yüan of the Liang). *Tōyōshi kenkyū*, VI, no. 5 (October 1941), 48–61.

MORI MIKISABURŌ. *Ryō no Bu tei* (Emperor Wu of the Liang). Kyoto: Heirakuji Shoten, 1956.

MORINO SHIGEO. "Kanbun tei no bunshōkan" (Emperor Chien-wen's View of Literary Composition). *Chūgoku chūsei bungaku kenkyū*, V (June 1966), 47–59.

——————. "Ryō no bungaku no yūgisei" (Literary Games of the Liang). *Chūgoku chūsei bungaku kenkyū*, VI (June 1967), 27–40.

——————. "Ryō-shō no bungaku shūdan" (Literary Salons in Early Liang). *Chūgoku bungaku-hō*, XXI (October 1966), 83–108.

OBI KOICHI. *Chūgoku bungaku ni arawareta shizen to shizenkan* (Nature and Its View Revealed in [medieval] Chinese Literature). Tokyo: Iwanami, 1962.

OZAWA MASAO. "Riku-chō shi ni okeru eibutsu to daiei" (*"Yung-wu"* and "T'i-yung" in Six Dynasties Poetry). *Nihon bungaku ken-kyū*, XXXVIII (1953).

SHIBA ROKURŌ. " 'Fu-toku' no imi ni tsuite" (On the Meaning of "Fu-te"). *Chūgoku bungaku-hō*, III (October 1955), 33–49.

SUZUKI TORAO. *Fushi taiyō* (Outline History of Rhymeprose). Tokyo: Fuzanbō, 1936.

TABEI FUMIO. "Riku-chō kyūtai no shi ni tsuite" (On the Palace-Style Poetry of the Six Dynasties Period). *Kanbun gakkai-hō*, XVIII (1959), 6–11.

TAKEDA RYOJI. "Kō Kei no ran ni tsuite no ikkōsatsu" (A Study of Hou Ching's Rebellion). *Shigaku*, XXIX, no. 3 (1956), 34–59.

T'ANG YUNG-T'UNG. *Han Wei Liang-Chin Nan-Pei-ch'ao fo-chiao shih* (History of Buddhism in the Han, Wei, Two Chin, and Northern and Southern Dynasties). 2 vols. Shanghai, 1938. Reprinted Taipei: Taiwan Commercial Press, 1965.

WANG CHUNG-LO. "Hou Ching luan Liang ch'ien-hou ti Nan-ch'ao cheng-chih chü-shih" (The Political Situation in the Southern Dynasties Before and After Hou Ching Disrupted the Liang). *Wen shih che hsüeh-pao* (1955), 50–63.

Appendix I: Selected Genealogy of the Hsiao Clan

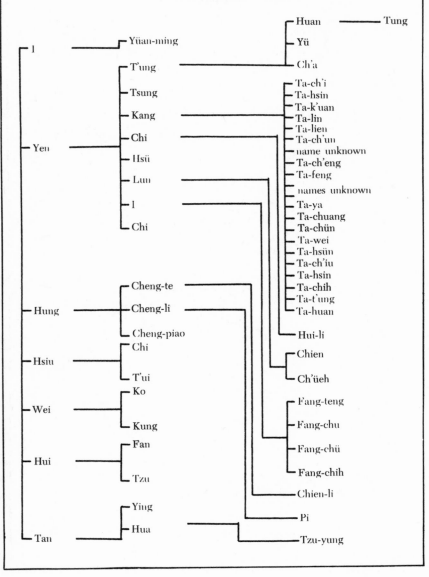

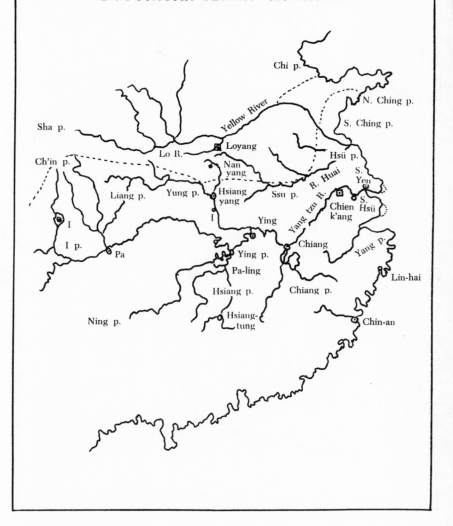

MAP 1

Sketch Map of Area of Hsiao Kang's Provincial Administration

Chi p.

Yellow River

N. Ching p.

S. Ching p.

Sha p.

Lo R.

Loyang

Hsü p.

Ch'in p.

Nan yang

S. Yen

Liang p.

Yung p.

Hsiang yang

Ssu p.

R. Huai

Chien k'ang

S. Hsü

I

I

Ying

Yang tzu R.

I p.

Pa

Ying p.

Chiang

Yang p.

Pa-ling

Lin-hai

Hsiang p.

Chiang p.

Ning p.

Hsiang-tung

Chin-an

MAP 2

Metropolitan Area of Chien-k'ang

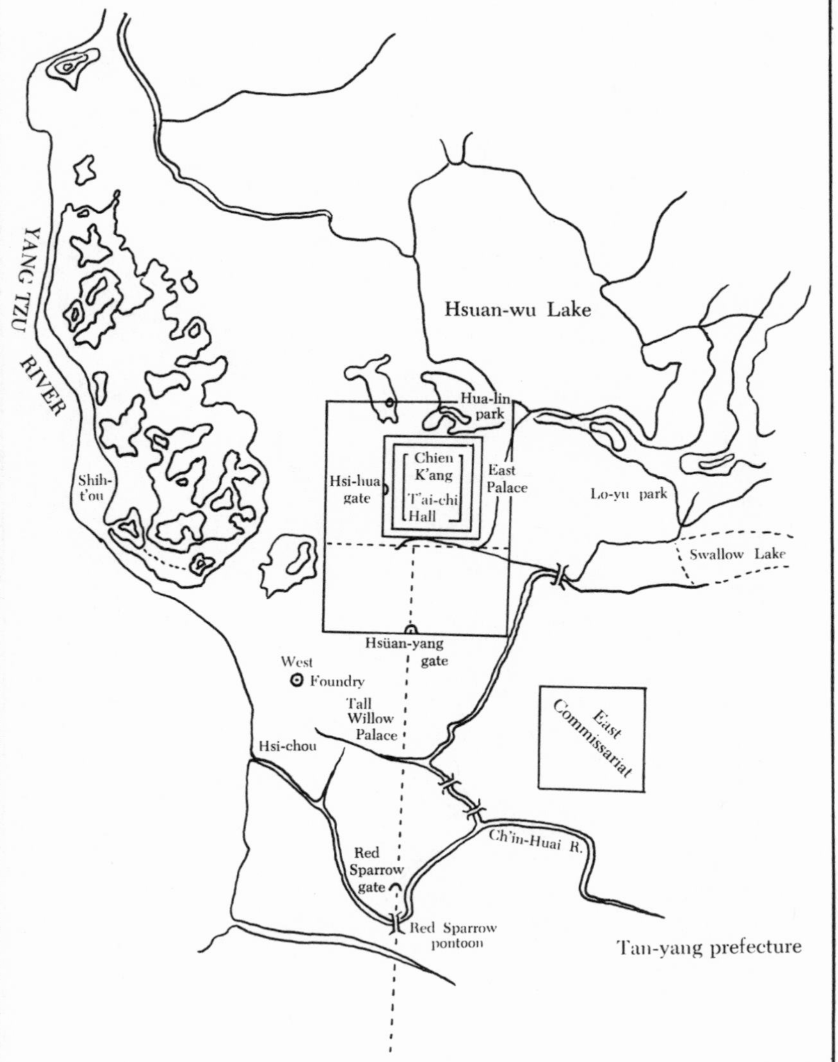

YANG TZU RIVER

Hsuan-wu Lake

Hua-lin park

Shih-t'ou

Hsi-hua gate

Chien K'ang T'ai-chi Hall

East Palace

Lo-yu park

Swallow Lake

Hsüan-yang gate

West

⊙ Foundry

Tall Willow Palace

East Commissariat

Hsi-chou

Red Sparrow gate

Ch'in-Huai R.

Red Sparrow pontoon

Tan-yang prefecture

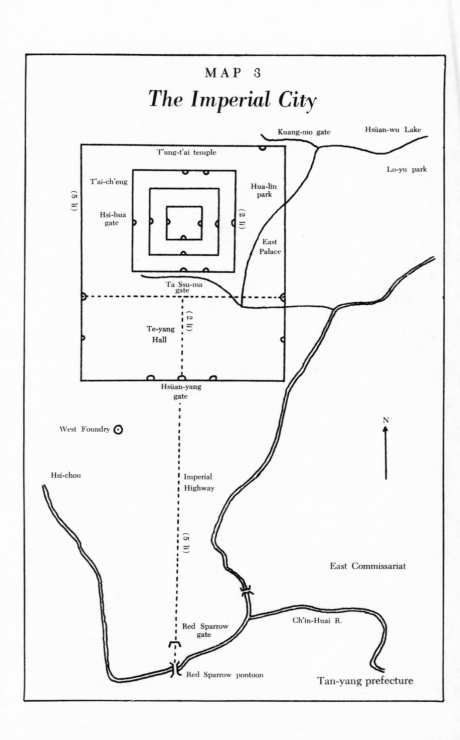

MAP 3

The Imperial City

Index

217